Gender and Justice

For Theo

Gender and Justice

New concepts and approaches

Edited by

Frances Heidensohn

WILLAN
PUBLISHING

Published by

Willan Publishing
Culmcott House
Mill Street, Uffculme
Cullompton, Devon
EX15 3AT, UK
Tel: +44(0)1884 840337
Fax: +44(0)1884 840251
e-mail: info@willanpublishing.co.uk
website: www.willanpublishing.co.uk

Published simultaneously in the USA and Canada by

Willan Publishing
c/o ISBS, 920 NE 58th Ave, Suite 300,
Portland, Oregon 97213-3786, USA
Tel: +001(0)503 287 3093
Fax: +001(0)503 280 8832
e-mail: info@isbs.com
website: www.isbs.com

Paperback
ISBN-13: 978-1-84392-199-8
ISBN-10: 1-84392-199-5

Hardback
ISBN-13: 978-1-84392-200-1
ISBN-10: 1-84392-200-2

British Library Cataloguing-in-Publication Data

A catalogue record for this book is available from the British Library

Typeset by GCS, Leighton Buzzard, Bedfordshire
Project managed by Deer Park Productions, Tavistock, Devon
Printed and bound by T.J. International Ltd, Padstow, Cornwall

Contents

Figures and Tables

Figures

Tables

Notes on the contributors

Frances Heidensohn is Visiting Professor, Department of Sociology, London School of Economics and Emeritus Professor of Social Policy, University of London. She has researched and written about gender, crime and justice for many years. Among her books are *Women and Crime* (1985/1996), *Women in Control? The Role of Women in Law Enforcement* (1992), *International Feminist Perspectives in Criminology* (with Nicole Rafter) (1995), *Sexual Politics and Social Control* (2000) and *Gender and Policing* (with Jennifer Brown) (2000). She was awarded the Sellin Glueck Award of the American Society of Criminology in 2004 for her international contributions to criminology.

Rachel Condry is a research fellow in the Law Department at the London School of Economics. She holds a British Academy post-doctoral fellowship award and is currently studying parenting and youth justice. She is the author of *Families Shamed: The Consequences of Crime for Relatives of Serious Offenders* (2007).

Kirstine Hansen is the research director of the Millennium Cohort Study at the Institute of Education, University of London. She was previously a lecturer in the Department of Social Policy, London School of Economics. Her recent publications include 'Education and the Crime-Age Profile', *British Journal of Criminology* and articles in the *Journal of Quantitative Criminology* and the *Oxford Bulletin of Economics and Statistics*.

Stephanie Hayman is senior lecturer in criminology at Kingston University. Her main area of research is women's imprisonment and she is the author of *Imprisoning our Sisters: The New Federal Women's Prisons in Canada* (2006) and co-author, with Tim Newburn, of *Policing, Surveillance and Social Control: CCTV and Police Monitoring of Suspects* (2002).

Nicola Hutson is a research fellow at the UK Observatory for the Promotion of Non-Violence, based at the University of Surrey. Her background is in social and developmental psychology. Her areas of interest include working with young offenders, violence and bullying in schools, and conflict resolution with children and young people.

Barbara Mason is a senior researcher at the London School of Economics. She spent most of her working life in business and studied criminology after taking early retirement. Her PhD thesis was an ethnographic study exploring the outcomes of an innovative penal experiment in a new women's prison in Ireland. Several articles based on this study appeared in 2006. She is also a magistrate and sits on the bench in north Surrey.

Carrie Anne Myers is a post-doctoral fellow at the UK Observatory for the Promotion of Non-Violence, University of Surrey. She has worked on several projects, including violence reduction in schools for the DfES, the mental health of young offenders for the prison service and the role of peer support systems in reducing bullying.

Oliver Phillips is reader in the School of Law, University of Westminster. He has lived much of his life in Zimbabwe and South Africa. He was a Rockefeller Fellow at the Program for the Study of Sexuality, Gender, Health and Human Rights at Columbia University. He has written widely on law, sexuality and HIV/AIDS in Southern Africa and has worked for a number of campaigning organisations for political and sexual rights in the region.

Joanna Phoenix is senior lecturer in sociology, Department of Social and Policy Sciences, University of Bath. She is the author of *Making Sense of Prostitution* (2001), *Illicit and Illegal: Sex, Regulation and Social Control* (with Sarah Oerton) (2005) as well as several articles and chapters on prostitution and its regulation. Her current research, funded by the Economic and Social Research Council, is on risk and need assessment in the context of youth justice.

Nicole Rafter is a senior research fellow at Northeastern University's College of Criminal Justice and an affiliated faculty member in Northeastern's Law, Policy and Society programme. She has been a Visiting Fellow at St John's College, Wolfson College and the Centre for Sociolegal Studies at Oxford University. She is a Fellow of the American Society of Criminology. Her recent books include *Shots in the Mirror: Crime Films and Society* (2006) and a new translation (with Mary Gibson) of Lombroso's *Criminal Woman* (2004) and *Criminal Man* (2006). Her current research is on a history of biological theories of crime.

Judith Rumgay is reader in the Department of Social Policy, London School of Economics. Formerly a probation officer, she is the author of *Crime, Punishment and the Drinking Offender* (1998), *The Addicted Offender: Developments in British Policy and Practice* (2000) and *Ladies of Lost Causes* (2006) as well as many articles and chapters. She directs the Griffins Fellowship programme at the LSE.

Mike Shiner is senior research officer, Mannheim Centre, London School of Economics. He has researched and written extensively about drugs, youth and crime. His recent publications include *Dealing with Disaffection: Young People, Mentoring and Social Inclusion* (with Tim Newburn) (2005), *Community Responses to Drugs* (with Betsy Thom *et al.*) (2004), *Doing it for Themselves: An Evaluation of Peer Approaches to Drug Prevention* (2000), and many articles and chapters.

Marisa Silvestri is senior lecturer in criminology at London South Bank University. She is the author of *Women in Charge: Policing, Gender and Leadership* (2003) and of *Gender, Crime and Human Rights* (2007). Her research interests include gender, policing and human rights.

Kate Steward is director of the Griffins Society, a voluntary organisation which identifies and promotes resettlement needs of female offenders by supporting practitioner-led research through its Fellowship programme based at the LSE. She has a long-standing interest in women in the criminal justice system and completed her PhD on the use of custodial remand for female offenders in 2004.

Acknowledgements

This book has a number of inspirations and sources. First, I have long been concerned with the ideas and issues it covers and was delighted to find so many new and younger scholars working on these topics. Many of them are linked to the London School of Economics as past or present staff or students. When compiling reading lists for courses, I was struck that most of this exciting and challenging material was not easily accessible. Questions about gender, justice and crime seem to be constantly in the public arena, whether they focus on young women getting drunk or taking drugs or the rising numbers of women going to prison or committing violent crimes. Masculinity has also been highlighted as an issue, with reports of macho behaviour in the military, law enforcement or professional sport.

Returning to the sociology department at the LSE as a visiting professor in 2004 provided me with a marvellous stimulus to produce this text and a most lively and supportive atmosphere in which to work. My thanks to Nikolas Rose for the invitation and most kind welcome and to Joyce Lorenstein and Tia Exelby for all their help. The LSE is one of the most interesting and important centres for the study of criminology today and I have been most fortunate to be able to share ideas and discussions and gain encouragement from all my colleagues there. I am especially grateful to Paul Rock, David Downes, Tim Newburn, Stan Cohen, Nikki Lacey, Dick Hobbs, Janet Foster, Robert Reiner, Anna Souhami, Jacqui Karn, Maurice Punch, Coretta Phillips, Iman Heflin and the regular members of the Tuesday seminars. My debt to all the contributors is immense, for their hard work, willingness to take part and for the spirit in which they have done so. Mary Eaton and Betsy Stanko were always ready with thoughtful advice and suggestions. Nicky Rafter has, as always, been the best of friends, offering encouragement, wisdom and support.

Brian Willan has been an exemplary publisher, proving again his star status in UK criminology. Jutta Schettler has provided incomparable skill and patience in preparing the manuscript for publication.

I am most appreciative of all the support and kindness I have received from everyone and trust that they, and all our readers, will find interest, challenges and some answers here.

Frances Heidensohn
London School of Economics
September 2006

Chapter I

New perspectives and established views

Frances Heidensohn

Gender and crime have been closely linked in criminological understanding for many decades. Textbooks include sections under this title; start a Google search and you will find links to websites covering relevant books, articles and news stories, with some offering to write essays on the topic (at a price). It was not always so. This high level of recognition has been largely achieved by the pioneering work of feminist criminologists who have contributed to the development and establishment of a series of new perspectives in the subject (Rafter and Heidensohn 1995). From very modest beginnings in the work of a few individuals, there grew a volume of activity so notable that Downes and Rock (1988), writing in the 1980s, described it as the development of the decade.

Considerable effort has been expended on defining the meaning of the term 'feminist criminology' (Gelsthorpe 2002; Naffine 1997). A neat and apt description is offered by a (male) criminologist who was not even born when the first articles in the field appeared:

> Since the early 1970s feminist perspectives have provided a critique of mainstream male criminology based on two principle observations: women are generally invisible in most ... work and, where they do appear, they are portrayed in ways that distort and marginalize their experiences. (Shiner 2005)

This critique began with an interest in women and crime and drew on two key sources. The first was the modern, or second-wave, feminist movement that offered a vocabulary and concepts to criticise and challenge mainstream academic discourse (Heidensohn 1996). A new generation of scholars applied these tools to a wide range of subjects with remarkable and lasting results. This process took longer in criminology where there were distinctive problems with the omission of gender from theories of crime and with the ways in which women's experiences of crime and criminal justice were marginalised and distorted in the field (Heidensohn 1968; Daly and Chesney-Lind 1988).

These moves had, after initial silence and incomprehension, considerable impact with Smart's (1977) pivotal text providing the breakthrough. After that point it became possible, and indeed necessary, to provide regular state-of-the-art reports in what was becoming an important subsection of criminology. By 1987, in an edited collection titled *Gender, Crime and Justice* (Carlen and Worrall 1987), it was possible to review the findings of a considerable number of studies and assert that 'we can now say much more confidently what women offenders are like and how they make sense of their own experiences' (Heidensohn 1987: 17). Much of mainstream criminology was still not taking note of this work and I had found three categories of response to the gender dimension and the questions it raised: 'continued denial, shamefaced awareness and born again acceptance' (1987: 23). In other words, there were more questions raised for criminology than there were answers or acceptance. Nevertheless, it was possible to summarise four major characteristics of female offenders based on the evidence of research. These were (1987: 17):

1 Economic rationality
2 Heterogeneity of their offences
3 Fear and impact of deviant stigma
4 The experience of double deviance and double jeopardy

Briefly, the first two findings contradicted the assumptions of most earlier work, that female offending was specialised and often sexually motivated. Instead, women's crimes were shown to be motivated by need (and sometimes greed) and to be as varied as males', having notably been involved in terrorism, for instance, in the 1980s.

Stigma had proved to be a powerful concept in understanding how 'women perceive themselves and are perceived as being damaged or spoiled by criminalisation' (1987: 19). 'Double deviance' described how many women found themselves twice punished for deviant behaviour: both by the criminal justice system and by informal sanctions from family and society. Both these notions are at odds with the view of much conventional criminology, that male chivalry protects women (Mannheim 1965).

A decade later, in another review, I recorded that 'the main features of female offending, of the treatment of women in the criminal justice system and of their experiences of social control have remained ... constant'. However, 'what has changed most of all is the *study of the topic itself*' (Heidensohn 1996: xiii, emphasis added). Again, four key headings could be used to list developments (1996: xiii):

1 Recognition
2 Expansion
3 Engendering the agenda
4 Deconstruction

The first two points are perhaps self-evident: the terms 'feminist criminology', 'gender and crime' and the 'gender gap' had achieved very widespread recognition. This was partly due to the dramatic expansion of the field: in research for the study cited above, Marisa Silvestri and I had located hundreds of relevant articles published in the previous decade, as well as numerous bibliographies and surveys of these topics (Heidensohn 1996: xiv). By 'engendering the agenda', I meant the ways in which debates had been influenced by feminist discourse – on domestic violence, sex crimes, and most interestingly, masculinity. 'Deconstructing categories' reflected the ways in which the category of 'women' had been challenged, with several writers arguing that black or other minority women do not share the same experiences as their white counterparts. These and many other surveys and texts suggest that the key questions for criminology remained broadly the same, focused on gender differences and their explanation in experiences in the criminal justice system.

Reviews of the current state of research and policy now appear regularly (as in the successive editions of the *Oxford Handbook*, for instance: Heidensohn 2002; Heidensohn and Gelsthorpe 2007). It can certainly no longer be argued that gender is invisible or ignored in criminology. There are a variety of views on the prospects for feminist criminology and its proponents: participants in one recent roundtable were pessimistic (Wincup *et al.* 2005). Yet the Division on Women and Crime of the American Society of Criminology launched a new journal in 2006 called *Feminist Criminology*; its contributors are generally confident: 'Feminist criminology now is routinely recognized by the broader discipline as a legitimate theoretical perspective ... feminist studies of crime are more commonplace

3

than ever before' (Burgess-Proctor 2006: 27). Whichever viewpoint one adopts, pessimistic or optimistic, it does appear that we now have an established, distinctive field with a significant role to play in criminology.

There are some notable features of the context in which gender and crime can be studied in the first part of the twenty-first century, as well as of such studies themselves. Once again, I suggest that these can be grouped under four headings:

1 The high profile of policies directed at female offending
2 The number of studies and critiques of the criminal justice system and women by established scholars
3 The involvement of the voluntary sector and NGOs in justice for women issues
4 Intense media interest

There have never before been more concerted and high-profile efforts directed at female offenders. From being a group who were usually portrayed as invisible and neglected, at best marginalised, they are now the focus of a series of programmes designed to co-ordinate 'work across departments and agencies to ensure that policies, services, programmes and other interventions respond more appropriately to the particular needs and characteristics of women offenders' (Home Office 2004: 3). This policy initiative, the Women's Offending Reduction Programme (WORP), was launched following extensive consultation on the government's Strategy for Women Offenders document (Home Office 2000). It was also explicitly made 'an important element of the Government's wider push towards improving gender equality' and linked to policies directed at that aim (Home Office 2004: 3). WORP was already the subject of regular reports on its progress; in addition, at the time of writing another review had been announced 'to take stock of the work being done and to look again at the measures in place to ensure that we are doing everything possible for the especially vulnerable group of women who come into contact with the criminal justice system' (House of Lords Hansard, 28 March 2006). This announcement followed two debates in the House of Lords in the preceding six months on women in prison (House of Lords Hansard, 28 October 2005 and 22 March 2006). In an unprecedented intervention, the first woman law lord devoted a public lecture to the topic of women and criminal justice and, after a full and feminist analysis of problems and concerns, argued that 'the criminal justice system could also ask itself whether it is indeed unjust to women. It could engage with the principled debate on the nature and purpose of punishment' (Hale 2005: 23).

There has continued to be a stream of books and articles published on gender and justice topics across the English-speaking world. These include edited collections (e.g. Carlen 2002; Carlen and Worrall 2004; Alder and Worrall 2004; Chesney-Lind and Pasko 2004; McIvor 2004), while major research council funds have also been devoted to the area (Liebling and Stanko 2001). As noted above, a new journal, *Feminist Criminology*, was launched in January 2006. One of the striking aspects of much of this output is that it comes from established scholars who have been writing about these subjects for some time.

Voluntary and charitable activity in support of female offenders is another robust tradition. First-wave feminists in the nineteenth and early twentieth centuries used their role in such organisations, which they themselves had generally founded, to campaign for matrons in prisons, for women's entry into policing and the repeal of sexually discriminating laws that penalised female prostitutes (Heidensohn 1992, 2000). In more recent times, the National Council of Women, the Prison Reform Trust and the Fawcett Society have all produced reports on women and the criminal justice system. The Fawcett Society has continued to monitor the issues raised in its initial reports and to initiate public debates. The Griffins Society, originally a charity providing hostels and aftercare to discharged female offenders, has transformed itself into a research, information and lobbying body (Rumgay 2006). At international level, the United Nations' Tenth Congress on Crime and Crime Prevention devoted one of its 'streams' to women and criminal justice (Ollus and Nevala 2001).

The media have always had an interest in women and crime, even though a distorted one. There does, however, seem to be even more disproportionate media interest in the twenty-first century. Horrifying cases, for instance of so-called 'happy slapping', involving girls, are given huge prominence (*Evening Standard*, 19 April 2006) and concerns about young women drinking heavily or using drugs are widely aired; the extensive and lurid treatment of the model Kate Moss in 2005–6 was one of the most sensationalised and stereotypical. A less stereotypical treatment of women in contact with the law has been evident in the reporting of a series of miscarriages of justice, which involved mothers wrongly convicted of murdering their children. Their cases have been presented very sympathetically (e.g. *Observer*, 20 February 2005); in notable contrast, the key expert witness in several of these convictions was harshly handled. A BBC drama based on one of these cases was shown in February 2005. While this was a play drawn from real life, there have been fictionalised representations of women's penal punishment, which have seemed exaggerated and extraordinary, especially the ITV series *Bad Girls*. Nevertheless, the founder of the charity Women in Prison, an ex-inmate herself, was the programme's advisor.

In sum, the settings in which questions about gender, crime and justice are studied, presented and discussed in the twenty-first century are different in important aspects from the past. There are positive features to note in the strength of research, as the content of this book shows, but there are concerns as well. Several of the same scholars who have analysed female offending and punishment have expressed anxieties about the very strength and significance of these developments. Snider (2003) has argued forcefully in support of what might be called the 'Pandora Problem' or the 'Falklands' Fate'. She insists that the worldwide trend of imprisoning more and more women is due in part to the knowledge produced, she examines 'how constructions of women developed by claims makers in feminist criminology have structured the ways in which women are now punished' (2003: 354). Feminist criminology, she argues, has produced 'components of the incarceration spiral' but it is vital to look 'beyond academe and ask not what discourses are produced but what discourses are heard by politicians, the public, and criminal justice professionals' (2003: 354). These are serious claims, although Snider concludes her discussion by arguing that 'since much of the institutional and ideological power remains in the hands of judges, wardens and parole officers', penal policies have not been shifted significantly (2003: 371).

More pessimistic views are expressed by Carlen (2002), who sees the state, despite attempts at reform, renewing 'carceral clawback' which means that more women are subjected to more punishment. She does not put responsibility for such negative outcomes directly onto feminist work, but notes the coincidence of the growth of punishment and the rise of feminist perspectives. Worrall is more explicit about the consequential links: 'Feminist critiques of welfarism in the 1980s resulted in moves towards "just deserts" for girls, which promised much ... but delivered greater criminalization and incarceration in the 1990s' (Worrall 2004: 56).

It is much more difficult to produce a short state-of-the-art summary about gender and crime some years into the twenty-first century than it was in the past. On the one hand, many of the questions originally posed by feminist criminologists are still being posed and debated. The 'gender gap' – the differences between male and female levels of recorded crime – is the focus of continued analysis, albeit often in secondary forms, as in analyses of relative increases in rates of violent crime (Steffensmeier *et al.* 2005). Theory questions, what Daly and Chesney-Lind (1988) call the 'generalisability problem' still abound, if also in unexpected forms. Miller and Messerschmidt, for instance, engaged in a lively debate in the pages of *Theoretical Criminology* about their respective work on masculinities, femininities and gangs and what theoretical assumptions underpin 'labelling gang girls as having "bad girl" femininities' (Miller 2002b: 478; see Messerschmidt 2002 and Miller 2002a for the original papers). Chesney-Lind herself has made a strong plea for more theorising since this is 'crucial to feminist criminology' (Chesney-Lind 2006: 21). The complex of concepts centred on equity of treatment in the criminal justice system – chivalry, stigma and double deviance – retain some of their power too. Worrall explores what she terms the 'search for equivalence ... in offending' which, she argues, has led to the creation of a spurious gender-neutrality that 'contains within it an asymmetrical moral judgement (or double standard). '"Women who kill", "female sex offenders, violent girls" and "women drug-dealers" are implicitly worse than their male counterparts because (and here we return full circle to a very old argument) they are "doubly deviant" – violating both the law and gender role expectations' (Worrall 2002: 49).

Together with Carlen, Worrall has also analysed trends in female convictions around the world; they begin by observing ironically that 'investigating these figures exposes a seemingly universal chivalry' (Carlen and Worrall 2004: 43). Goodwin and McIvor observed in their study of women on community service orders that 'despite their preferences for community service rather than a prison sentence, the public nature of community service was disliked by a number of women in [this] study, with [its] perception of public shaming ... some women ... experience a degree of stigma as a result of being placed on a community service order' (McIvor 2004: 134).

Many more approaches and issues are, of course, being covered in the study of gender and crime, but the persistence of these original themes is striking. In this text we present a series of chapters that cover new research in the field. This selection is distinguished by the predominance of younger scholars among the contributors. Almost all report on recently conducted empirical studies, several on relatively unexplored topics; the rest propose new theoretical perspectives to renew or challenge existing feminist criminologies.

A wide range of research methods is deployed in these studies: qualitative methods predominate, with, typically, participant observation and/or ethnography (Rachel Condry, Carrie Anne Myers, Barbara Mason, Kate Steward) employed. To these, the authors add interviews with inmates or pupils, staff and policy-makers. Extensive analyses of documents and archives support more directly available sources (Stephanie Hayman, Judith Rumgay, Barbara Mason, Rachel Condry, Kate Steward). Official discourse is analysed as well as more informal cultures (Joanna Phoenix, Stephanie Hayman, Oliver Phillips). Kirstine Hansen carried out a secondary analysis of existing survey data. The theory chapters range from Lombroso to human rights (Nicole Rafter, Marisa Silvestri, Oliver Phillips).

While these approaches may be typical of traditional and established feminist work, there are some novel features. Hansen considers economic factors and labour market features related to crime; Condry presents an analysis of vicarious victimisation and stigma among the families of serious offenders. The issues raised are a complex mixture of the established feminist agenda: the gender gap, equity in the criminal justice system, penal regimes and their impact on women. But there are considerable variations and developments on these themes. Steward finds some evidence of chivalry in courts' handling of women on remand, but notes other factors at work too. Myers' observations of bullying in a rural school record not a gender divide, nor gender gap, but that boys and girls take part together.

The book is divided into three parts. Part One includes chapters on gender and offending behaviour; Part Two covers gender and the criminal justice system; Part Three presents a selection of new concepts and approaches applied to this field. A short introduction outlines the key topics and questions raised in each part. This selection is not meant to be exhaustive; its length is necessarily limited by what one volume can contain. We have not included studies of policing nor of victims, both of which have been extensively researched and written about (Heidensohn 1992; Brown and Heidensohn 2000; Silvestri 2003; Walklate 2004; Zedner 2007). The range of topics covered is considerable, the research presented of very high quality.

While central questions from the feminist criminology agenda are considered by the authors here, they all indicate how much these original themes have been extended, reinterpreted and answered in new and distinctive ways. It is no longer possible to encompass the whole of this field in a single volume – it is too vast, diverse and complex. We can, however, show some of the strength, variety and vitality of what is being produced. Surprisingly, perhaps, gender and justice are flourishing as topics for research, yet at the same time there are increasing concerns about many of the items on the related policy agenda. In short, this is a flourishing field of criminology, as the following chapters show.

References

Alder, C. and Worrall, A. (eds) (2004) *Girls' Violence*, Albany: SUNY Press.

Brown, J. and Heidensohn, F. (2000) *Gender and Policing*, Basingstoke: Palgrave/Macmillan.

Burgess-Proctor, A. (2006) 'Intersections of Race, Class, Gender and Crime: Future Directions for Feminist Criminology', *Feminist Criminology*, 1(1): 27–47.

Carlen, P. (ed.) (2002) *Women and Punishment*, Cullompton: Willan Publishing.

Carlen, P. and Worrall, A. (eds) (1987) *Gender, Crime and Justice*, Milton Keynes: Open University Press.

Carlen, P. and Worrall, A. (eds) (2004) *Analysing Women's Imprisonment*, Cullompton: Willan Publishing.

Chesney-Lind, M. (2006) 'Patriarchy, Crime and Justice: Feminist Criminology', *Feminist Criminology*, 1(1): 6–26.

Chesney-Lind, M. and Pasko, L. (2004) *The Female Offender*, Thousand Oaks, CA: Sage.

Daly, K. and Chesney-Lind, M. (1988) 'Feminism and Criminology', *Justice Quarterly*, 5(4): 498–538.

Downes, D. and Rock, P. (1988) *Understanding Deviance*, 2nd edn, Oxford: Clarendon Press.

Gelsthorpe, L. (2002) 'Feminism and Criminology', in M. Maguire *et al.* (eds) *The Oxford Handbook of Criminology*, 3rd edn, Oxford: Oxford University Press.

Hale, B. (2005) 'The Sinners and the Sinned Against: Women in the Criminal Justice System', Longford Lecture (December).

Heidensohn, F. (1968) 'The Deviance of Women: A Critique and an Enquiry', *British Journal of Sociology*, 19(2): 160–75.

Heidensohn, F. (1987) 'Questions for Criminology', in P. Carlen and A. Worrall (eds) *Gender, Crime and Justice*, Milton Keynes: Open University Press.

Heidensohn, F. (1992) *Women in Control? The Role of Women in Law Enforcement*, Oxford: Clarendon Press.

Heidensohn, F. (1996) *Women and Crime*, 2nd edn, Basingstoke: Macmillan.

Heidensohn, F. (1998) 'Translations and Refutations', in S. Holdaway and P. Rock (eds) *Thinking About Criminology*, London: UCL Press.

Heidensohn, F. (2000) *Sexual Politics and Social Control*, Buckingham: Open University Press.

Heidensohn, F. (2002) 'Gender and Crime', in M. Maguire *et al.* (eds) *The Oxford Handbook of Criminology*, 3rd edn, Oxford: Oxford University Press.

Heidensohn, F. and Gelsthorpe, L. (2007) 'Gender and Crime', in M. Maguire *et al.* (eds) *The Oxford Handbook of Criminology*, 4th edn, Oxford: Oxford University Press.

Home Office (2000) *Women's Offending Reduction Programme Report.*

Home Office (2004) *Women's Offending Reduction Programme Report 2002–2005.*

Liebling, A. and Stanko, B. (eds) (2001) 'Special Issue: Methodological Dilemmas of Research', *British Journal of Criminology*, 41: 3.

Maguire, M., Morgan, R. and Reiner, R. (eds) (1997, 2002, 2007) *The Oxford Handbook of Criminology*, 2nd, 3rd and 4th edns, Oxford: Oxford University Press.

McIvor, G. (2004) 'Service with a Smile? Women and Community Punishment', in G. McIvor (ed.). *Women Who Offend*, London: Jessica Kingsley.

McIvor, G. (ed.) (2004) *Women Who Offend*, London: Jessica Kingsley.

Mannheim, H. (1965) *Comparative Criminology*, London: Routledge.

Messerschmidt, J. (2002) 'On Gang Girls, Gender and Structured Action Theory: A Reply to Miller', *Theoretical Criminology*, 6(4): 461–75.

Miller, J. (2002a) 'The Strengths and Limits of "Doing Gender" for Understanding Street Crime', *Theoretical Criminology*, 6(4): 433–60.

Miller, J. (2002b) 'Reply to Messerschmidt', *Theoretical Criminology*, 6(4): 477–80.

Naffine, N. (1997) *Feminism and Criminology*, Cambridge: Polity.

Ollus, N. and Nevala, S. (eds) (2001) *Women in the Criminal Justice System: International Examples*, Helsinki: HEUNI.

Rafter, N. and Heidensohn, F. (eds) (1995) *International Feminist Perspectives in Criminology*, Buckingham: Open University Press.

Rumgay, J. (2006) *Ladies of Lost Causes*, Toronto: de Sitter.

Shiner, M. (2005) Personal communication.

Silvestri, M. (2003) *Women in Charge*, Cullompton: Willan Publishing.

Smart, C. (1976) *Women, Crime and Criminology*, London: Routledge.

Snider, L. (2003) 'Constituting the Punishable Woman: Atavistic Man Incorporates Postmodern Woman', *British Journal of Criminology*, 2: 354–78.

Steffensmeier, D., Schwartz, J., Zhong. H. and Ackerman, J. (2005) 'An Assessment of Recent Trends in Girls' Violence Using Diverse Longitudinal Sources: Is the Gender Gap Closing?', *Criminology*, 43(2): 355–405.

Walklate, S. (2004) *Gender, Crime and Criminal Justice*, 2nd edn, Cullompton: Willan Publishing.

Wincup, E. *et al.* (2005) *Roundtable on Feminist Criminology*, British Society of Criminology Conference, Leeds University, July.

Worrall, A. (2004) 'Twisted Sisters, Ladettes, and the New Penology: The Social Construction of "Violent Girls"', in C. Alder and A. Worrall (eds) *Girls' Violence*, Albany: SUNY Press.

Zedner, L. (2007) 'Victims', in M. Maguire *et al.* (eds) *The Oxford Handbook of Criminology*, 4th edn, Oxford: Oxford University Press.

Introduction

Frances Heidensohn

The 'problem' of the gender gap in recorded crime rates was the stimulus to the earliest essays in feminist criminology (Heidensohn 1968). There were two aspects to be explained: why was there such a profound and extensive difference between female and male registered criminality and why had most criminologists, especially those of the modern era, largely ignored this? Not only had they failed to deal with this significant feature, they had also neglected women's offending *per se* (Heidensohn 1985).

Decades on from that initial critique, we can find, as outlined in Chapter 1, many accounts of female offending, and, increasingly, of male offending interpreted through a gender lens (Connell and Messerschmidt 2005). Debates about the gender gap are still current, but they have been enlivened by the older 'liberation causes crime' arguments, which now manifest themselves in more recent concerns about convergence.

Three of the chapters in this section contribute to these discussions. Mike Shiner challenges interpretations of data on drug use and suggests that the similarities between young men and women have been exaggerated. He notes the importance of 'domestic transitions' in young people's drug use. Kirstine Hansen too explores differences between female and male crime rates and provides a novel 'take' on the liberation and crime controversy (Adler 1975) by looking at women's increased entry into the labour market and its association with rising crime rates. Both of these studies are based on the secondary analysis of large data-sets and consider changes over time. Carrie Anne Myers' focus is on bullying in one school and draws on her detailed ethnography as well as on interviews. She does find some 'convergence' in that boys and girls admit to bullying and observes that mixed bullying is the most important of the forms she found.

All three authors make comparisons between males and females, a feature that has become much more common since the pioneer days of work on gender. Shiner and Hansen represent examples in Britain of another trend, characteristic of US work, of the use of large data sets for this kind of analysis (e.g. Steffensmeier *et al.* 2005, 2006; Heimer and Kruttschnitt 2006). Myers' school-based ethnography is more in keeping with earlier feminist work, although one of her findings, that boys were doubly victimised by bullying is not. Of course, Stanko and Hobdell (1993) recorded similar observations in their study of men as victims.

The remaining two contributions to this section are less directly comparative and raise the twin issues of stigma and of double deviance. Rachel Condry looks at a relatively unexplored area, that of the lives of the relatives of serious offenders and how they are affected by vicarious stigmatisation. Significantly, no doubt, she did not set out solely to study female relatives, but in practice found only women taking on supportive roles. Hers is an institutionally derived sample and required a great deal of time and patience on her part to gain the confidence of her subjects, making clear parallels with studies of female offenders (Heidensohn 1996).

Joanna Phoenix approaches the question of prostitution as a core theme in feminist scholarship and activism and argues that the regulation of the lives of women in prostitution is much deeper and more far-reaching in the twenty-first century than it was in the twentieth. She argues that official discourse, in employing the language of victimisation, has produced new definitions of the problems of prostitution, which place it almost entirely in relation to criminal men.

All five authors in this section add to our understanding of concepts and theory in the context of gender. Shiner challenges pioneers of feminist theory such as Smart and insists that postmodernism leads to misinterpretations of drug-taking. Hansen employs rational choice and economic theories in order to dissect links between labour markets and crime rates. Myers develops the notion of double victimisation in her portrayal of boys bullied at school. Condry extends the concept of stigma to encompass the relatives of serious offenders. Phoenix shows how problem (re)definition is the key to understanding how deviant women may be regulated. In sum, if the original debates to which all these scholars contribute are drawn from the agenda of the pioneer feminist criminology, they have equally explored, enhanced and contradicted them.

References

Adler, F. (1975) *Sisters in Crime*, New York: McGraw-Hill.

Connell, J. and Messerschmidt, J. (2005) 'Hegemonic Masculinity: Rethinking the Concept', *Gender and Society*, 19(6): 829–59.

Heidensohn, F. (1968) 'The Deviance of Women: A Critique and an Enquiry', *British Journal of Sociology*, 19(2): 160–75.

Heidensohn, F. (1985) *Women and Crime*, Basingstoke: Macmillan.

Heidensohn, F. (1996) *Women and Crime*, 2nd edn, Basingstoke: Macmillan.

Heimer, K. and Kruttschnitt, C. (eds) (2006) *Gender and Crime*, New York: New York University Press.

Stanko, B. and Hobdell, K. (1993) 'Assault on Men: Masculinity and Male Victims', *British Journal of Criminology*, 33(3): 400–15.

Steffensmeier, D., Schwartz, J., Zhong, H. and Ackerman, J. (2005) 'An Assessment of Recent Trends in Girls' Violence Using Diverse Longitudinal Sources: Is the Gender Gap Closing?', *Criminology*, 43(2): 355–405.

Steffensmeier, D., Schwartz, J., Zhong, H., Ackerman, J. and Agha, S. (2006) 'Gender Gap Trends for Violent Crimes, 1980 to 2003', *Feminist Criminology*, 1(1): 72–98.

Chapter 2

A dubious equality? Drug use and the discovery of gender

Michael Shiner

> Now the social climate surrounding drug use has changed so much that sniffing, swallowing and smoking powders, potions and pills at work, rest and at play has become part of 'having it all' for 'Cosmo girl' and many another 'modern girl' culture (or so we may well believe from media tales of fashion models, movie and pop stars and other representatives of 'girl power'). (Henderson 1999: 36)

The relationship between criminology and feminism has not been an easy one. For much of its history criminology was apparently oblivious to issues of gender, and women were neither seen nor heard. Unsurprisingly, such patriarchal arrangements came under fire with the rise of modern feminism and feminists began to engage with criminology on the basis that it needed to be changed (Gelsthorpe 2002; Heidensohn 2002). Thirty years on and criminology is certainly a very different subject from what it once was, but some feminists have been left frustrated by the direction it has taken and have called for a parting of the ways. Early feminist critiques, such as that offered by Carol Smart (1976), argued that women were largely invisible in most criminological work and that where they did appear they were portrayed in a stereotypical manner that distorted and marginalised their experience. Of particular concern was the way that thinking about female deviance represented a 'throwback to the earliest stage of criminological evolution' (Downes and Rock 2003: 294), which focused on biological or psychological 'nature' and ignored any rational or purposive motivations. Concern about the invisibility or misrepresentation of women's experiences have remained central to feminist perspectives and it has been argued that the shortcomings of 'mainstream' criminology cannot be remedied by simply 'inserting' women into theories that were formed on a patriarchal basis (Gelsthorpe and Morris 1988). While some feminists have continued to work within criminology, others have called for an abandoning of the subject on the grounds that it has little to offer feminism. Those who have urged such a move have tended to be drawn towards postmodernism, which they consider to be more consistent with feminist goals (Smart 1990; Young 1994).

In the course of this chapter I will reflect on some of the main themes to emerge from feminist dialogues with criminology by focusing on illicit drug use. I will begin by considering relevant theoretical developments before going on to consider some key empirical questions. The concluding section will assess the broader implications for feminist perspectives and criminology.

Criminology and the sociology of drug use

The sociology of drug use first came to prominence in the 1960s and early 1970s, with the rise of new deviancy theories. These theories presented a serious and sustained challenge to the 'correctionalist' orientation of 'mainstream' criminology and dismissed the idea that there was a distinct, unambiguously deviant, minority whose behaviour could be explained as a result of individual pathology or social dysfunction (Matza 1969). Rejecting their allocated role as assistants in the quest to free society from 'troublesome activities', new deviancy theorists advocated an 'appreciative' stance that was committed to faithful representation and understanding the world as it is seen by the subject. In terms of their substantive interests, these theorists frequently expressed unease about the extension of social control into morally ambiguous areas and tended to focus on examples of rule-breaking which were designed to elicit a liberal response (Cohen 1971). As a 'victimless crime' drug use was ideally suited to their wider purpose.

Howard Becker was a hugely influential figure in the development of new deviancy theories, and, in the *Outsiders* (1963) produced one of the two most widely cited American criminological writings of the time (Downes and Rock 2003). Reflecting his experiences as a jazz musician and activist in the campaign to legalise marijuana, Becker devoted two chapters of *Outsiders* to the moral career of the marijuana user, each of which was based on interviews with 50 users, half of whom were professional musicians. Becker rejected the idea that marijuana use could be explained in terms of particular psychological traits and developed the hypothesis that users learn to view marijuana as something that can give them pleasure. In doing so he showed how users have to contend with powerful forces of social control and how participation in the user group helps to disable these attempts at control.

Becker's work helped set the tone for much of the early sociology of drug use. His emphasis on subcultural perspectives was developed by Harold Finestone (1964), while his focus on social control was continued by Edwin Schur (1965) and Troy Duster (1970). More than anybody, however, it was Jock Young who most fully realised the implications that new deviancy theories had for illicit drug use. In *The Drugtakers*, Young mounted a sustained attack on the 'absolutist' monolith that dominated contemporary understandings and viewed drug use as a disease that spread on the basis of individual pathology and social dysfunction. Among other things, Young objected to the way that such perspectives reduced individual motivation to a set of symptoms and ignored the functional and meaningful nature of such behaviour. Drawing on the work of Matza and Sykes (1961), Young argued that drug use does not exist outside of the conventional value system, but may be readily understood in terms of widely accepted 'subterranean' values, which emphasise excitement, spontaneity and individuality. What was particularly distinctive about Young's analysis was the way it linked subterranean values to the broader political economy of 'late industrial' or 'post-industrial' societies. Subterranean values were held to be identical to the customary definition of play and were contrasted with formal values, which were said to be consistent with the structure of modern industry because they served to maintain diligent, repetitive work and assist the realisation of long-term productive goals. Rather than forming isolated moral regions, however, these value systems were considered to be mutually dependent upon one another, albeit with subterranean values being subsumed under the ethos of productivity (Young 1971: 128):

Leisure is concerned with consumption and work with production; a keynote of our bifurcated society, therefore, is that individuals within it must constantly consume in order to keep pace with the productive capacity of the economy. They must produce in order to consume, and consume in order to produce.

According to the dominant ethos of productivity subterranean values can only be expressed legitimately if the individual has earned the right to do so by working hard and being productive. Young people provide something of an exception to this general rule, however, because they are in the privileged position of not having to justify their play through productivity, though they are expected to invest in their future through education and training.

Based on the distinction between formal and subterranean values, Young (1971: 124) argued that drug use can be readily explained in terms of 'factors existing in wider society'. Not only was the use of 'psychotropic' drugs described as being 'almost ubiquitous in our society' but it was also considered to provide a 'vehicle which enhances the ease of transition from the world of formal values to the world of subterranean values' (1971: 135). The type and quality of drugs used were thought to vary, however, and a key distinction was drawn between alcohol and other psychotropic drugs. While alcohol was commonly used to gain access to that area of subterranean values that is typically subsumed under the cycle of productivity, other drugs offered a route to 'more radical accentuations of subterranean reality' (1971: 137).

Although new deviancy theories were presented as a radical alternative to 'mainstream' criminology they were criticised for replicating some of the shortcomings of established perspectives. In particular, feminist commentators were quick to point to the continued invisibility of women in these accounts (Heidensohn 1989). In a pointed criticism of Becker's work, for example, Marcia Millman (1982: 260) noted that he 'certainly never asked the wives of jazz musicians what they thought about their husbands' occupations, much less quoted them as authorities on the subject'.

Postmodernity and the discovery of gender

New deviancy theories enjoyed a relatively brief period of ascendancy within British criminology, before being supplanted by neo-Marxist concerns about the link between capitalism and crime (Downes 1988). Expressive deviance was considered peripheral to such weighty concerns and drug use attracted little sociological interest until the arrival of 'rave' in the late 1980s and early 1990s. By itself, it has been suggested, 'rave culture has revitalised the sociological literature on youth culture, and in particular has provoked a revisionist view of its history challenging the hegemony of the key writers of previous decades' (Shapiro 1999: 18). The same might be said in relation to the sociology of drug use, as recent contributions to this field have been consciously distanced from what came before. Most notably, given the current context, these contributions have broken away from criminology and have included an explicit focus on gender.

The call for new perspectives has been developed most fully by Howard Parker, Fiona Measham and Judith Aldridge, who have argued that existing explanations have 'simply been left behind by the pace of social and behavioural change' (Parker *et al.* 1998: 20–21). Recreational drug use, they note, has become too widespread to be explained convincingly in terms of psychosocial disorders or alienated youth subcultures. Rather, such behaviour is said to be undergoing a process of normalisation, whereby it is moving from the margins to the mainstream of British youth culture. In developing this thesis, Parker *et al.* (1995: 25) have distanced their analysis from previous formulations by rejecting subcultural theory and linking normalisation to the onset of postmodernity, suggesting that 'perhaps drugs *consumption* best depicts what is under way; for illegal drugs have become products which are grown, manufactured, packaged and marketed through an enterprise culture whereby the legitimate and illicit markets have merged'.

Normalisation, it is claimed, has undermined the distinct profile once associated with drug use. Boundaries between users and non-users are said to have been blurred by the rapid closure of the 'gender gap' and the disintegration of traditional class distinctions. Young women experiment with drugs in similar numbers to young men; being 'middle class' no longer predicts school-based abstinence; and being 'black' or 'Asian' does not predict higher than average rates of adolescent drug use. As such, 'the withering of traditional sociological predictor variables is in political terms, 'the most challenging aspect of normalisation' (Parker *et al.* 1998: 154).

Recent developments in the sociology of drug use have also seen the emergence of explicitly feminist perspectives. Drawing on a mixture of postmodern theory and traditional feminist concerns about the marginalisation and misrepresentation of women's experiences, these perspectives have sought to give women a 'voice' (Hinchcliff 2001). In a neat summation of the feminist critique, Sheila Henderson (1999: 37) argued:

This, predominantly medical and psychological, literature presented a picture of drug use in which drug users just happened to be male (if you bothered to notice) and women hardly figured. When they did, they appeared as sicker, more deviant, more psychologically disturbed than their male peers: as weak and pathetic creatures. Women's drug use figured as a 'deviation' from 'normal' femininity due to mental or physical deficiencies, or disease.

When Henderson (1999: 41) began to examine the relationship between gender and drug use in the context of dance culture in the early 1990s she was faced by a 'somewhat empty tool-kit': the young women who participated in dance events were 'like the chalk to the cheese of the prevailing images of femininity within other studies of drug use'. This mismatch, it was argued, highlighted the need for new perspectives which allowed for the possibility that women are active social agents and not merely passive subjects of male power. As a counterpoint to the puritanical (female) victim mentality, feminist perspectives have tended to emphasise similarities between male and female drug use. Thus we are told that women 'have achieved the (dubious) equality of consuming as many illegal mind-changing substances as the next man' (Henderson 1999: 36); have 'participated in dance events as often as men' (Hinchcliff 2001: 456); and 'use drugs in ways which have previously been considered predominantly male' (Hinchcliff 2001: 466). In their attempts to explain this apparent equality, feminist commentators have drawn on developments in cultural studies, arguing that certain types of drug use can best be understood as a form of consumption. Where traditional explanations of women's drug use emphasised coercion and unhappiness, recent feminist accounts have emphasised choice and pleasure. Young women, we are told, do not use drugs in the context of dance culture because they are forced to by men and nor are they leading unhappy lives as result. They are, rather, 'self-confident' women who choose to use drugs as part of a lifestyle that involves a commitment to consumption and mass pleasure-seeking and through which they make sense of their place in the world (Henderson 1999; Hinchcliff 2001).

Surveying the gender gap

National surveys of drug use have been conducted routinely by the Home Office since the early 1990s. The British Crime Survey has included detailed questions about such behaviour since 1992 and provides the principal basis on which the government monitors trends in use (see, for example, Ramsay and Percy 1996; Roe 2005). Similar questions were also included in the 1992/93 and 1998/99 Youth Lifestyles Survey (Graham and Bowling 1995; Flood-Page *et al.* 2000). The following analysis is based largely on the 1998 BCS and 1998/99 YLS and it is important to note, at the outset, that levels of drug use have remained remarkably stable since these surveys were conducted (see Roe 2005). Although the BCS and YLS share a similar methodology they cover different sections of the population. The BCS is an adult survey, which typically collects drug use data from 16 to 59 year olds, while the 1998/99 YLS focused on 12 to 30 year olds. Reflecting the focus of recent debates about gender and drug use, the following analysis concentrates on young adults' use of 'recreational' drugs. For the purposes of this paper, young adults are defined as those aged 16 to 30 years, while the term 'recreational' drugs refers to cannabis, the hallucinants[1] and cocaine.

The 1998 BCS and 1998/99 YLS confirmed that illicit drug use has become fairly widespread among young women, while also pointing to significant differences between the sexes (see Table 2.1). Approximately one and a half times as many young men as young women had recently used cannabis, twice as many had recently used a hallucinant and two or three times as many had recently used cocaine. Less striking differences were evident in relation to

Table 2.1 Prevalence of drug use among young adults by sex (percentages)

	Cannabis			Hallucinants			Cocaine			
	Never	Past	Recent	Never	Past	Recent	Never	Past	Recent	*n*
BCS		**			**			**		
Male	49	22	29	66	20	14	92	4	4	*1137*
Female	63	20	17	78	15	7	96	2	2	*1688*
YLS		**			**			**		
Male	44	19	37	58	23	19	86	6	9	*1570*
Female	57	19	24	72	18	10	94	3	3	*1887*

Source: BCS (1998) and YLS (1998/99) ** p < .01
Note: Recent drug use refers to that which had taken place during the previous 12 months, while past use refers to that which had taken place at an earlier time.

past use although the ratio of past to recent users does suggest that female users were more likely to have stopped using drugs than male users. Further analysis confirmed the statistical significance of these differences in relation to cannabis and the hallucinants, though not cocaine.[2]

Although drug use continues to be less prevalent among young women than young men it is possible that gender differences have become less marked over time. Some sense of whether this is the case can be gained by comparing the various sweeps of the BCS. The 1992 sweep found that almost one and a half times as many males as females in the 16 to 29 age group had used an illicit drug at some point and that almost twice as many had done so in the previous 12 months (Mott and Mirrlees-Black 1995). Subsequent sweeps have continued to report very similar differences and this suggests that the gender gap is a long-standing and fairly stable feature of early adulthood.[3] The lack of comparable data prior to the early 1990s clearly creates difficulties in assessing possible changes

Figure 2.1 Prevalence of drug use by age and sex (percentage that ever used cannabis, the hallucinants and/or cocaine)

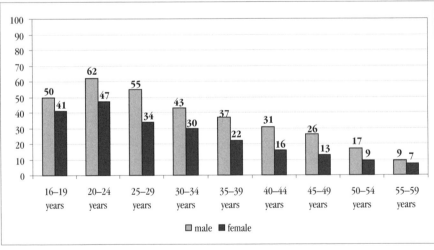

$n = 9,805$

Source: BCS (1998)

Note: Differences between the sexes were statistically significant for all age groups except 55-59 year olds (p < .05 for 16-19 year olds; p < .01 for each group in the 20-54 age range and p > .05 for 55-59 year olds).

over a longer period, but recent surveys can be used to make some comments about the nature of likely changes over time. Assuming that most people who use drugs do so during adolescence and early adulthood – and all the indications are that they do – then changes over time will be reflected in differences between age cohorts (Shiner and Newburn 1999). If the gender gap has closed in the way that some commentators suggest then differences between the sexes should be most marked among older groups and then converge sharply among younger groups. The results of the 1998 BCS did not follow this pattern, however, but pointed instead to a similar general trend among males and females (see Figure 2.1). The ratio of male to female users did vary between 1.2 and 2.0 depending on age, but these variations were not consistent with a sudden narrowing of the gender gap. Further analysis confirmed that the relationship between drug use and age was similar for males and females.[4]

Drugs, gender and early adult transitions

The observation that crime is mostly committed by young people has prompted suggestions that any theory of criminal offending should seek to explain how such behaviour fits with the life course, from infancy to old age (Smith 2002). It is precisely this that John Laub and Robert Sampson have sought to explain in their 'age-graded theory of informal social control' (Sampson and Laub 1993; Laub and Sampson 2003). In essence, Laub and Sampson argue that persistent offending is explained by a lack of social controls, few structured routine activities and purposeful human agency, while desistance from such behaviour is explained by a confluence of social controls, structured routine activities and purposeful human agency. Drawing on the work of new deviancy theorists, such as David Matza and Howard Becker, crime is considered to be a vehicle for demonstrating freedom and agency – it is purposeful, systematic and meaningful, attractive because it offers a source of excitement. At the same time, however, Laub and Sampson maintain that these 'agential processes' are reciprocally linked to situations and larger structures: that is to say, situations and structures are considered to be partly determined by the choices that individuals make, yet simultaneously constrain, modify and limit the choices that are available to them. Because situations are said to vary in the extent to which they constrain behavioural choices, persistence and desistance from crime are considered to be the result of 'situated choice'. More specifically,

Laub and Sampson argue that desistance is facilitated by 'turning points' or changes in situational and structural life circumstances. A good marriage or a stable job are said to have the potential to reshape life-course trajectories by reordering short-term situational inducements to crime and redirecting long-term commitments to conformity. While emphasising the importance of social ties across all stages of the life-course, Laub and Sampson note that the influence of social bonds varies with age and life experiences and that social controls become more salient as people get older. It follows, therefore, that adolescence is a time of relative freedom. The bonds that tie children to family and school have weakened and are yet to be replaced by a new set of adult relationships and associated commitments. As a result young people are generally less constrained during this phase of the life-course than at any other time and are freer to engage in acts of delinquency and deviance (see also Coleman and Hendry 1999).

It is particularly noteworthy, given the current context, that Laub and Sampson's empirical analysis was based on an exclusively male sample. Despite this, their theory has considerable potential as a means of explaining some notable differences between male and female offending.

Females are generally considered to mature more quickly than males and tend to adopt explicitly adult roles at an earlier age, particularly within the domestic sphere (Coleman and Hendry 1999; Rutter et al. 1998). Both the 1998 BCS and 1998/99 YLS confirmed that women tend to leave the parental home and form families of their own at a younger age than men.[5] One in ten women in the 18 to 22 age group were either married or were cohabiting and had children, compared to 1 in 30 or 1 in 50 men, depending on the survey. Many men do appear to 'settle down' during the course of their mid-to-late twenties, however, and this results in much less marked differences between the sexes. Both surveys found that almost half the men in the 27 to 30 age group were either married or were cohabiting, with children, which was only marginally less than the proportion of women. A further one in four men in this age group were cohabiting (without children) and/or buying their own home. Crucially, therefore, most men make significant moves towards adulthood during the course of their twenties, but tend to take longer to complete them than women.

In view of these differences, it is perhaps unsurprising that men appear to 'grow out of crime' more slowly than women. The peak age of offending for males is generally higher than for females (Newburn

2002) and this disparity has been linked to early adult transitions. Based on the 1992 YLS, Graham and Bowling (1995) note that the proportion of females who were actively involved in offending began to decline from the late teens onwards, and that for women desistance was closely associated with leaving home and school, forming partnerships and new families and becoming economically independent. The situation among males was rather less clear-cut. On the one hand, men in their early twenties committed fewer and less serious offences than their teenage counterparts, but relatively few of them had stopped offending altogether. Overall, the proportion of males who were actively involved in offending remained fairly stable across the 14 to 25 year age range and appeared to be relatively unaffected by the vicissitudes of early adulthood: 'Thus, it appears to be the case that not only do many young men fail to successfully make the transition to adulthood by their mid-twenties', but 'those who do appear to be no more likely to desist than those who do not' (Graham and Bowling 1995: 64–5). Similar analysis, conducted on the basis of the 1998/99 YLS, reinforced the conclusion that women 'grow out' of crime at an earlier age than men although it also indicated that the proportion of men who were actively involved in offending began to decline from the age of 22 years (Flood-Page et al. 2000).

Drug use was specifically excluded from these analyses, but certain similarities were noted between this and other forms of offending. The 1992 YLS indicated that the proportion of females who used illicit drugs peaked among 17 year olds, but then fell away quite sharply, while the proportion of males who engaged in such behaviour continued to increase up to the age of 20, before falling away at a more modest rate (Graham and Bowling 1995). As a result of these differences, male users were found to outnumber female users from the age of 18, though not before. A similar pattern was noted on the basis of the 1992 BCS, which extended the usual adult sample to include 12 to 15 year olds (Mott and Mirrlees-Black 1995). When the same basic pattern was identified by the 1998/99 YLS it was suggested that females 'grow out' of drug use, as well as other forms of 'anti-social behaviour', at an earlier age than males (Flood-Page et al. 2000; and see Figure 2.2).

For all the claims that have been made about normalisation and the closing gender gap, moreover, the North West Cohort Study actually found that gender differences began to emerge as members of the cohort entered early adulthood (Parker et al. 1998; Williams and Parker 2001). At 14 and 15 years of age the proportion of males and females who had used illicit drugs in the last month was very

Figure 2.2 Prevalence of recent drug use by age and sex (percentage that used cannabis, the hallucinants and/or cocaine in the last 12 months)

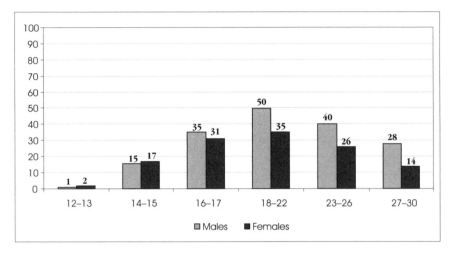

Source: YLS (1998) $n = 4,585$

Notes

1 Differences between the sexes were not statistically significant among 12 to 17 year olds (p > .05 for each group), but were significant among 18 to 30 year olds (p < .01 for each group).

2 Similar differences were evident from the 1998 BCS. Male users outnumbered female users by three-to-two among 18 to 22 year olds (p < .01), two-to-one among 23 to 26 year olds (p < .01) and almost three-to-one among 27 to 30 year olds (p < .01). Once again, differences among 16 and 17 year olds were not significant (p > .05).

similar, but notable differences began to emerge thereafter. At 18 years of age, 45 per cent of males and 28 per cent of females had used drugs in the last month and at 21 years of age 39 per cent and 25 per cent had done so respectively.

Further analysis indicated that this emerging gender gap can be readily understood in the context of early adult transitions. Multivariate models based on the 1998 BCS and 1998/99 YLS indicated that age and domestic circumstances were significantly associated with drug use independently of one another and a range of other variables.[6] Getting older and 'settling down' both tended to reduce the probability of recent drug use and increased the probability of desistance. Crucially, these effects were found to be similar regardless of sex.[7] Most notably, perhaps, forming stable partnerships that were reinforced by marriage and/or shared parental responsibilities reduced the probability of drug use for both males and females. What did vary, however, was the timing of these developments and this helps to explain the appearance of a gender gap during early adulthood. Most men do not get married or have children until after their mid-twenties and this provides the basis for an extended adolescence, which leaves considerable room for illicit drug use. Women's lifestyle choices appear to be rather more limited by comparison because they tend to 'settle down' more quickly, thereby establishing a domestic context that is less conducive to such behaviour.

Conclusion

The analysis presented in this chapter highlights the need for gendered perspectives in relation to illicit drug use but also raises important questions about the nature of such perspectives. It is a slightly curious feature of recent accounts that the discovery of gender has been accompanied by an emphasis on the similarities between male and female drug use. Thus we have been told that the normalisation of drug use has been accompanied by a rapid closure of the gender gap and that young women use drugs at a similar rate to young men and for broadly similar reasons. On close inspection, national drugs surveys confirm that recreational drug use is fairly widespread among young women but also point to a continuing gender gap. The proportion of males and females who use drugs is very similar up to the age of 17 years or so, at which point male users begin to outnumber female users. As such, it seems that females 'grow out' of drug use, as well as other forms of offending, at an earlier age than males. The challenge for gendered perspectives, therefore, is to explain both the similarities and differences between male and female drug use.

Criminology has more to offer in this context than many might think. Recent developments in the sociology of drug use, including the emergence of gendered perspectives, have been strongly influenced by postmodern theory and have largely broken away from criminology. The need for, and desirability of, this move remains unclear, however, and may be challenged on a number of grounds. Most of the key postmodern themes were pre-empted by new deviancy theories (Cohen 1997; Young 1999) and, by extension, much that has recently been written about drug use can be found in earlier work. The rejection of explanations that view deviance as the result of individual pathology or social dysfunction, the emphasis on the meaningful and purposive nature of such behaviour, and the focus on consumption and pleasure-seeking were all central to the work of new deviancy theorists and to related developments in the early sociology of drug use. Given the gender-blindness of this earlier work, feminist perspectives have clearly made an important contribution to our understanding of drug use, but this contribution could have been made within the framework of existing theories. Where recently developed perspectives struggle to account for differences between male and female drug use, moreover, life-course criminology appears to offer a basis for explaining such differences. As noted by Downes and Rock (2003: 313), 'older, apparently male-centred theories have a good deal of utility in explaining female crime' and are more relevant to the pursuit of feminist criminologists than is generally recognised. As such, it seems that criminology and feminism have rather more to offer one another than is often supposed.

Notes

1 The term hallucinants was coined by Ramsay and Percy (1996) to refer to those drugs that are most closely associated with the 'dance' scene and includes ecstasy, amphetamines, LSD, magic mushrooms and amyl nitrate.

2 Non-users were excluded from these analyses in order to assess the desistance rate. What was being compared, therefore, was the proportion of users who had last used a particular drug or set of drugs over a year ago.

3 Five separate sweeps of the BCS were carried out between 1992 and 2000 and on each occasion detailed information was published about the extent of drug use among young adults aged 16 to 29 (see Ramsay and Percy 1996; Ramsay and Spiller 1997; Ramsay and Partridge 1999; Ramsay et al. 2001). Each of these sweeps indicated that for every young woman who had ever used illicit drugs there were 1.3 or 1.4 young men who had done so. The corresponding figure for recent use hovered between 1.5 and 1.8. A similar figure of 1.6 was produced by the 2004/05 BCS although this was not directly comparable with the earlier figures because it was based on a slightly narrower age range, made up of 16 to 24 year olds (Roe 2005).

4 Logistic regression was used to specify a model with drug use as the dependent variable and age and sex as the independent variables. An Interaction term was included between the independent variables and showed that the effects associated with age did not vary significantly by sex.

5 Both surveys indicated that there were significant differences in the domestic circumstances of men and women aged 18 to 22 years, 23 to 26 years and 27 to 30 years (p < .01 for each age group). No such differences were evident among 16 or 17 year olds, the vast majority of whom were living with their parents (p > .05).

6 This analysis concentrated on young adults aged 16 to 30 years and was based on a multinomial logistic regression procedure. Separate models were developed for cannabis, the hallucinants and cocaine and each model distinguished between non-use, past use and recent use. A range of independent or predictor variables were included in the models, which related to demographic characteristics (age, sex, ethnicity, etc.), lifestyle choices (participation in the night-time economy, drinking style, etc.) and life course characteristics (work status, domestic circumstances, etc.). These models indicated that age and domestic circumstances were significant predictors of drug use. Work status had less of an effect although there was some evidence that unemployment and other forms of marginalisation from the labour market increased the probability of recent drug use (Shiner 2006).

7 A series of interaction terms were included in the models which formally tested whether age and domestic circumstances had a significantly different effect on men than women.

References

Becker, H. S. (1963) *Outsiders: Studies in the Sociology of Deviance*, London: Macmillan.

Cohen, S. (1971) *Images of Deviance*, Harmondsworth: Penguin.

Cohen, S. (1997) 'Intellectual Scepticism and Political Commitment', in P. Walton and J. Young (eds) *The New Criminology Revisited*, London: Macmillan.

Coleman, J.C. and Hendry, L. (1999) *The Nature of Adolescence*, London: Routledge.

Downes, D. (1988) 'The Sociology of Crime and Social Control in Britain, 1960–1987', *British Journal of Criminology*, 28(2): 175–187.

Downes, D. and Rock, P. (2003) *Understanding Deviance*, Oxford: Oxford University Press.

Duster, T. (1970) *The Legalisation of Morality*, New York: The Free Press.

Finestone, H. (1964) 'Cats, Kicks and Colour', in H. Becker (ed.) *The Other Side*, New York: Free Press.

Flood-Page, C., Campbell, S., Harrington, V., and Miller, J. (2000) *Youth Crime: Findings from the 1998/1999 Youth Lifestyles Survey*, London: Home Office.

Gelsthorpe, L. (2002) 'Feminism and Criminology', in M. Maguire, R. Morgan and R. Reiner (eds) *The Oxford Handbook of Criminology*, 3rd edn, Oxford: Oxford University Press.

Gelsthorpe, L. and Morris, A. (1988) 'Feminism and Criminology in Britain', *British Journal of Criminology*, 28(2): 93–110.

Graham, J. and Bowling, B. (1995) *Young People and Crime*, London: Home Office.

Heidensohn, F. (1989) *Crime and Society*, London: Macmillan.

Heidensohn, F. (2002) 'Gender and Crime', in M. Maguire, R. Morgan and R. Reiner (eds) *The Oxford Handbook of Criminology*, 3rd edn, Oxford: Oxford University Press.

Henderson, S. (1999) 'The Question of Gender', in N. South (ed.) *Drugs: Cultures, Controls and Everyday Life*, London: Sage.

Hinchcliff, S. (2001) 'The Meaning of Ecstasy Use and Clubbing to Women in the late 1990s', *International Journal of Drug Policy*, 12: 455–68.

Laub, J. H. and Sampson, R. J. (2003) *Shared Beginnings, Divergent Lives: Delinquent Boys to Age 70*, Cambridge, MA: Harvard University Press.

Matza, D. (1969) *Becoming Deviant*, Englewood Cliffs, NJ: Prentice-Hall.

Matza, D. and Sykes, G.M. (1961) 'Juvenile Delinquency and Subterranean Values', *American Sociological Review*, 26: 712–19.

Millman, M. (1982) 'Images of Deviant Men and Women', in M. Evans (ed.) *The Women Question*, London: Fontana.

Mott, J. and Mirrlees-Black, C. (1995) *Self-reported Drug Misuse in England and Wales: Findings from the 1992 BCS*, London: Home Office.

Newburn, T. (2002) 'Young People, Crime and Youth Justice', in M. Maguire, R. Morgan and R. Reiner (eds) *The Oxford Handbook of Criminology*, 3rd edn, Oxford: Oxford University Press.

Parker, H., Aldridge, J., and Measham, F. (1998) *Illegal Leisure: The Normalization of Adolescent Recreational Drug Use*, London: Routledge.

Parker, H., Measham, F., and Aldridge, J. (1995) *Drugs Futures: Changing Patterns of Drug Use Amongst English Youth*, London: Institute for the Study of Drug Dependence.

Ramsay, M. and Partridge, S. (1999) *Drug Misuse Declared in 1998: Results From the British Crime Survey*, London: Home Office.

Ramsay, M. and Percy, A. (1996) *Drug Misuse Declared: Results of the 1994 British Crime Survey*, London: Home Office.

Ramsay, M. and Spiller, A. (1997) *Drug Misuse Declared: Results of the 1996 British Crime Survey*, London: Home Office.

Ramsay, M., Baker, P., Goulden, C., Sharp, C., and Sondhi, A. (2001) *Drug Misuse Declared in 2000: Results From the British Crime Survey*, London: Home Office.

Roe, S. (2005) *Drug Misuse Declared: Findings from the 2004/5 British Crime Survey*, London: Home Office.

Rutter, M., Giller, H., and Hagell, A. (1998) *Antisocial Behaviour by Young People*, Cambridge: Cambridge University Press.

Sampson, R. J. and Laub, J. H. (1993) *Crime in the Making: Pathways and Turning Points Through Life*, Cambridge, MA: Harvard University Press.

Schur, E. (1965) *Crimes Without Victims*, Englewood Cliffs, NJ: Prentice Hall.

Shapiro, H. (1999) 'Dances with Drugs: Pop Music, Drugs and Youth Culture', in N. South (ed.) *Drugs: Cultures, Controls and Everyday Life*, London: Sage.

Shiner, M. (2006) *Drug Use and Social Change: Secondary Analysis of the British Crime Survey (1994–8) and Youth Lifestyle Survey (1998)*, unpublished PhD Thesis, London School of Economics and Political Science.

Shiner, M. and Newburn, T. (1999) 'Taking Tea With Noel: The Place and Meaning of Drug Use in Everyday Life', in N. South (ed.) *Drugs: Cultures, Controls and Everyday Life*, London: Sage.

Smart, C. (1976) *Women, Crime and Criminology*, London: Routledge and Kegan Paul.

Smart, C. (1990) 'Feminist Approaches to Criminology or Postmodern Woman Meets Atavistic Man', in L. Gelsthorpe and A. Morris (eds) *Feminist Perspectives in Criminology*, Buckingham: Open University Press.

Smith, D.J. (2002) 'Crime and the Life Course', in M. Maguire, R. Morgan, and R. Reiner (eds) *The Oxford Handbook of Criminology*, 3rd edn, Oxford: Oxford University Press.

Williams, L. and Parker, H. (2001) 'Alcohol, Cannabis, Ecstasy and Cocaine: Drugs of Reasoned Choice Among Young Adult Recreational Drug Users in England', *International Journal of Drug Policy*, 12: 397–413.

Young, A. (1994) 'Feminism and the Body of Criminology', in D. Farrington and S. Walklate (eds) *Offenders and Victims: Theory and Policy*, London: British Society of Criminology and ISTD.

Young, J. (1971) *The Drugtakers: The Social Meaning of Drug Use*, London: MacGibbon & Kee.

Young, J. (1999) *The Exclusive Society: Social Exclusion, Crime and Difference in Late Modernity*, London: Sage.

Chapter 3

Gender differences in self-reported offending

Kirstine Hansen

Introduction

'The associations between gender and crime are profound, persistent, and paradoxical. For as long as observation of offending has been made, it has been noted that men and women differ in their offence rates and patterns' (Heidensohn 2002: 491). Criminologists have long been interested in examining the different propensities with which males and females commit crime. Indeed, the gap in offending between males and females has been the focus of much empirical and theoretical criminology. Early feminists theorised that as the position of women changed over time we would see a shift in the gender gap in offending. However, as criminologists applied these theories to empirical analyses they have been unable to account for either the gender gap in offending or the relatively static nature of the gender gap over time. Gender-specific theories, developed later to address these specific concerns, have fared little better and questions concerning the gender gap in offending, posed decades ago, remain key in modern criminology (Heidensohn 2002). It is an examination of the gender gap in self-reported offending that constitutes the main focus of this chapter.

Early theories were based on the idea that as the position of women improved their rate of offending would alter and the gender gap in offending would shift. Since then there has been a large increase in the relative position of women in society. Their employment rate has increased (Hansen 2006), the gap between male and female earnings has reduced (Harkness 1996; Blau and Kahn 1997, 2000) and girls are now out-performing boys at most stages of the education sequence (Machin and McNally 2005). At the same time, trends in family structures have seen later marriages, rising divorce rates, the increase of births outside of marriage, the growth of single-parent families and an increase in female-headed households.

We would usually think (as the early criminologists in this area did) that changes like those described above would result in a shift in the crime rate, because factors such as education, employment, income and family have been found to be strong predictors of criminal involvement (Gould *et al.* 2002; Hansen 2003; Hansen and Machin 2002, 2006; Lochner and Moretti 2004; Machin and Meghir 2004). As changes in these determinants of crime are likely to differentially affect men and women, we would expect to see shifts in the propensity of men and women to offend. As a result we would expect to see movement in the gender gap in offending over time.

This chapter uses data on self-reported offending to look at shifts in the gender gap in offending over time. The analysis shows no consistent pattern over time in the aggregate gender gap, but finds both increases and decreases in the gender gap for certain groups of people. The results highlight the fact that if we are interested in examining the gender gap in offending we need to look at specific groups of women (and men) who are likely to be differentially affected by changes in society and are also differentially likely to offend.

Why would we expect to see a movement in the gender gap in offending?

Predictions as to what might happen to the gender gap in offending, when there are changes in the relative economic and social conditions faced by males and females thought to be correlated with offending, have been put forward by criminologists since at least the 1950s. Early work in this area argued that equality for women would result in shifts in female participation in crime (Smart 1977). As their position improved in society and they gained mobility, power and confidence, women would develop attitudes traditionally thought to be more masculine, such as risk-taking and competitiveness, which are positively related to crime (Adler 1975; Simon 1975). In societies where women have reduced the gap between themselves and men in other arenas we would therefore expect to see relatively small gender gaps in offending.

While this theory is largely considered outdated and even disproved (Chesney-Lind 2006; Smart 1979; Steffensmeier 1995), other theories also predict that as female positions in society shift, so too does female involvement in crime. Some of these theories relate to female success in the labour market, others to changes in the family and the interaction of the two areas. For example, from a criminal opportunities perspective increasing female employment rates and a growing female presence in the public sphere is associated with increased opportunities to offend outside the home and to establish networks and contacts that may facilitate criminal interactions.

Others argue that employment not only brings opportunities for women but also increased responsibilities as earners and providers. This is particularly true in recent periods where later marriages, increasing divorce rates and the rise in births outside of marriage have resulted in the growth of female-headed households – where women are the sole or main contributor to the family income. The responsibility that accompanies the need to achieve financial success and security for their families, it is argued, places increased strain (Merton 1957) on women that in the past was confined to the male breadwinner. In addition to this economic strain women in today's society are likely to experience greater role strain (Berger 1989; Dubeck and Dunn 2002) where women have trouble maintaining a sense of identity and self when their roles change, but norms regarding the appropriate behaviour of women do not or change at a slower pace (Bianchi 1995).

Control theories (Hirschi 1969) have also been used to predict a reduced gender gap in crime in modern society. Steffensmeier *et al.* (2006) argue that the deterioration of control mechanisms such as the family and community, which have been correlated with male crime in the past, may now be having a lagged effect on female crime. Indeed, later marriages, rising divorce rates and relatively high levels of single-mother households may affect female crime more than male crime as females are the ones who predominantly take responsibility for the home sphere, even when they are also working (Lundberg 2005).

These theories all predict that changes in the position of women witnessed over the last 30 or 40 years should result in women committing more crime than in the past, leading to a reduction in the gender gap in offending over time. However, rational choice theory (Becker 1968; Ehrlich 1973) predicts the very opposite. As women become more successful in terms of their education and labour market status they will commit less crime because economic success is negatively related to crime.

All these theories predict a shift in female crime that would either reduce or increase the gender gap in offending. Their predictions do not appear to be borne out by the empirical evidence, which finds relatively little movement in the gap between male and female offending rates over time (Barclay 1995; Hansen 2006; Heidensohn 2002; Steffensmeier *et al.* 2006).

The need to look beneath the surface

Failure to observe shifts in the aggregate gender gap in offending, despite changes in factors considered to be determinants of crime, does not mean that shifts in these factors have no impact on crime. Indeed, a large body of literature has repeatedly found that education (Hansen 2003; Lochner 2004), employment (or unemployment) (Cook and Zarkin 1985; Land *et al.* 1990) and wages (Gould *et al.* 2002; Hansen and Machin 2002, 2006; Machin and Meghir 2004) are robust determinants of crime. It may just be that treating all women as a homogeneous group and expecting to see shifts in the rate of offending of this group compared to all males is misleading. First, it ignores what is happening to men and the male crime rate, and second by looking at the relative stability of the gender gap in offending in the aggregate picture, specific relationships for certain groups of men and women are lost.

The changes that have been occurring in the family, in education and in the labour market are extremely unlikely to have affected women but had no impact on men. Indeed, while there has been a lot of attention paid to the fact that women have made gains in terms of education, employment and income, there has been relatively little attention to the fact that, in relative terms, where there are winners there are also losers. And in a number of places women's gains have been made at the cost of men.

Recent patterns of change in the labour market[1] shifted the focus of the economy away from manufacturing and towards the service sector. This not only created increased demand for women (Blumberg 1978; Hakim 1992, 1998; Huber 1990; Oppenheimer 1970, 1973) but also forced a number of men to seek employment in a sector where they had to compete with women, sometimes for jobs that were traditionally thought of as female, such as check-out operators in supermarkets (Hakim 1998) and office staff. In this way, more women in the labour market has, in places, increased competition for jobs and certain men, particularly those in low-paid jobs, have seen relative declines in their wages (Hansen 2006). Lower male wages, particularly for those men at the bottom of the employment structure, are positively associated with male crime (Hansen 2006).

Moreover, many absent fathers face high levels of both financial and emotional strain in maintaining the family home and their relationships with their children despite the fact that they are no longer living as part of that family. It could also be argued that males (just as much as females) are likely to feel gender role strain as they try to adapt to a society where the male breadwinner, head of the family role is less important. For all of these reasons it seems unrealistic to assume that societal shifts would have an impact on female crime, but not on the crime committed by males. If instead societal changes are reflected in both male and female offending rates then we may well see no difference in the gender gap over time despite the fact that the determinants of crime are shifting.

A second and related issue is that much of the work on the gender gap in offending, both theoretical and empirical, has treated women (and men) as a homogeneous group. However, as others (such as Burgess-Proctor 2006) have argued women (and men) are a diverse group and while it is true that women have on average made gains in certain areas, it is not true that these gains have been equally spread across all women.

The women who have benefited the most from employment and wage gains have been those with the most education who work full-time, while the men who have seen relative losses in these areas are those who are unskilled (Juhn 1992; Nickell and Bell 1995). This may be particularly concerning as it is these low-skilled males who are most likely to be on the margins of crime (Hansen 2006; Hansen and Machin 2002, 2006).

It is therefore clear that these societal shifts have affected both males and females and have done so differentially across different groups of males and females. In particular, changes in education have played an important part in determining which women benefit from increased labour market opportunities, which men lose out and who offends. Therefore, when considering the impact of the changing position of women in society on crime and the gender crime gap it would seem important to take into account the role of education.

The remainder of this chapter empirically examines the gender gap in offending in self-reported data for different age groups to see whether the aggregate gap between men and women has shifted over time with societal changes. Then the gender gap in offending is examined separately for three groups with different levels of education. If education is important we would expect to see different gender gaps in offending across the different educational groups even if no picture emerges from the aggregate gender gap. Finally, a number of variables, known to be related to crime, are examined to see what effect they have on the gender gap in offending for the different groups. If any of the variables are able to account for the gender gap for any of the groups we will see a reduction in the gap for that particular group.

Data

The data used in this chapter come from the 2003 Crime and Justice Survey. These data were collected for the Home Office by BMRB Social Research and the National Centre for Social Research to measure the prevalence of offending and drug use in the population of England and Wales. The survey includes information on 10,085 core individuals aged 10 to 65 as well as an additional 1,886 respondents from ethnic minority groups.

A problem with much of the work on the gender gap in offending in the past is that it has relied on official arrest or convictions data as the gender of the offender is only known if the offender has been identified. But as Heidensohn (2002) points out, this is only true in a very small percentage of cases. Moreover, the gender gap in offending produced by official statistics may be more a reflection of police activity and court processing procedures than any real trends in gender-specific offending (Steffensmeier *et al.* 2006).

As the data used in this chapter are self-reported survey data they are not affected by the bias associated with the selection and processing of individuals by the criminal justice system. However, there are also some problems associated with self-report surveys. For example, respondents may conceal or exaggerate their involvement in crime, or may answer in a way they think the interviewer wants them to. Moreover, because some of the information is being asked retrospectively, respondents may not remember accurately events that happened in the past, or may say that they happened at the specific time the researcher is asking about when in reality it was before or after that date (Brantingham and Brantingham 1984). Despite the potential problems, these data offer a very rich source of information on individual offending at a national level not found elsewhere in the UK.

Descriptive statistics

The respondents in the survey are grouped together by age to construct pseudo-cohorts. This makes it possible to look at the gender gap over time despite the fact that the data are cross-sectional. The cohorts are constructed into three groups: the youngest, aged 16 to 29, represents those growing up in the 1990s and 2000s; the next group are those aged between 30 and 45, represents those growing up predominantly in the 1970s and 1980s; while the oldest cohort includes those who grew up in the 1950s and 1960s and were aged between 46 and 66 when they were interviewed in 2003.

These groups growing up in different eras should have different experiences of the position of men and women in society. We would therefore expect to see differences in the gender gap in offending between these different age groups. In particular, we might expect to see the gap decrease over younger age cohorts as the relative position of women has improved. The youngest cohort growing up in the most recent time period with the least inequality between males and females should have the smallest gender gap in offending. However, as we can see from Table 3.1, which shows numbers (and percentages) of both men and women who report that they have ever committed a crime, this is not the case. For each cohort more men offend than women, but the gap between the two does not reduce over time. In fact, it is the oldest cohort that has the smallest gender gap in offending (at 17.8 percentage points lower for women than men).

Table 3.1 Numbers and percentages of offences committed by gender and age

	All ages	16–29	30–45	46–66
Any offence ever	42.2% 2819	55.9% 1216	45.4% 932	29.9% 671
Males	53.1% 1681	67.9% 688	58.3% 576	38.6% 417
Female	31.3% 1138	44.4% 528	32.7% 356	20.8% 254
Percentage point gender gap	21.8	23.5	25.6	17.8

This concurs with other research in this area which fails to find a decline in the aggregate gender gap in offending across time. However, when the gender gap within the age cohorts is broken down by educational level (Figure 3.1) an interesting picture emerges. Figure 3.1 shows clear differences in the gender gap in offending over time for different educational groups. For those with no qualifications the gender gap is smaller for the youngest group and increases across the age groups. For the most educated group the relationship appears to work the other way round – with the gender gap greatest for the younger group and declining with age.

These descriptive results suggest that there may be important educational differences in the gender gap in offending. This is important because we know that the least educated are more likely to be involved in crime (Hansen 2003; Lochner and Moretti 2004). This relationship can be examined in more detail by carrying out regression analysis of the relationship between crime and gender for the different age cohorts and different education levels.

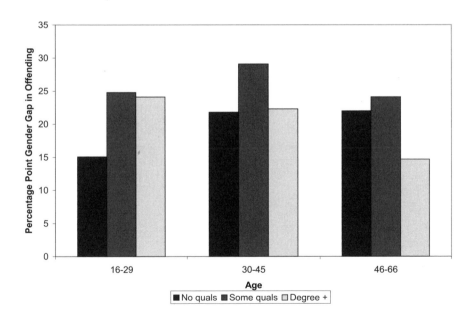

Figure 3.1 The gender gap in offending by age and education level

Statistical results

This section uses regression models to examine differences in the gender gap in offending over time by education levels. As respondents say that they either commit a crime or they do not the regression model utilised is a maximum likelihood probit[2] model (Gujarati 1995). This model is based on the assumption that the probability distribution in question, i.e. the probability of committing an offence, is normal and predicts probability Y=1 (i.e. committing an offence) compared to Y=0 (not committing an offence).

Results of the basic model

The regressions are run separately for each age cohort and for each education group. The results of the probit regressions are shown in Table 3.2. It shows probit coefficient estimates (with standard errors in curved parentheses and associated marginal effects in square parentheses). The basic model is simply a probit regression of gender on crime. The marginal effect for the gender variable shows the differential probability of a female committing a crime as compared to a male. For example, in column 1 for the no qualifications group this probability is −16.4 percentage points. We have seen from the descriptive statistics that women commit less crime for all age groups and at all levels of education, so we would expect the coefficient on this variable to be negative. We can see from Table 3.2 that this is the case for all age and education levels.

Table 3.2 shows separate estimates for the different education groups within each age cohort. Column 1 shows the basic results for those with no qualifications, column 3 for those with some qualifications and column 5 for those with a degree. The results for the youngest cohort appear at the top of the table, the 30 to 45 year olds in the middle and the results for the oldest cohort (those aged 46 to 66) appear in the bottom panels. In each case the coefficient on gender attracts a negative coefficient statistically significant at a greater than 1 per cent level.

We can think of this as the raw gender gap in offending, where the larger in magnitude the estimated marginal effect is, the greater is the gender gap in offending. These results support the findings of the descriptive statistics. For those with no qualifications the gender gap in offending is smallest for the youngest cohort, but for those with a degree the gap is largest for the youngest cohort. This raw gender gap is the gap that would exist if gender were the only determinant of crime. In reality, however, there are a range of variables that theory and past empirical work inform us may influence crime and possibly account for, or contribute to, the gender gap in offending.

Explanatory variables

The data are rich in regard to explanatory variables, so the model is able to control for a range of individual, lifestyle, attitude, family and labour market factors that may affect the relationship of primary interest between gender and offending. The first incorporated into the model is whether an individual is non-white. Graham and Bowling (1995) and Flood-Page et al. (2000) found whites and blacks had similar rates of criminal participation, but Asians had a lower rate of offending. We would ideally like to differentiate between different ethnicities, but unfortunately there are too few observations. The model also takes account of whether individuals have experienced any form of victimisation. This not only has been found to be a strong predictor of involvement in offending (Mcara 2001), but may also explain gender differences in crime (Rivera and Widom 1990).

The next set of explanatory variables examined relate to lifestyles and control for whether individuals have ever taken drugs and whether they are heavy alcohol users. In a recent Home Office study, 65 per cent of arrestees whose urine was tested, tested positive for drugs (Holloway et al. 2004). There are also strong links between alcohol and offending, particularly violent offences. In 2001 and 2002, 47 per cent of all victims of violence described their assailant as being under the influence of alcohol at the time (Flood-Page and Taylor 2003). We can think of these as risky behaviour. Also included in the model is a measure of risk-taking attitudes. This is important because risk-taking is not only usually thought to be positively associated with crime, it is also something, according to the gender equality theorists, we should expect to see shifts in among women.

A third set of explanatory variables added to the model relate to family and friends. Whether an individual has at least one family member and/or friend living in the area has been included as a proxy for social bonds and informal social control, which it has been argued, differ by gender (Hagan et al. 1979; Hagan 1990; Heidensohn 1996; Mawby 1981; see Heidensohn 2002 for a good discussion). Another measure of informal social control was added to the model by including a variable that measures the number of social networks an individual has. This aims to measure involvement in, and therefore attachment to, the community.

Table 3.2 Regression showing the gender gap in offending by age and education level

	No qualifications		Some qualifications		Degree +	
	(1)	(2)	(3)	(4)	(5)	(6)
	Gender and crime	Plus all other controls	Gender and crime	Plus all other controls	Gender and crime	Plus all other controls
16 to 29 year olds						
Female coefficient	-.429*** (.166) [-.164]	-.249 (.198) [-.095]	-.627*** (.071) [-.241]	-.507*** (.078) [-.194]	-.531*** (.104) [-.255]	-.594*** (-.115) [-.232]
Other controls	No	Yes	No	Yes	No	Yes
Pseudo R squared	.020	.215	.044	.180	.032	.175
Observations	252	252	1299	1299	606	606

30 to 45 year olds

Female coefficient	-.592*** (.143) [-.220]	-.599*** (.166) [-.220]	-.754*** (.085) [-.292]	-.681*** (.093) [-.264]	-.598*** (.093) [-.235]	-.582*** (.102) [-.228]
Other controls	No	Yes	No	Yes	No	Yes
R squared	.039	.175	.063	.170	.040	.168
Observations	340	340	927	927	757	757

46 to 66 year olds

Female coefficient	-.590*** (.091) [-. 173]	-.591*** (.102) [-.164]	-.627*** (.105) [-.222]	-.494*** (.116) [-.172]	-.338*** (.103) [-.130]	-.385*** (.109) [-.147]
Other controls	No	Yes	No	Yes	No	Yes
R squared	.041	.166	.045	.150	.016	.097
Observations	987	987	646	646	619	619

*** 1% significance level, ** 5%, * 10%. ( ) Standard errors [ ] Marginal effects

Another important characteristic related to offending is whether an individual is married. Married individuals are less likely to offend and when they do marriage often encourages desistence (Farrington 1995; Sampson and Laub 1990). The model also controls for whether an individual has family and/or friends who are offenders. Whether through learning or opportunity, research in the past has found this to be a very strong predictor of offending (Farrington 1995; Hansen 2003; Nagin and Land 1993).

The final set of explanatory variables included in the model relate to the labour market. There have been a number of studies that examine the labour market and crime (see Box 1987; Freeman 1983, 1999; Chiricos 1987). Although there is no consensus, many studies find that, at least to some extent, crime is related to unemployment (Cook and Zarkin 1985; Land *et al.* 1990) and low wages (Gould *et al.* 2002; Hansen and Machin 2002, 2006; Machin and Meghir 2004). In this analysis, because we are interested in increasing female employment, the model controls for whether an individual is employed and whether the individual has low household income.[3]

Results of the full model

We would expect that if differences in these variables are able to account for the difference in offending between males and females the gender gap in the original model will be reduced. We can see from Table 3.2 that this is the case for some groups, but not for others. There are a number of groups where the inclusion of these other variables has very little effect on the gender gap in offending. This is the case for the 30 to 45 year olds with no qualifications where the coefficient remains practically the same after the inclusion of the control variables, suggesting that despite differences across the genders in some of the control variables they are unable to account for the gender gap in offending for this particular group. For another group (the 46 to 66 year olds educated to degree level) controlling for differences in these other factors actually increases the size of the original gender gap from −.13 to −.15.

For most groups the inclusion of the control variables slightly reduces the estimated gender gap, but the gap remains statistically significant. This suggests that the gender gap cannot be accounted for by these observable differences in the characteristics controlled for. For only one group does controlling for the additional characteristics make any significant impact on the gender gap in offending. Once the control variables are added to the model for the youngest cohort with no qualifications, the original gender gap of −.16 is almost halved in magnitude and is reduced to statistical insignificance.

If one looks for systematic patterns by age or education, there is no consistent story. For the youngest cohort education plays an important role in the gender gap in offending which appears to be linear in nature, the gender gap in offending being smallest for those with the least education and largest for those with the most. Once all the variables are controlled for in the full model there is no statistically significant gender gap in offending for the least qualified group. For those with some qualifications there remains a 19 percentage point gender gap in offending in the full model and for the most educated group the gap in offending is 23 percentage points (both of which are statistically significant at a greater than 1 per cent level).

For the older cohorts, those aged 30 to 45 and those aged 46 to 66, educational differences do not seem to contribute to the gender gap in offending. For the 30 to 45 year olds the gender gap hardly varies by education group at all in the full model – ranging from a 22 to 26 percentage point gender gap all of which are statistically significant at a greater than 1 per cent level. For the older group the gender gap in offending in the full model is smaller and has even less variation, ranging from a 15 to 17 percentage point gap.

If we examine the relationship within educational group there is again no consistent story. For those with a degree the gender gap appears to have increased over time, being greatest for the youngest cohort (at 23 percentage points) and smallest for the oldest cohort (at 15 percentage points). Although, for those with fewer qualifications than this there is no systematic movement of the gender gap over time.

What contribution do the explanatory variables make?

Table 3.2 shows the effect that the explanatory variables have on the gender gap in offending for each of the groups examined in the full model. But it is also interesting to consider which of the variables are more important. We know from Table 3.2 that for some groups considered the explanatory variables make very little contribution to the gender gap in offending, while for others the explanatory variables play a more important role. This is particularly true for the youngest, least qualified group where differences in the explanatory variables are able to fully account for the original raw gender gap. We can examine which variables matter for which age and education group by looking at the coefficients on the explanatory variables.

The coefficients on the explanatory variables are shown in Appendices 3.1 to 3.3 at the end of this chapter. For the most recent cohort (Appendix 1), whether an individual has ever been a victim of crime is a robust determinant of their involvement in crime for all education groups. Experiencing some form of victimisation makes individuals between 11 and 16 percentage points more likely to be involved in offending depending on their education level. Drug-taking has a larger effect on the probability of committing crime for this young age group, but the effect is roughly the same at all levels of education. If an individual takes drugs they are around 30 to 33 percentage points more likely to offend.

We can see from Appendix 3.1 that some explanatory variables matter for some educational groups but not for others. For example, heavy alcohol use is associated with the probability of offending for the more educated groups, but is statistically insignificant for those with no qualifications. Risk-taking attitudes are important for those with a degree but not for those in the other education groups. Having friends and/or family members who offend is a strong predictor of offending for the least qualified but is not associated with offending for those with a degree.

For the second cohort, aged 30 to 45 (see Appendix 3.2) three explanatory variables are important at all educational levels: being non-white, having experienced victimisation and having taken drugs. In terms of magnitude, taking drugs has the greatest effect on the probability of offending, which is similar for all groups (ranging from 29 to 33 percentage points). The size of the impact of the other two variables is smaller but more variation is shown by education level. For example, experiencing victimisation increases the probability of offending for those with a degree by 8 percentage points (significant at the 5 per cent level), but has a greater effect on offending for those with no qualifications and those with some qualifications (increasing the probability of offending by 14 and 15 percentage points respectively). For all levels of education being non-white is associated with a decrease in the probability of offending, but the effect is greatest for those with a degree (22 percentage points) than for those with no qualifications (16 percentage points) and some qualifications (15 percentage points).

As with the younger cohort, heavy alcohol use is associated with a higher probability of offending for the more educated groups but not for the group with no qualifications. But unlike the previous cohort the coefficient on risk-taking attitudes is only statistically significant for those with some qualifications and having friends and/or family members who offend only predicts a higher probability of offending for the most educated group.

The results for the older cohort, aged 46 to 66, are given in Appendix 3.3. For this group there are two explanatory variables that consistently increase the probability of offending: taking drugs and heavy alcohol use. In terms of magnitude, drug-taking is the most important, increasing the probability of offending by 26 percentage points for those with a degree, 34 percentage points for those with some qualifications and 45 percentage points for those with no qualifications (all significant at a greater than 1 per cent level). Heavy alcohol use is most associated with offending for those with some qualifications, increasing the probability of offending by 21 percentage points. For the other educational groups heavy alcohol use increases the probability of offending by 12 and 11 percentage points respectively for those with no qualifications and those with a degree. The latter result is only significant at the 10 per cent level. In addition, for this age group experiencing victimisation is associated with an increased probability of offending for those with no qualifications and those with a degree.

The only explanatory variable that predicts increased probability of offending for all age and education groups is drug-taking. But its effect varies considerably across the different groups ranging from increasing the probability of offending by 26 to 45 percentage points depending on age and education level.

Discussion and interpretation

It is clear from the results that it is not enough to consider whether the gender gap in offending has shifted over time. There is a lot of heterogeneity in terms of the estimated gender gaps by age cohort and education group. For example, we would have expected to see the youngest cohort with a lower gender gap in offending across all levels of education than the older cohorts if the data were following predictions made by gender equality theories. Or a greater gap for the youngest cohort if the data supported the rational choice theories. However, in reality we see no consistent pattern across the groups.

Like other work in this area, the results presented here suggest that conventional theories are not able to account for the gender gap in offending. Gender specific theories, which take account of differences in previous victimisation, differential social control or different attitudes, fare little better. While some of the variables that proxy for these theories are able to account for some of the gender gap for some groups, they do not fully explain them.

The results also show that educational differences do not help to explain the gender gap for all groups either. Measured education does appear to be important for some groups, especially for the young. Indeed, the results show for the most recent cohort the gender gap in offending increases with educational level. For those with no qualifications there is no statistically significant gender gap in offending at all. The importance of education for the youngest cohort may reflect shifts in the education system that have resulted in increased educational inequality. With growing numbers of young people passing exams and going on to higher education there is an increasing penalty for those who are left behind with no qualifications.

In a society where inequalities along the lines of education, employment and income are increasingly a concern, both theory and empirical research concerning the gender gap in offending need to take account of these factors. The changes in modern society may make it less appropriate for research to examine differences between males and females while ignoring differences within groups of women and men in terms of other characteristics.

This is not a new way of thinking. There is a well-established body of criminological research that has shown that educational, employment and income inequalities are robust determinants of crime. However, most of this sort of research has looked at these inequalities while paying little attention to gender, while criminologists interested in gender have focused on differences between men and women rather than focusing on differences within these groups.

For feminist criminology (or for criminologists interested in gender more broadly) this research suggests a need for a more sophisticated range of theories, able to incorporate the changing nature of inequality in society. Early feminist theories that examine women's 'shared' experiences are no longer appropriate. The idea that all women are subordinated by a hegemonic male power is also now outdated (Connell and Messerschmidt 2005). Nor is it productive to continue to ask what it is about maleness that is criminogenic (Cain 1990) or about femaleness that is not. Instead we need to know what it is about the situations of some men and women that make them commit crimes (or not).

To do this, research needs to recognise that there are differences between groups of women and men as well as differences between men and women. Indeed, changes in inequality witnessed during the 1980s and 1990s have altered the social structure of society in a way that may mean that in places, differences between groups of women and men are as important, or even more important, than differences between the genders. This is an area that clearly needs more investigation. The findings of this chapter suggest that a potential starting point for any such future investigation may be the work of black and global feminists (Gelsthorpe 2002) who draw attention to the importance of inequalities in areas such as class, race, economy and ecology (Bulbeck 1998; Smith 2000) and the way these interact with gender to produce gender differences in offending.

Acknowledgement

I would like to thank Frances Heidensohn and Stephen Machin for helpful comments on an earlier draft of this article.

Notes

1 There are debates on the main cause of this restructuring. It is widely believed that skill biased technological change was the driving factor behind the movement (see Berman *et al.* 1998); other explanations include the reduction of international trade barriers, or institutional changes such as de-unionisation (Freeman 1992).
2 The analysis was also carried out using a maximum likelihood logit model, which gave very similar results. Logit models are closely related to probits but are based on a logistic distribution rather than a normal distribution.
3 Measured if they are in the bottom 30 per cent of the household income distribution.

References

Adler, F. (1975) *Sisters in Crime*, New York: McGraw-Hill.
Barclay, G. (1995) *Digest 3: Information on the Criminal Justice System in England and Wales*, London: Home Office.
Becker, G. (1968) 'Crime and Punishment: An Economic Approach', *Journal of Political Economy*, 76: 175–209.

Berger, R. (1989) 'Female Delinquency in the Emancipation Era: A Review of the Literature', *Sex Roles*, 21: 375–99.

Berman, E., J. Bound, J. and Machin, S. (1998) 'Implications of Skill Biased Technological Change: International Evidence', *Quarterly Journal of Economics*, 113: 1245–79.

Bianchi, S. (1995) 'Changing Economic Roles of Men and Women', in R. Farley (ed.) *State of the Union: American in the 1990s*, New York: Russell-Sage.

Blau, F. and Kahn, L. (1997) 'Swimming Upstream: Trends in the Gender Wage Differential in the 1980s', *Journal of Labour Economics*, 15: 1–42.

Blau, F. and Kahn, L. (2000) 'Gender Differences in Pay', *Journal of Economic Perspectives*, 14: 79–99.

Blumberg, R. (1978) *Stratification: Socio-economic and Sexual Inequality*, Iowa: William C. Brown.

Box, S. (1987) *Recession, Crime and Punishment*, London: Macmillan.

Bulbeck, C. (1998) *Re-orientating Western Feminisms: Women's Diversity in a Post Colonial World*, Cambridge: Cambridge University Press.

Burgess-Proctor, A. (2006) 'Intersection of Race, Class, Gender and Crime', *Feminist Criminology*, 1(1): 27–47.

Brantingham, P. and Brantingham, P. (1984) *Patterns in Crime*, New York: Macmillan.

Cain, M. (1990) 'Towards Transgression: New Directions in Feminist Criminology', *International Journal of Sociology and Law*, 18: 1–18.

Chesney-Lind, M. (2006) 'Patriarchy, Crime, and Justice: Feminist Criminology in an Era of Backlash', *Feminist Criminology*, 1: 6–26.

Chiricos, T. (1987) 'Rates of Crime and Unemployment: An Analysis of Aggregate Research Evidence', *Social Problems*, 34: 187–211.

Connell, R. and Messerschmidt, J. (2005) 'Hegemonic Masculinity: Rethinking the Concept', *Gender and Society*, 19: 829–59.

Cook, P. and Zarkin, G. (1985) 'Crime and the Business Cycle', *Journal of Legal Studies*, XVI: 115–29.

Dubeck, P. and Dunn, D. (2002) *Workplace/Women's Place: An Anthology*, Los Angeles: Roxbury.

Ehrlich, I. (1973) 'Participation in Illegitimate Activities: A Theoretical and Empirical Investigation', *Journal of Political Economy*, 81: 521–63.

Farrington, D. (1995) 'The Development of Offending and Anti-Social Behaviour from Childhood: Key Findings from the Cambridge Study in Delinquent Development', *Journal of Child Psychology and Psychiatry*, 360: 929–64.

Flood-Page, C., Campbell, S., Harrington, V. and Miller, J. (2000) *Youth Crime: Findings from the 1998/99 Youth Lifestyles Survey*, Home Office Research Study 209, London: Home Office.

Flood-Page, F., Taylor, J. (2003) *Crime in England and Wales 2001/2002: supplementary volume*. London: Home Office Research Development and Statistics Directorate.

Freeman, R. (1983) 'Crime and Unemployment', in J. Q. Wilson (ed.) *Crime and Public Policy*, San Francisco: Institute for Contemporary Studies.

Freeman, R. (1992) 'Is Declining Unionisation in the US Good, Bad or Irrelevant?', in M. Lawrence and P. B. Voos (eds) *Unions and Economic Competitiveness*, Armonk, NY: ME Sharpe.

Freeman, R. (1999) 'The Economics of Crime', in O. Ashenfelter and D. Card (eds) *Handbook of Labor Economics*, Netherlands: North Holland Press.

Gelsthorpe, L. (2002) 'Feminism and Criminology', in M. Maguire, R. Morgan and R. Reiner (eds) *The Oxford Handbook of Criminology*, 3rd edn, Oxford: Oxford University Press.

Gould, E., Weinberg, B. and Mustard, D. (2002) 'Crime Rates and Local Labor Market Opportunities in the United States: 1979–1995', *Review of Economics and Statistics*, 84: 45–61.

Graham, J. and Bowling, B. (1995) *Young People and Crime*, Home Office Research Study 145, London: Home Office.

Gujarati, D. N. (1995) *Basic Econometrics*, New York: McGraw-Hill.

Hagan, J. (1990) 'The Structuration of Gender and Deviance: A Power Control Theory of Vulnerability to Crime and the Search for Deviant Role Exits', *Canadian Review of Sociology and Anthropology*, 27: 137–56.

Hagan, J., Simpson, J. and Gillis, A. (1979) 'The Sexual Stratification of Social Control: A Gender Based Perspective on Crime and Delinquency', *British Journal of Sociology*, 30: 25–38.

Hakim, C. (1992) 'Explaining Trends in Occupational Segregation: The Measure, Causes and Consequences of the Sexual Division of Labour', *European Sociological Review*, 8: 127–52.

Hakim, C. (1998) *Social Change and Innovation in the Labour Market*, Oxford: Oxford University Press.

Hansen, K. (2003) 'Education and the Crime-Age Profile', *British Journal of Criminology*, 43: 141–68.

Hansen, K. (2006) 'Male Crime and Rising Female Employment', mimeo.

Hansen, K. and Machin, S. (2002) 'Spatial Crime Patterns and the Introduction of the UK Minimum Wage', *Oxford Bulletin of Economics and Statistics*, 64: 677–97.

Hansen, K. and Machin, S. (2006) 'Crime and the Minimum Wage', forthcoming, *Journal of Quantitative Criminology*.

Harkness, S. (1996) 'The Gender Earnings Gap: Evidence from the UK', *Fiscal Studies*, 17: 1–36.

Heidensohn, F. (1996) *Women and Crime*, 2nd edn, Basingstoke: Macmillan.

Heidensohn, F. (2002) 'Gender and Crime', in M. Maguire, R. Morgan and R. Reiner (eds) *The Oxford Handbook of Criminology*, 3rd edn, Oxford: Oxford University Press.

Hirschi, T. (1969) *Causes of Delinquency*, Berkeley, CA: University of California Press.

Holloway, K., Bennett, T. and Lower, C. (2004) *Trends in Drug Use and Offending: The Results of the New-Adam Programme 1999–2002*, Home Office Findings 219, London: Home Office.

Huber, J. (1990) 'Macro-Micro Links in Gender Stratification', *American Sociological Review*, 55: 1–10.

Juhn, C. (1992) 'The Decline in Male Labor Market Participation: The Role of Declining Market Opportunities', *Quarterly Journal of Economics*, 107: 79–121.

Land, K. C., McCall, P. L. and Cohen, L. E. (1990) 'Structural Covariates of Homicide Rates: Are there any Invariances Across Time and Social Space?', *American Journal of Sociology*, 95: 922–63.

Lochner, L. (2004) 'Education, Work, and Crime: A Human Capital Approach', *International Economic Review*, 45(3), August: 811–43.

Lochner, L. and Moretti, E. (2004) 'The Effect of Education on Crime: Evidence from Prison Inmates, Arrests, and Self-Reports', *American Economic Review*, 94: 155–89.

Lundberg, S. (2005) 'Gender and Household Decision-Making', lecture notes from the University of Siena International School of Economic XVIII Workshop on Gender and Economics, July, Certosa di Pontignano.

Machin, S. and Meghir, C. (2004) 'Crime and Economic Incentives', *Journal of Human Resources*, 39: 958–79.

Machin, S. and McNally, S. (2005) 'Gender and Student Achievement in English Schools', *Oxford Review of Economic Policy*, 21: 357–72.

Mawby, R. (1981) 'Sex and Crime: The Results of a Self-Report Study', *British Journal of Criminology*, 31(4): 525.

Mcara, L. (2001) 'Parenting Style linked to Teenage Delinquency Rates', ESRC press release.

Merton, R. (1957) *Social Theory and Social Structure*, New York: Free Press.

Nagin, D. and Land, K. (1993) 'Age, Criminal Careers, and Population Heterogeneity: Specification and Estimation of a Non-parametric, Mixed Poisson Model', *Criminology*, 31: 327–62.

Nickell, S. and Bell, B. (1995) 'The Collapse in Demand for the Unskilled and Unemployment across the OECD', *Oxford Review of Economic Policy*, 11: 40–62.

Oppenheimer, V. (1970) *The Female Labor Force in the United States*, Berkeley, CA: University of California Press.

Oppenheimer, V. (1973) 'Demographic Influence of Female Employment and the Status of Women', *American Journal of Sociology*, 78: 184–99.

Rivera, B. and Widom, C. (1990) 'Childhood Victimisation and Violent Offending', *Violence and Victims*, 5: 19–35.

Sampson, R. and Lamb, J. (1990) 'Crime and Deviance over the Life Course: The Salience of Adult Social Bonds', *American Sociological Review*, 5: 609–27.

Simon, I. (1975) *The Contemporary Woman and Crime*, Washington, DC: National Institute of Mental Health.

Smart, C. (1977) *Women, Crime and Criminology*, London: Routledge.

Smith, B. (2000) *Global Feminisms Since 1945*, London: Routledge.

Steffensmeier, D (1995) 'Trends in Female Crime: It's Still a Man's World', in B. Raffel Price and N. Sokoloff (eds) *The Criminal Justice System and Women*, New York: McGraw-Hill.

Steffensmeier, D., Zhong, H., Ackerman, J., Schwartz, J. and Agha, S. (2006) 'Gender Gap Trends for Violent Crimes 1980 to 2003', *Feminist Criminology*, 1(1): 72–98.

Appendix 3.1 Regression showing the gender gap in offending for 16–29 year olds

	No qualifications		Some qualifications		Degree +	
	(1)	(2)	(3)	(4)	(5)	(6)
	Gender and crime	Plus all other controls	Gender and crime	Plus all other controls	Gender and crime	Plus all other controls
Female coefficient	-.429*** (.166) [-.164]	-.249 (.198) [-.095]	-.627*** (.071) [-.241]	-.507*** (.078) [-.194]	-.531*** (.104) [-.255]	-.594*** (.115) [-.232]
Non white		-.306 (.341) [-.120]		.283** (.158) [.105]		-.096 (.168) [-.038]
Been a victim		.430** (.187) [.162]		.283*** (.079) [.109]		.410*** (.117) [.160]
Taken drugs		.810*** (.189) [.304]		.869*** (.081) [.327]		.866*** (.116) [.335]
Heavy alcohol user		.291 (.197) [.111]		.272*** (.080) [.105]		.402*** (.118) [.159]
Risk-taking attitudes		.100 (.183) [.038]		.065 (.080) [.025]		.361*** (.123) [.141]

Family and friends in the area		.058 (.273) [.023]		-.010 (.141) [-.004]		.049 (.161) [.019]
Friends and family offenders		599*** (.197) [.223]		.346*** (.083) [.131]		.199 (.154) [.078]
Married		-.140 (.193) [-.054]		-.150* (.092) [-.058]		.195* (.124) [.077]
Number of social networks		.021 (.228) [.008]		.168*** (.056) [.066]		-.006 (.068) [-.002]
Employed		-117 (.201) [-.045]		-.066 (.105) [-.026]		.321 (.215) [.124]
Low household income		-.069 (.184) [-.027]		.026 (.076) [.010]		.043 (.114) [.017]
Pseudo R squared	.020	.215	.044	.180	.032	.175
Observations	252	252	1299	1299	606	606

*** 1% significance level, ** 5%, * 10% ( ) Standard errors [ ] Marginal effects

Appendix 3.2 Regression showing the gender gap in offending for 30–45 year olds

	No qualifications		Some qualifications		Degree +	
	(1)	(2)	(3)	(4)	(5)	(6)
	Gender and crime	Plus all other controls	Gender and crime	Plus all other controls	Gender and crime	Plus all other controls
Female coefficient	-.592*** (.143) [-.220]	-.599*** (.166) [-.220]	-.754*** (0.85) [-.292]	-.681*** (0.93) [-.264]	-.598*** (0.093) [-.235]	-.582*** (.102) [-.228]
Non white		-.476** (.276) [-.164]		-.407** (.214) [-.151]		-.556*** (.165) [-.217]
Been a victim		.367** (.165) [.140]		.373*** (.099) [.147]		.193* (.107) [.076]
Taken drugs		.883*** (.158) [.334]		.720*** (.095) [.296]		.752*** (.102) [.292]
Heavy alcohol user		.182 (.174) [.070]		.215** (.103) [.085]		.424*** (.111) [.166]
Risk-taking attitudes		.036 (.165) [.013]		.284*** (.112) [.109]		.087 (.117) [.035]

Family and friends in the area	-.012 (.143) [-.004]		-.090 (.151) [-.035]		-.581** (.291) [-.227]
Friends and family offenders	.353** (.177) [.137]		.161 (.138) [.064]		.116 (.210) [.044]
Married	-.009 (.106) [-.0032]		-.081 (.098) [-.032]		-.094 (.161) [-.036]
Number of social networks	.120** (0.57) [.048]		.062 (0.66) [.024]		.210 (.150) [.078]
Employed	.061 (.147) [.024]		-.150 (.124) [-.058]		0.51 (.181) [.019]
Low household income	.154 (.100) [-.061]		-.120 (.092) [-.047]		-.040 (.151) [-.015]
Pseudo R squared	0.168	.040	0.170	.063	0.175	0.039
Observations	757	757	927	927	340	340

*** 1% significance level, ** 5%, * 10% ( ) Standard errors. [ ] Marginal effects

Appendix 3.3 Regression of showing the gender gap in offending for 46–66 year olds

	No qualifications		Some qualifications		Degree +	
	(1)	(2)	(3)	(4)	(5)	(6)
	Gender and crime	Plus all other controls	Gender and crime	Plus all other controls	Gender and crime	Plus all other controls
Female coefficient	-.590*** (.091) [-.173]	-.591*** (.102) [-.164]	-.627*** (.105) [-.222]	-.494*** (.116) [-.172]	-.338*** (.103) [-.130]	-.385*** (.109) [-.147]
Non white		-.352 (.339) [-.082]		-.336 (.373) [-.104]		-.994*** (.311) [-.300]
Been a victim		.400*** (.118) [.121]		.080 (.137) [.028]		.306** (.126) [.119]
Taken drugs		1.263*** (.153) [.448]		.895*** (.145) [.336]		.663*** (.123) [.258]
Heavy alcohol user		.378*** (.127) [.115]		.567*** (.144) [.210]		.271* (.139) [.106]
Risk taking attitudes		-.005 (.110) [.001]		.213 (.140) [.076]		.140 (.140) [.054]

	(1)	(2)	(3)	(4)	(5)	(6)
Family and friends in the area	-.038 (.173) [-.15]		-.138 (.186) [-.049]		-.118 (.163) [-.034]	
Friends and family offenders	.064 (.223) [.025]		-.180 (.226) [-.064]		.414** (.188) [.130]	
Married	-.087 (.118) [-.034]		-.216* (.120) [-.076]		-.118 (.104) [-.033]	
Number of social networks	.023 (.052) [.009]		.109 (.074) [.038]		.095 (.088) [.026]	
Employed	.102 (.122) [.040]		.008 (.124) [.003]		.211** (.100) [.058]	
Low household income	.053 (.109) [.021]		-.126 (.113) [-.043]		.135 (.098) [.037]	
Pseudo R squared	.097	.016	.150	.045	0.166	.041
Observations	619	619	646	646	987	987

*** 1% significance level, ** 5%, * 10% ( ) Standard errors [ ] Marginal effects

Chapter 4

Schoolbags at dawn

Carrie Anne Myers

Introduction

Bullying is a universal term. It is used in everyday language and encompasses a number of events. It can be seen as an umbrella for a range of verbal, psychological, physical and violent interactions. It is a topic that has been traditionally studied within the domains of psychology and education. Such studies have been quantitative in nature and have informed education policy. The study that is the subject of this chapter considered incidents of school violence and school bullying within a criminological and sociological framework. It was the product of four years of qualitative research and gave the pupils who took part 'a voice', rather than responding by tick box on yet another bullying questionnaire. I will argue that a number of feminist questions do provide a useful analytical framework. However, I will also argue that some of these questions need to be expanded and that ultimately gender is just one of many concepts to consider. School bullying must be viewed in its 'whole context' and gender should not be looked at in isolation. Otherwise there is a danger of excluding the role of the male pupils at the expense of the female ones.

A number of core traditional feminist arguments are revisited and expanded on within this chapter. The 'double deviance' (Carlen 1983) label often attributed to female offenders is still very relevant, but I would argue requires expansion to consider the 'double victim' status of the male pupils. This leads on to the consideration of the concept of invisibility. Early feminist arguments used to claim that girls are absent from the majority of delinquent studies and that there is a gap in research acknowledging the presence and role of women (Heidensohn 1996). This chapter will demonstrate that this early view may, by serendipity, have been correct. While ignoring girls in the research process is wrong, to be a feminist researcher and only consider girls and women is also incorrect. Rather than split the genders, this research considered a particular adolescent population in a small, rural comprehensive school that I called Bayview, as a united group. I will show how, regardless of gender, all pupils were involved in bullying. The roles assumed in acts of bullying were performed by both male and female pupils, on a daily basis.

The subcultures of female friendship groups are also considered. McRobbie and Garber stated that 'girl culture, from our preliminary investigations, is so well insulated as to operate to effectively exclude not only other "undesirable" girls – but also boys, adults, teachers, and researchers' (1976: 222).

This chapter highlights that it was indeed the case that the female pupils 'did their own thing' but they were very much present in all levels of friendship group and were closely allied to the male pupils. By reconsidering the original arguments made by McRobbie and Garber, this work expands on the questions they raised and revisits female subcultural activity 30 years on.

This chapter also asks new questions by entering an arena that is predominantly researched within other academic disciplines. School bullying has not traditionally been studied within a feminist criminological framework. There are studies that have focused on bullying within the prison system, and more specifically female inmates, that have demonstrated that bullying is widespread, often subtle in nature and consequently difficult for staff to detect (Loucks 2004). This chapter expands on such findings and suggests that bullying among females in a different organisational context follows similar patterns, and demonstrates that girls take part in all forms of school bullying. Furthermore, if the extent of school bullying is to be understood within a criminological framework then a feminist argument can help to contextualise the experience for both bullies and victims of bullying.

Ten years ago, schoolgirl bullies were targeted by the media as another bane of civilised society; 'proof', it was maintained, of an emerging generation of gymslip delinquents (Kirsta 1994). A decade on and little has changed. The assault on 19 October 2005 of Shanni Naylor, who was attacked by a female peer in the classroom with the blade of a pencil sharpener and scarred for life, was reported as a consequence of female bullying. Typical moral panics ensued in the media and on 11 November 2005 the attack on Natashia Jackman with a pair of scissors by a 14-year-old girl in the canteen at a school in Surrey hit the headlines. Again this assault was publicised as an example of school bullying and an indication of how teenage girls are becoming increasingly more violent. However, it is not merely the case that girls are becoming 'more' violent. Girls have always attacked other girls in the playground, but it is just now entering the public domain, and being publicised as much as the extreme male attacks that occur within schools. Female 'bullying' as a phenomenon has been 'criminalised' in the media, highlighting that the significance of gender has to be considered in incidents of school bullying.

Studies into female delinquency tend to focus on the extremes rather than the day-to-day experiences. Such portrayal of extreme bullying is adding to the representation of women as increasingly violent and is obscuring the realities of the topic. Indeed, feminists have expressed caution when considering violence perpetrated by women (Alder and Worrall 2004). Furthermore, feminist criminologists have argued that 'it is striking that we do not have notions of "normal" uses of force and violence by women and girls. This contrasts markedly with the ways we deal with male behaviours such as rough play and fighting' (Heidensohn 2001). The focus on extreme depiction of female bullying has led to an oversight of the more mundane daily occurrences of female interactions that happen daily in the playground.

McRobbie and Garber argued that 'it is always the violent aspects of a phenomenon which qualify as newsworthy ... precisely the areas of sub-cultural activity from which women have tended to be excluded' (1976: 212). This will help to contextualise the work. Was this still the case in the twenty-first century or was it more a case that as a number of women move into the study of criminology they are able to account for the actions of females? Did my gender enable me to uncover the actions of both male and female pupils without excluding one of the sexes?

Through examining both male and female bullying techniques I uncovered complicated bullying relationships both within and between the genders. I shall now present these findings.

Male and female techniques of bullying

Previous research has documented the direct/indirect nature of school bullying, with boys opting for more direct and physical methods and girls more indirect (Bjorkvist *et al.* 1992; Ahmad and Smith 1994). Since direct bullying is 'easier' and more 'obvious' to observe, it has been argued that it is a possibility that girls' bullying has been underestimated in the past (Smith and Sharp 1994). Nonetheless, I would argue that this generalisation appears to be oversimplified. I wanted to analyse the extent of bullying across the genders at Bayview School and to see if the techniques used were direct or indirect, whether there were any clear gender differences, or whether the techniques or victims were selected regardless of gender, supporting feminist observations by Lees (1993) who argued: 'While bullying and fighting by boys are recognised phenomena, investigation of the extent of girls' involvement in such activities has yet to be seriously undertaken.'

The pupils confirmed that bullying was a problem and I found three key forms of victimisation at Bayview School: male on male, female on female and mixed. The dominant form was the mixed variety. I will now explain these bullying techniques in turn.

Male victimisation: big boys can't cry

To begin with, male victims of bullying will be considered. The boys at this school had higher rates of victimisation than the girls. Furthermore, male victims often used self-denial and normalisation techniques as a coping mechanism to deal with their situation. A feminist perspective was applied to male victims as a useful way of exploring the significance of their victim status. Male on male victimisation occurred daily and had a profound effect on its victims.

> **Q**: What form did the bullying take?
> **A**: Oh, it was like small things like, you sort of didn't notice but it was annoying and worrying that they [his bullies] had like been there [to his home] and so I don't know ... like people just running across just like for the fact that they'd done it ... and we've got like an acre of land and like, they'd be pulling up vegetables and things like that, cos they used to do just vandalising it in general and stealing things. I know someone, I think it was actually at the time of the bullying, they just pulled out this moneybox that my dad had made and broke it up and chucked it in the river down the bottom of our road. So it was just, it was like, it was coming closer all the time, and before

long it was like prank calls on the door and prank phone calls.
It was just pretty scary actually.

Q: And was all of this down to one boy that you had met from
primary school?

A: Yeah, and his actual little clique sort of thing that were
actually doing it. His little group of people.

Q: All boys?

A: Yes, all boys.

(*'Brian', 15 years old*)

'Brian' suffered victimisation both on and off the school premises, and
his aggressors were boys. A popular myth about bullying between
boys is that it tends to be of a violent nature, and once there has
been a fight to 'clear the air' the situation is more often than not
resolved. 'Brian' endured victimisation for two and a half years and
was an example of a 'typical' male victim of bullying at Bayview
School.

The following account given by 'Bill', bullied because his father
was a vicar, highlights the complex nature of patterns of male
victimisation further.

Q: What happened when you were bullied?

A: It was a really bad year. I got a bad report, didn't do well
in any subjects I usually do well in. And I just, I got it full
stop. I mean I sometimes, I sometimes, you know, they'd say
something and I'd turn around and say shut up or it would
just escalate and then I'd be in trouble. Yeah, I must have been
in the office about five times. It's all sorted out now. I'm you
know, I'm in a group, I'm not unpopular, well I'm not popular
… yeah, it's all sorted out.

Q: And who was it egging you on or making you mad?

A: Yeah, it was all boys really.

Q: All boys?

A: I was taking on people I just couldn't beat, or they'd be in
a really big group and I just wouldn't think, it would just be,
I was just reckless. But I've learnt to deal with it. And I don't
get teased any more cos they realise that, you know, Dad's just
a human vicar and he's, he does come into assemblies and talk,
which I didn't think was, I was a bit nervous but I'm always
nervous during assembly, but it's really made it better. But he's
involved in the committee of the skate club and Rivers End

youth project, he runs the Christian youth group. Yeah, that's improved it.

Q: So in year seven, was that almost like a bullying period, you went through, would you classify it as bullying?

A: Not really, um, I would, it would usually be a one-on-one. It wouldn't be kids piling in, it would just be sort of and the other thing, I would come back with a comment and that would make them cross and then would fight back. It wasn't bullying, yeah, bullying in some sense, there were a few people doing it but it was my fault because I came back and fought. And I wouldn't have had that problem if I had just left it. Yeah, should have just left it, not reacted.

Q: So were you being a bit oversensitive, do you think?

A: Um, I thought I could win every, every time, I thought I could stamp out the problem if, you know, by saying a comment or fighting back. Yeah, but it's all sorted.

As a consequence of the verbal provocation received at school, 'Bill' reacted in a violent way once he had been pushed to his limit. The boys were engaging in both verbal and physical forms of bullying and direct and indirect methods at Bayview School. The boys interviewed reported more incidents of victimisation than their female counterparts. Furthermore, there was often a denial that what was happening to them was bullying. This suggests that to admit to victimisation leaves one with a stigmatised label so a tactic to counteract this is to engage in self-blame and processes that normalise the bullying behaviour. The extent to which male victimisation is experienced among this age group, that is, the 11 to 16 year olds, is an under-researched area within criminology. Feminist criminologists demonstrate how male victims 'play down' their experience of victimisation as it may threaten their masculinity to talk about themselves as weak and powerless (Stanko and Hobdell 1993).

Feminist criminologists argue that female offenders are regarded as 'double deviants' (Carlen 1983; Carlen and Worrall 1987), both for offending and for offending against the gendered ideal of femininity. I would argue by extension that male victims are 'double victims'. First, they have been victimised, and second, they have suffered from the workings of the gendered norms of masculinity. The idea of victimisation is predominantly a feminised term. 'Brian' and 'Bill' openly discussed their victimisation during the process of long, often highly emotional, one-on-one interviews. Their experiences demonstrate the necessity to look at how bullying is dealt with within schools and to consider that male victims of school bullying does not take the form of a simple 'fight and clear the air'.

Female victimisation: sugar and spice and all things nice?

Female against female patterns of bullying were verbal at Bayview School. 'Demelza', aged 15, who was a victim of bullying, described what it was like to be a victim of female peers and the complex friendship levels within the peer groups.

> **A**: There's the popular people, you know if you talk to them they kind of block you out. Er, there's the people who are quite popular and then there's the people who are outside all the time [laughs nervously]. The popular people, I don't know [laughs] I think being pretty and thin, but they are usually really horrible people, nasty to each other.
> **Q**: And what makes you not popular?
> **A**: Being different [laughs], like me.
> **Q**: Would you say you were on the outside, then?
> **A**: Yeah, definitely.
> **Q**: So, why do the popular people think they are so special?
> **A**: Um, some of them are clever, they just pretend they are not, they drink and smoke and I think they have more social lives than anybody else.
> **Q**: And do they pick on the other people?
> **A**: There is someone they usually pick on, which is really cruel.
> **Q**: What do they do to them?
> **A**: Just take the piss out of her completely all the time. She's really, really thin, she's like emaciated and, um, she's got quite big teeth and, er, speaks a bit like weird? And they just take the mick out of her all the time for it.
> **Q**: So would you say they bully?
> **A**: Yeah, yeah, I would. It can be awful.

Along with bullying verbally girls ostracised individuals from their peer group and would ignore them and isolate them. This was a common form of bullying among female pupils.

> **A**: I used to be friendly with some people and I broke up with one person and then all the others decided to back that one person, so they are really nasty to me now.

Q: How are they nasty?

A: Name calling.

Q: And is anybody on your side?

A: Yeah, a couple of people.

Q: So why did you break friends with them, was it a big disagreement?

A: No, but, um, we were playing a game where you shove at people and I shoved one of my friends and she hit her head very slightly and she so she went and told her mum and her mum said I wasn't allowed to come over to her house again and then all of the others sided with her and then it went from there.

Q: And it's still going on?

A: Yeah.

Q: How long ago did this happen?

A: When term started, about six weeks ago. I know that they're doing it because like, everyone said that I said stuff about them.

Q: But you didn't?

A: No, I didn't and they are all going on one side and they are getting other people on their side because they're like, popular people? And I'm not really getting very many people.

Q: What do your friends think about it? The friends you've got?

A: Um … they are trying to be friends with the other people as well because they don't want to break up with them and go through the same thing as me.

Q: Is this just a girl thing?

A: Just girls.

(*'Stephanie', 13 years old*)

Female on female victimisation followed existing patterns uncovered in previous research (Slee and Rigby 1993). It was discreet in nature in that girls would often be excluded from their peer group. It was a problem and every girl interviewed had either experienced or been involved in bullying while at Bayview School. As I have argued, gendered explanations are required to highlight the plight of male adolescent victims. They are also essential to uncover the true picture of discreet female bullying. Female bullying occurred in 'hidden' forms and as a result it is difficult to detect and quantify, something that feminist criminologists have highlighted in relation to female criminality. Furthermore, discretion will result in an unknown quantity of female on female victimisation.

To pursue the analysis further I wanted to know what a 'typical' female bully's characteristics were. How did she look? Why was she in a position to be so critical? A description of a female bully was offered by 'Fudge', a girl aged 13:

> Yeah, she is a bully, she is a bully. She just criticises everybody else, she's got like a nice figure and everything. I don't think she's pretty really but everybody else might think she's pretty but just like, she's really like has big boobs and she's always walking around like this and always like trying to sing. And she cannot sing, I'll tell ya. It's really bad. She nicks peoples clothes, like if you give her a top, she won't give it back. I gave her a top one time, to borrow, and she never gave it back. So I kept on asking and said, 'Can I have my top, please?' She said, 'No', like that. Yeah, like she takes everybody's clothes. She maybe looks, thinks she looks nice, she might have boobs but she's some little, like little troll.

The girl described here was clearly attractive and 'pretty', this is consistent with other research that has documented hierarchies among female pupils at schools (see Phillips 1994, 2003; Artz 2004). However, she also had a nasty side to her personality: pretty, yet a thief!

A number of pupils claimed that the bullies were 'popular':

> A: Our year (year 11) are kind of bonding more together now but, um, you do get like the popular girls and you do get the people that no one really talks to, the little group that hangs around together. And you get like the people that are friends with the popular people, the people that are like, in between, who are friends with everyone, like that kind of category, I try to fall in there.
> Q: What do you have to do or be to be popular?
> A: I think you have to be really pretty [laughs], um, have a lot of, well maybe have a bit of money, like have all the brand names and ... just be really nice and everyone gets on with you I suppose [laughs], but quite a few of the popular girls all grew up together, and they come to this school and make

friends with the other pretty popular girls and they just form one group. There's about 10 of them, that all are together.

Q: Is there anyone who these girls pick on?

A: Yeah [laughs] there is one girl who is picked on, yeah. Well, she's always trying to fit in, she's like a loner and she was trying to fit in with everyone and kept trying to talk to anyone and was like very annoying [laughs], no, I don't think she'll ever be popular [laughs].

('Rosie', 16 years old)

These contradictions were almost impossible to assess. The 'pretty', 'attractive', 'popular' pupils were the bullies. There was a form of hierarchy maintenance and those girls 'at the top' had to keep their fellow pupils in their place by way of bullying. A self-confessed bully offered an opinion of why such behaviour is engaged in:

You just know it's horrible, but you're just meant to do it, you know, to be cool, you've got to pick on a few people. But we're not that bad. No one ever hit anyone, or I mean a lot of people talk to the, like talk to the victims. There's one that is, he knows he always gets picked on and he won't let anyone talk to him if they've been picking on him either. I go and talk to him and he's like no, go away, but he won't let anyone in. That's why he's picked on.

('Emily', 15 years old)

Through interview the single-sex bullying patterns came to light and it became clear that, contrary to previous research, the behaviour and bullying patterns of the two genders were much more complicated than 'direct' or 'indirect' forms. The most interesting form was the uniting of the genders into mixed peer groups to bully together.

Mixed victimisation – a uniting of the genders

The dominant style of bullying technique at Bayview School was mixed, whereby boys and girls would unite and victimise together:

Q: And do boys and girls do the same?

A: Yeah, definitely ... they are all doing similar sorts of things, all teasing, like.

Q: And do boys ever pick on girls or is it just boys on boys and girls on girls?

A: Um, yeah, some of the boys like the more popular boys pick on the like unpopular girls and like make rude comments about them.

(*'Rosie', 16 years old*)

A: Everyone does it. Um, I suppose you could call it bullying. You know, some people really say nasty things about her but some people just ignore her. You know, it's like mainly the boys are out to bully her and call her names and stuff. The girls just, you know, ignore her.

Q: Why do you bully her?

A: She's just like, she's really skinny and she's like really lanky, she's got like really big hair and she's got like really big buck teeth and stuff … Um, I suppose you could call it bullying. You know, some people really say nasty things about her but some people just ignore her. You know, it's like mainly the boys are out to bully her and call her names and stuff. The girls just, you know, ignore her.

(*'Chantel', 15 years old*)

A: People in our year used to pick on other people in our year and like start calling them names and stuff for no real reason? And, yeah, cos I remember being in year 7, 8, and 9 on the more unpopular side [laughs] and yeah couldn't like understand. They never used to pick on me but they used, some of them, the popular people in our year used to like bully people and like call them names and just start like push them around and stuff. And it was kinda like mixed, yeah, definitely mixed, it's not just boys picking on boys or girls picking on girls.

Q: Who tended to be the victims of it, why were they picking on them?

A: They tended to be like smaller people or like they were like fat or something and like really tall and skinny and it's just people who look odd might add to the fact they get picked on. But I think now everyone in our year definitely has calmed down a lot and just accepted the fact we have to go to school and do everything and there's no point making more trouble for ourselves.

(*'Rachel', 16 years old*)

Mixed bullying was the most indiscreet form of bullying that took place and more often than not would involve the public humiliation of victims. Bullying that transcended gender was united in an exercise in 'saving face' before one's peers. This is important for two reasons. First, there was a theme of diffusion to soften the impact of the action. If the whole peer group are involved in the victimisation, then more subtle, indirect, private instances of bullying go unnoticed or are undermined in comparison to the ritualistic mixed forms of bullying. Second, the importance of peer group and friendship networks requires consideration. Although the pupils expressed in interview the instances of bullying, the teachers were rarely informed. All the pupils observed an unwritten code of silence surrounding any form of bullying.

The students who participated in this kind of behaviour were assuming a bystander role, in that they were present and aware of the scenario but took no action to stop it. Such forms of bullying are highly problematic, especially in a small school like Bayview. Rivers End, the setting for this research, is a small town and the problems that occur within the school leak out beyond the school premises, making it difficult to segregate roles and identities. Therefore, if one is a victim at Bayview School one is more than likely to be a victim in the wider community. There are no opportunities for individuals to make friends with pupils from other schools. The nearest secondary school is approximately five miles away.

It could be argued that there was a crowd mentality surrounding the plight of the bullied victims:

> There's a couple of boys in my form and people leave them out because they are very, very intelligent and one's got long teeth, they call him goof tooth and things like that. Um, I don't want to be dragged into it, but people drag me into it, calling them names and that, but I don't want to, because I've grown up with them in primary school, since like class one and I know them really well and I know they're not like losers or anything, I know they're really nice. They get picked on a lot.
> ('Jamie', 11 years old)

What is interesting is that 'Jamie' documented being a victim of bullying herself and found her position very distressing, yet here she openly admits to following the crowd and bullying these boys with the rest of her peers. She claimed that she was 'dragged' into the bullying, yet it could be the case that she bullies to 'save face' in front of her peers. It appeared that there were no circumstances when pupils tried to protect the victims of bullying. Nonetheless, the overall view of bullying at this particular school was that it was a taken for granted occurrence. As 'Rosie' concluded:

> I think wherever you go there's going to be bullying, cos you always get people that no one will talk to and that everyone like teases. I wouldn't say it was a huge issue here, there's no big bullying really. Er, people may get teased, like certain people may get picked on for certain reasons, but, yeah, you always get that, that's life.

Conclusion

Bullying was clearly a problem at the school studied. Unlike previous research into the phenomenon of school bullying, I considered the interactions and opinions of both the male and female pupils in order that 'both sides of the story' could be factored into the equation. In order to do this a qualitative approach was adopted and through asking questions about the day-to-day practices of bullying, the less extreme cases were highlighted and the more 'mundane' ones articulated.

Previous feminist criminologists have often criticised traditional criminological research and claimed that the accounts presented in academic texts often

> define the delinquent as unmistakably and exclusively male. Indeed, when girls feature in these accounts it is to provide the appropriate counterpoints to the dominant male theme. There is no balance or equality in these accounts, female figures are whisked on and off the stage, a small cast of extras without whom the plot cannot go forward but who have no lines to say. (Heidensohn 1996: 133)

One could argue that this is because the plethora of existing criminological work has been carried out and written by men and it is easier to write about what one knows. Therefore one could argue that female researchers can integrate women into their research more easily. One can draw on personal experience, deconstruct the female participation and present accurate portraits of how adolescent and adult women are involved in criminal activity (Daly and Chesney-Lind 2004). Consequently in my research the female pupils' unique bullying styles were exposed. They also upheld the code of silence and observed the social rule that one should never 'grass' on a peer. Without understanding the roles of the females in this particular piece of work crucial elements would have been missing in trying to comprehend the pupil interactions within the school.

These findings build upon McRobbie and Garber's argument that 'The important question then, may not be the absence or presence of girls in the male sub-cultures, but the complementary ways in which girls interact among themselves and with each other to form a distinctive culture of their own' (1976: 219). I would suggest that in order to understand the interactions of pupils at a mixed gendered school the separate female culture needs to be uncovered but the male culture still requires attention and any united groups have to be analysed. Rather than split the genders I looked at them together and found much of the interaction often had sexual undertones. This is consistent with previous research that has found that violent girls' social interactions involve a constant battle for dominance of girls over girls in search of male attention (Artz 2004). This can also be viewed as particularly relevant in relation to the plight of victims at the hands of mixed groups whereby victims were often attacked for being immature, late developers, or ugly and different from the stated peer group 'norm'. Bullying is an attack on the vulnerable and there was a consensus among the pupils that they should be intolerant of differences. Surely in this instance one could argue that *everyone* was being delinquent. This could mean that such subtle uniting of the genders should be a future consideration in contemporary feminist criminological research.

Lees (1993) suggested that the way masculinity and femininity are constituted changes in different historical periods. Expanding on this argument and line of thought could help to explain the 'uniting of the genders' that occurred at Bayview School. The pupils still behaved in masculine and feminine ways but they were not in opposition all the time and they did not always assume 'traditional' gender roles. Once again, could this be a sign of the times in which the research was conducted?

Gender was not the primary lens of the research but as the fieldwork progressed it could not be ignored. From this research the complexities of female bullying were observed and documented. I would argue that the female pupils were active participants in incidents of school bullying and could be viewed as 'knowing catalysts'. Furthermore, the girls observed the code of silence, and thus were operating in the same way as the boys. It emerged that the unwritten rules of the peer groups were more important than the official rules of the school and this was something that was subscribed to regardless of gender.

I have argued that one gender should not be prioritised or analysed over and above the other. Through this research, the extent of male bullying and plight of male victimisation was uncovered. The traditional view that boys have a fight and clear the air, and it will all be 'forgotten in the morning', is a severe underestimation of what it means to be a male pupil at school, victimised day in, day out, by one's peer group.

In conclusion I would argue that by splitting the genders, research has been focused inappropriately. Girls and boys were very much present at all levels of the friendship group; whether they were bullies, victims or bystanders they were united in subcultural activities. It is no longer a case of girls versus boys but of an interconnectedness of the genders in all aspects of their day-to-day lives. Future research needs to differentiate within the genders as well as between them. The notion of being a 'female' pupil was not a united existence. To talk about girls as a united group obscures the differences between the female pupils. These differences were articulated by both male and female pupils, but research rarely taps into categories within categories. Therefore, if the 'true' extent of mundane, day-to-day bullying incidents is ever to be understood and reduced, the power and complexities of the peer group networks have to be considered. Such findings may not make front page news but these incidents are very much the reality of daily schooling experiences for female and male pupils.

References

Alder, C. and Worrall, A. (2004) 'A Contemporary Crisis?', in C. Alder and A. Worrall (eds) *Girls' Violence: Myths and Realities*, New York: State University of New York Press.

Alder, C. and Worrall, A. (eds) (2004) *Girls' Violence: Myths and Realities*, New York: State University of New York Press.

Ahmad, Y. and Smith, P. K. (1994) 'Bullying in Schools and the Issue of Sex Differences', in J. Archer (ed.) *Male Violence*, London: Routledge.

Artz, S. (2004) 'Violence in the School Yard: School Girls' Use of Violence', in C. Adler and A. Worrall (eds) *Girls' Violence: Myths and Realities*, New York: State University of New York Press.

Bjorkvist, K., Lagerspetz, K. M. J. and Kaukainen, A. (1992) 'Do Girls Manipulate and Boys Fight? Developmental Trends in Regard to Direct and Indirect Aggression', *Aggressive Behaviour*, 18: 117–27.

Carlen, P. (1983) *Women's Imprisonment*, London: Routledge.

Carlen, P. and Worrall, A. (eds) (1987) *Gender, Crime and Justice*, Milton Keynes: Open University Press.

Daly, K. and Chesney-Lind, H. (2004) 'Feminism and Criminology' in P. J. Schram and B. Koons-Witt (eds) *Gendered In(Justice): Theory and Practice in Feminist Criminology*, Illinois: Wakeland Press.

Heidensohn, F. (1996) *Women and Crime*, 2nd edn, London: Macmillan (1st edn 1985).

Heidensohn, F. (2001) 'Women and Violence: Myths and Reality in the 21st Century', *Criminal Justice Matters*, 42: 20.

Kirsta, A. (1994) *Deadlier than the Male: Violence and Aggression in Women*, London: HarperCollins.

Lees, S. (1993) *Sugar and Spice: Sexuality and Adolescent Girls*, London: Penguin.

Loucks, N. (2004) 'Women in Prison', in G. McIvor (ed.) *Women Who Offend*, London: Jessica Kingsley.

McIvor, G. (ed.) (2004) *Women Who Offend*, London: Jessica Kingsley.

McRobbie, A. and Garber, J. (1976) 'Girls and Subcultures', in S. Hall and T. Jefferson (eds) *Resistance Through Rituals: Youth Subcultures in Post War Britain*, London: Hutchinson.

Phillips, C. E. (1994) *Aggressive Behaviour Amongst Young People: School Bullying and Physical Fighting*, unpublished PhD thesis, Manchester University.

Phillips, C. E. (2003) 'Who's Who in the Pecking Order? Aggression and "Normal Violence" in the Lives of Girls and Boys', *British Journal of Criminology*, 43: 710–28.

Slee, P. T. and Rigby, K. 1993. 'Australian School Children's Self Appraisal of Interpersonal Relations: the Bullying Experience', *Child Psychiatry and Human Development* 23: 273–82.

Smith, P. K. and Sharp, S. (1994) 'The Problem of School Bullying', in P. K. Smith and S. Sharp (eds) *School Bullying: Insights and Perspectives*, London: Routledge.

Stanko, E. A. and Hobdell, K. (1993) 'Assault on Men: Masculinity and Male Victimization', *British Journal of Criminology*, 33: 400–15.

Chapter 5

Regulating prostitution: controlling women's lives

Joanna Phoenix

The gendered nature of prostitution and the violence, exploitation and criminalisation that women experience when selling sex have been contentious issues for the last couple of decades, for academics and feminist campaigners alike. The debates have centred on a relatively limited range of questions focused on how to explain or conceptualise prostitution. What remains unquestioned, however, is that it is the women in prostitution who bear the brunt of regulation and punishment. Based on decades of empirical research, the last 30 years have seen a concerted effort by feminist scholars and campaigners to bring pressure on successive governments to address the vulnerability faced by women in prostitution. The aim of this chapter is to examine how prostitution – or rather street prostitution – is contemporarily regulated and the gendered nature and impact of that regulation.

The argument of this chapter is that the women who make up the majority of individuals selling sex in this country now find themselves subject to an interlocking system of regulation that variously defines them in policy as offenders; threats to public sexual health; victims of child abuse and, vulnerable women who must be compelled to seek help. Each policy definition gives rise to a set of interventions aimed at changing, or working with, different aspects of women's lives. In this way, defining women as a threat to public sexual health brings with it harm minimisation programmes aimed at educating women into working more 'safely'; while defining women as offenders brings with it criminal justice interventions. These various policy definitions create an interlocking system of regulation because they are not mutually exclusive. A woman can be defined as a victim as well as an offender, a vulnerable woman and a threat to public sexual health. As a result the way in which prostitution is regulated is capable of much deeper, lesser accountable and more far-reaching interventions into the lives of women in prostitution than the system of regulation that was in place throughout the majority of the twentieth century. Whereas in the 1980s a woman in prostitution may have only faced a fine, now she is liable to the full range of criminal justice disposals. But it does not end there; she is also likely to face being compelled to undertake programmes in which her relationships and the choices she makes in her life outside prostitution are subject to scrutiny and intervention.

In order to make this argument, this chapter is divided into five main sections. In the first section I outline some of the empirical realities of involvement in prostitution in Britain in the twenty-first century. The second section describes how prostitution-related criminal justice sanctions are based on the idea that prostitution is a problem of public nuisance. Following on from this, I detail how the re-emergence of the notion that prostitution is a threat to public sexual health effectively split the regulation of prostitution between punitive criminal justice sanctions and educative health-based interventions. I then outline the way that new definitions of young people's involvement in prostitution impacted on the regulatory framework. Defining prostitution as a matter of child sexual abuse generated a third layer of intervention and further split the regulation of prostitution between statutory and non-statutory social services, sexual health outreach and criminal justice. The final section addresses recent Home Office proposals for reforming the regulation of prostitution. These reforms are based on the idea that women in prostitution are vulnerable victims of unscrupulous and criminal men and what is proposed is a system of 'enforcement plus support' in which women are compelled into welfare-based services that aim to change the types of choices they make.[1] Failure to do so then warrants even stronger criminal justice sanctions. It should be noted that the main focus of this chapter is the ways in which the regulation of prostitution impacts on street-working women.

Empirical realities

There can be no understanding of women's involvement in or the regulation of prostitution that does not take account of women's socio-economic status more generally. As McLeod (1982) pointed out, there are economic push and pull factors that help to structure the sorts of choices women can and do make with regard to whether they sell sex. Prostituting is, above all, an economic activity and involvement in it is usually conditioned by the economic situation in which women find themselves. Despite the claim that modernity and the drive for 'equality' has freed women from their economic dependency on male relatives, increased the range of economic opportunities for women and permitted a life that is not based on domesticity and familialism, empirical evidence indicates that women's lives are still circumscribed by the same dynamics of inequality that have existed for centuries. These dynamics continue to structure women's poverty and their economic dependency on men. Recent research compiled by the Equal Opportunities Commission reports that 'average hourly earnings for women working full-time are 18% lower than for men working full-time, and for women working part-time hourly earnings are 40% lower' (EOC 2003: 1). Significantly, 44 per cent of women who are economically active are part-time workers in comparison to only 11 per cent of economically active men (EOC 2003: 1). In this way, women's access to financial security, social security benefits, housing, pensions and so on are still mediated by and through their relationships with men. And for some women, such dependency bears a heavy burden. Regardless of years of campaigning and successive policy reforms, domestic violence continues. An examination of ten domestic violence prevalence studies across Europe has indicated that one in four women will experience domestic violence over their lifetimes and between 6 per cent and 10 per cent of women suffer domestic violence in the course of a given year (Council of Europe 2002). The significance of the persistence of domestic abuse is simple: many women find themselves locked into violent and unhappy relationships because of their economic dependency. Leaving these relationships brings with it the risks of poverty.

The burdens of violence and poverty are not spread equally among women in the UK. Other forms of social inequalities combine with women's individual class position so that some women can avert the risks of poverty and violence while at the same time limiting other women's ability to avoid the same risks. Ordinary women whose lives are largely unremarkable and mundane experience social and economic dependency on men who may, or may not, let them down, leave them or abuse them, or from whom they may be desperate to escape. Such women find themselves in a struggle to survive on meagre incomes or social security benefits as they negotiate the difficulties of unemployment, underemployment, homelessness, housing difficulties, childcare problems and so on. Time and again, empirical studies confirm that women working from the streets have just such backgrounds. They are like many other working-class women in that they face the risks of violence and poverty and make choices in their struggle to survive. Some of the choices are commonplace, such as claiming benefits, whereas others are more extraordinary, such as engaging in prostitution (Phoenix 2001; O'Neill 2001; Saunders 2005).

Contemporary detailed ethnographic studies of prostitution have provided descriptions not just of women's poverty, but the numerous other economic and social problems encountered. For many researchers, feminist and non-feminist alike, the 'bottom line' is that involvement in prostitution is always economic need (Carlen 1996; Melrose *et al* 1999; O'Neill 2001; Phoenix 2001). While adult women in prostitution regularly cite inadequate benefits or income, drug and alcohol problems, homelessness and housing difficulties as some of the primary reasons for getting into prostitution to begin with, the situation for young women is even more grim. Two decades of social policy reform has meant that there are few or no social benefits that the young can claim: entrance into the legitimate labour force and the provision of social security benefits are all age-restricted (Hill and Tisdall 1997). It should come as no surprise, therefore, that adult and young women report that involvement in prostitution provides them with a means to get money to buy things that they cannot otherwise afford (such as consumables), to fund drug and alcohol problems (both their own and their partner's) and as a means of supporting themselves and any dependants they may have while avoiding begging or other criminogenic activities that attract (up to now) much harsher and higher levels of punishment.

Research also tells another tale, and that is of the widespread practice of extorting money from women in prostitution via the use of threats, intimidation and violence or indeed through the coercion of charm and love (Barnardo's 1998; Phoenix 2001). Ethnographic research demonstrates the regularity by which women in prostitution experience physical attacks and sexual assaults, often severe and resulting in hospitalisations, broken bones, bruises and burns, of being kidnapped and of having most if not all of the money earned taken by boyfriends, partners, pimps and a host of other men. And the violence and exploitation does not end there. Individuals working as prostitutes also tell researchers about harassment from neighbours in the areas in which they work as well as from the police themselves.

In this respect, while street prostitution might well provide women with a strategy to survive the shattering effects of poverty and social problems, it also exposes them to risks that further entrap them in that poverty and exacerbate the social difficulties they experience. So for instance, recent qualitative research has described the way in which working in prostitution leads to even greater levels of dependency on men, and through economic exploitation (often by these men), greater levels of poverty that ultimately adversely impacts on women's longer term physical, sexual and mental health (Ward *et al.* 1999) and increasing their risks of drug and alcohol problems (May *et al.* 1999).

When discussing women's involvement in prostitution it is important to recognise the gendered nature of the experiences and inequalities that prostitute women have. It is also important to acknowledge that not all prostitution is the same. Some women are more able to control their working environments than others (Saunders 2005). Specifically the experiences of poverty, social welfare and health problems and violence are more typical of those women working from the streets and not necessarily shared by those who either work indoors in saunas and brothels or who work within escort agencies. So, for example, women working in saunas talk about the way in which simply working with other women helps to protect them from the threat of predatory violence (Saunders 2005). In comparison, street-working women regularly report that changes in the law with regard to kerb-crawling have lessened the time that they can spend assessing a potential client and therefore increase their risks of punter violence (Church *et al.* 2001). And, as Saunders (2005) and Phoenix (2001) have argued, the experience and social organisation of prostitution is shaped not just by marketability of sex, i.e. the commodification process, but through the various ways in which prostitution is regulated and policed through formal criminal justice and social policies.

In sum, nearly two centuries of research has shown that, especially in relation to street work, women in prostitution tend to have a multiplicity of social and economic difficulties. For them, prostitution presents the possibility of surviving poverty, of becoming independent, of securing their own financial futures. However, such security and independence is often illusory. Instead, street-working women often experience greater levels of poverty as well as greater levels and prevalence of violence and exploitation than they might have experienced before. In short, involvement in prostitution often generates the very dynamics that fuel the sorts of social and economic problems that drove the women into prostitution. The rest of this chapter examines the different ways that (street-based) prostitution is regulated and controlled.

Regulating nuisance: managing prostitution through criminal justice sanctions

The regulation of prostitution is constituted and shaped by the way that 'the problem' is defined because how a problem is defined necessarily suggests what should be done to address it. Any changes in definition or understanding of 'the problem', when officially recognised by government or non-governmental voluntary organisations, usually results in a call to implement different kinds of intervention or strategies to deal with the problem. Since the 1950s, the UK has practised what can be called a form of negative regulationism with regard to prostitution. The policing of prostitution through the use of criminal justice seeks only to sanction the more 'disruptive' aspects of prostitution and its associated activities. In this way, the objective of formal criminal justice is not to abolish prostitution, but rather to 'manage' it. Thus, selling sex is not illegal, but many activities connected with it are, such as loitering or soliciting in public places for the purposes of prostitution. This approach was engineered by the Wolfenden Report, which recommended that private sexuality and morality was not an appropriate object of legal control. In its preamble, the Wolfenden Committee asserted that the purpose of the criminal law is

> to preserve public order and decency, to protect the citizen from what is offensive or injurious and to provide sufficient safeguards against exploitation and corruption of others, particularly those who are specially vulnerable because they are young, weak in body or mind, inexperienced or, in a state of special physical, official or economic dependence. (Home Office 1957: 9–10)

The Wolfenden Committee then continued:

> It is not in our view the function of the law to intervene in the private lives of citizens, or to seek to enforce any particular pattern of behaviour, further than is necessary to carry out the purposes we have outlined. It follows that we do not believe

it to be a function of the law to attempt to cover all the fields of sexual behaviour. Certain forms of sexual behaviour are regarded by many as sinful, morally wrong, or objectionable for reasons of conscience, or of religious or cultural tradition; and such actions may be reprobated on these grounds. But the criminal law does not cover all such actions at the present time: for instance, adultery and fornication are not offences for which a person can be punished by the criminal law. Nor indeed is prostitution as such. (Home Office 1957: 10)

In this way, the Wolfenden Report defined the problem of prostitution as a matter of private morality. The only exceptions were to be activities and behaviours that caused an affront to public decency or a public nuisance. The Wolfenden Committee was clear:

ordinary citizens who live in these areas [i.e. those in which street prostitution takes place] cannot, in going about their daily business, avoid the sight of a state of affairs which seems to them to be an affront to public order and decency. (Home Office 1957: 82)

For this reason, Wolfenden Committee asserted that the law should focus on street prostitution rather than the clients (or even indoor prostitution) because:

the simple fact is that prostitutes do parade themselves more habitually and openly than their prospective customers, and do by their continual presence affront the sense of decency of the ordinary citizen. In doing so they create a nuisance which, in our view, the law is entitled to recognise and deal with. (Home Office 1957: 87)

The result of the Wolfenden Report has been a system of regulation which makes it illegal to loiter or solicit in a public place for the purposes of prostitution and uses 'prostitutes' cautions' in which women (and only women) suspected of loitering or soliciting for prostitution are given two cautions before being charged as a common prostitute. The Wolfenden Committee also recommended that the punishment of prostitution-related offences should start with a fine and become progressively more severe, culminating with imprisonment for up to three months.[2] Using the criminal justice system in such a way to regulate prostitution has remained unchanged in the interceding 50 years, with the exception of a sentencing guidance issued in 1982 that altered the punishment of soliciting or loitering to fines only.

One of the problems managing prostitution in such a way is that the burden of control has disproportionately fallen on street-working women. By so clearly defining the problem of prostitution to be a problem of the visibility of prostitute women, the Wolfenden Committee effectively created a special and unique category of offenders ('common prostitutes') who are deemed fit to receive more punitive measures. The Street Offences Act 1959 (which implemented the Wolfenden recommendations) also created an exceptional and discriminatory situation in which the general legal maxim of 'innocent until proven guilty' is displaced through a procedural system in which women are tried not on the evidence against them but on their previous criminal records and the cautions they have received. Simply the opinions of police officers on two occasions that a woman is soliciting or loitering is sufficient to charge her with being a common prostitute. It was not until 1986 that legal reform took place to extend criminal justice interventions to 'kerb-crawlers', and even then the police were not given any powers of arrest until 2001. Any cautions or charges interventions can only take place if a man is 'persistently' kerb-crawling, that is on three or more occasions.

More than this, and as Self (2003) has argued, the regulation of prostitution, despite official rhetoric to the contrary, has always been about regulating the moral choices of a small group of women. The Wolfenden framework protects the morality of some understood as 'decent', 'ordinary' citizens while punishing the those of others – women in prostitution who are thereby not 'decent' or 'ordinary'. Notions of what is offensive, 'indecent' or an affront to women working in prostitution, as opposed to those who are not, are excluded from the calculation of what is seen to be a nuisance and therefore in need of regulation. Because the women are classified as immoral and indecent themselves, they cannot be victims of immoral or indecent behaviour.

A second problem of the Wolfenden framework is the comparative under-enforcement of provisions designed to protect women working in prostitution (Matthews 1986; Edwards 1997; Phoenix 2001; Saunders 2005). Take, for example, the provision in the Sexual Offences Act 1956 against 'living off the earnings of prostitution', i.e. pimping, and 'exercising control over a prostitute', i.e. brothel-keeping. The focus of legal and police attention on the visible aspects of prostitution has enabled these less visible and less public activities to go virtually unregulated (Matthews 1986). In 2003, 30 convictions and four cautions were secured for living off earnings of prostitution or exercising control over a prostitute. The same year saw 2,627 convictions and 902 cautions for soliciting or loitering in a public place for the purposes of prostitution (source: Office for Criminal Justice Reform, Home Office).

Edwards (1997) is direct and argues that the failure to police proscriptions against exploitation is an example of the inequality of treatment that the law gives to women in prostitution. Smart (1995) and Phoenix (2001) have also noted that such provisions fail to differentiate between those individuals who extort, exploit, control and/or intimidate women in prostitution and those who simply share money and resources. More, current practice requires that the victims of exploitation and violence give evidence against the very individuals who threaten and abuse them – a situation that inhibits many of the victims from coming forward (Phoenix and Oerton 2005).

A final problem of the Wolfenden framework is the way in which fining women for prostitution-related offences creates a revolving door and exacerbates the poverty many women experience. In order to pay their fines, the women resort to prostitution, or in many cases merely let their fines accrue and then face prison sentences for fine-defaulting (see Matthews 1986 and Phoenix 2001). In this way the burden of regulation and punishment falls disproportionately to the one group least able to afford it – street-working poor women.

Regulating threats to public sexual health: managing prostitution through outreach programmes and the decline in criminal justice interventions

Throughout the 1980s and 1990s and in response to the concern about an HIV/AIDs pandemic, fears grew about the impact of prostitution (and more specifically, prostitutes' bodies (cf. Spongberg 1997)) on the sexual health of the 'innocent' and 'moral' general populace. Such concerns were not new.[3] In the mid nineteenth century, the idea that street-working women posed a threat to the sexual health of the nation underpinned the Contagious Diseases Acts of 1864, 1866 and 1869. These Acts enabled the police to force women they suspected of being prostitutes to undergo medical inspections to ensure that they were 'clean' in garrison towns. Although the Acts were repealed before the end of the nineteenth century, the measures were enacted again at the beginning of the First World War with the passing of the Defence of the Realm Act (1914), when the government had grave concerns as to the sexual health of the army. While the concern that 'unclean prostitutes' would infect the general population faded away in the period following the First World War, the arrival of the HIV/AIDS pandemic in the 1980s gave it renewed vigour. Popular media and public discussion drew on the stereotype of a 'junkie whore' – a syringe-using, drug-addicted woman selling sex from the streets. These women were seen as reservoirs of sexual disease. At the time, various calls were made to restrict their freedom of movement, or segregate them. Such was the climate of hostility towards women in prostitution that several commentators accused the media of conducting and fuelling a witch hunt (Roberts 1992; O'Neill 2001; ECP 1997). For instance, in 1992 the *Sunday Express* reported that the King's Cross police alleged that three-quarters of the women working in the area were infected with the AIDs virus. The allegation was found to be untrue and based only on the opinion of various arresting officers as to whether individual women might be infected (ECP 1997).

During the 1990s, however, there was shift of viewpoint in the way in which prostitution and threats to public sexual health were related. Focus moved from prostitute bodies *per se* to the specific behaviours and the lifestyles of women in prostitution. As a result, a plethora of new services developed with the aim of producing a change in women's behaviour (Phoenix 2001). The methods used are educative. The new sexual health agenda has as its ultimate aim reducing the harm of prostitution (i.e. the spread of sexually transmitted infections) to both the individual woman and the general populace. Throughout the early 1990s, considerable resources were made available to genito-urinary clinics and sexual health outreach projects to work with women in prostitution. The types of interventions that sexual health outreach projects, in particular, offer seek to re-educate them about their 'high-risk' behaviours. In order to do so, most sexual health outreach projects adopt a multi-agency approach in which everything from general and sexual health concerns, drugs and alcohol abuse and misuse, housing and homelessness and domestic violence are addressed. Women are brought into the service either by referral from another agency or through personal contact. Involvement with sexual health outreach projects is on a non-judgemental, voluntary and anonymous basis. Importantly, outreach projects also liaise with the police about community issues regarding prostitution and the arrest and prosecution of violent punters and men who are exploiting women. For example, during the 1990s the SAFE Project in Birmingham provided not only sexual health education but gave women condoms; took them to the genito-urinary clinic; helped them access other multi-agency projects and services; went with the women to court; pioneered the 'Ugly Mugs Scheme', in which identifying information about violent and dangerous punters was passed from woman to woman; liaised with police about these violent punters; and helped the police deal with community issues caused by a vociferous vigilante movement (i.e. the Streetwatch and Care Association). By the mid 1990s most major cities in the UK had sexual health outreach projects. Accompanying this growth, there has been a notable decline in criminal justice interventions. By 1999, the police scaled down their direct regulation across the country and instead worked in conjunction with the outreach projects to help produce a more 'manageable' street trade. This change can be seen in the remarkable decrease in the number of women being arrested and convicted for loitering or soliciting in public for the purposes of prostitution. In 1989 there were over 15,739 women cautioned or convicted for soliciting. By 2002 this number had fallen to 4,102 (source: Offending and Criminal Justice Group, Home Office; see also Matthews 2005). By 2003, the number had fallen still further to just under 3,000 (source: Criminal Justice Reform Group, Home Office).

To summarise, then, concerns about how prostitution might threaten public sexual health has resulted in the growth and establishment of sexual health outreach projects. While these projects are not part of the formal system of regulating prostitution, they nevertheless play an important role. Policing and punishment have dramatically reduced as formal criminal justice interventions give way to a health agenda. That said, the welfare services offered by sexual health outreach projects, while still focused on women's prostituting activities, have not *replaced* criminal justice mechanisms for regulating prostitution. Traditional methods of arrest, charge and punishment coexist (albeit in a reduced capacity) with the harm minimisation approaches of sexual health outreach.

Regulating the coercion of children: intervening in prostitution through child protection work

By the mid to late 1990s the dominance of the health agenda *vis-à-vis* regulating prostitution was challenged by a growing awareness and concern about the age of some of the people involved in prostitution.

Major children's charities ran campaigns calling for a change in the way in which girls in prostitution were treated. The Children's Society pointed out the anomaly of charging and convicting girls under the age of sexual consent for prostitution-related offences (Lee and O'Brien 1995). Barnardo's published a report entitled *Whose Daughter Next?* in which it was argued that girls in prostitution are the victims of exploitation and child abuse no matter what their circumstances and should be treated as such: they should be referred to social services and not criminalised. Pressure eventually led to the Department of Health and Home Office jointly issuing a guidance document in May 2000, entitled *Safeguarding Children in Prostitution*. This guidance directs all individuals working with young people in prostitution to think of them not as potential offenders but as victims. The claim is that no child (legally defined as anyone under the age of 18 years old) can consent to being involved in prostitution, that most young people are coerced into it and that at any rate the men who either entrap them in prostitution or buy sex from them are child sexual abusers and should be prosecuted.

> The Government recognises that the vast majority of children do not voluntarily enter prostitution. They are coerced, enticed or utterly desperate. We need to ensure that local agencies act quickly and sensitively in the best interests of the children concerned ... They should treat such children as children in need, who may be suffering, or may be likely to suffer significant harm. (DOH/HO 2000: 3)

These changing ideas about 'the problem' of prostitution further split the way that prostitution is regulated. Sexual health outreach programmes continue to work with adult women and provide general welfare and health services, but have reported difficulties in sustaining their work with anyone under the age of 18 as the involvement in prostitution of such people is now defined as a child protection issue and has the potential to contravene the strict confidentiality ethos of many sexual health outreach projects (see Phoenix 2002 for a fuller explanation). Instead, a plethora of multi-agency teams now exist to meet the needs of young people. These multi-agency teams frequently are little more than new constellations of existing statutory social services and voluntary children's services and are most often funded by the big children's charities. Projects such as SECOS in Middlesbrough or BASE in Bristol – both funded by Barnardo's – work very closely with social services and the local police. Such approaches are not without difficulties. First, voluntary organisations and social services now have a legal obligation to exit young people from prostitution in a context where no extra funding resources have been provided. Second, a culture of legal liability ensures that workers are highly anxious about being blamed if any specific girl does not leave prostitution, or gets severely hurt while involved in prostitution. Third, the complex needs of young people are not easily accommodated by the methods of working developed to deal with the abuse and neglect of much younger children by family members or relatives. In this context, many agencies can offer little more than 'working with where the young person is at' through self-esteem work, counselling and advocacy. In the five years since the introduction of this guidance, many young women in prostitution have ended up incarcerated in secure units, not as a punishment for their involvement in prostitution but as a means of limiting the liability to the organisation and the individual professional when girls continue to sell sex.

Government guidance to treat young people in prostitution as victims of child abuse has created yet another layer in the regulation of prostitution and has extended the type of control in which young women find themselves enmeshed. Adopting a child protection strategy for dealing with young women's involvement in prostitution focuses attention and intervention not simply on a girl's prostituting activities but on her wider relationships and deeper psychological state of being. Such focus is generated by the necessity that organisations assess both the girl's status as victim (to specific men) and her motivation to change. Official policy recommends that where a girl is not a victim and continues to sell sex, then the use of criminal justice sanctions is approved. Therefore, any particular girl's motivation and status as victim is all-important.

> However it would be wrong to say that a boy or girl under 18 *never* freely chooses to continue to solicit, loiter or importune … and does not knowingly break the law … The criminal justice process should only be considered if the child persistently and voluntarily continues to solicit, loiter or importune for the purposes of prostitution. (DOH/HO 2000: 27–8, emphasis in original)

Young people in prostitution are thereby caught within three interlocking systems of regulation: (i) social welfare based services for abused children, which frequently offer these young people more of the same social services interventions that they have already experienced and often rejected; (ii) harm minimisation, re-educative programmes of sexual health outreach (where such programmes choose to continue to work with young people); and (iii) criminal justice sanctions when nothing else works.

Regulating victimisation and vulnerability: abolishing street prostitution through 'enforcement plus support'

Guidance on young people in prostitution challenged the dominance of the health agenda by defining prostitution as being a problem of the child abuse, victimisation and the exploitation of vulnerable girls. Of course, this definition is not particularly new. A long tradition of feminist thinking has also defined prostitution in relation to male sexual violence. However, such understandings have not been officially recognised – until now. In 2004, the Home Office began a consultation process about reforming prostitution-related legislation, which ended in January 2006. The initial document, *Paying the Price*, and the resulting reform recommendations, *A Coordinated Prostitution Strategy and a Summary of Responses to Paying the Price*, signal a change from negative regulationism to an abolitionist agenda in which both soft law (guidance, Home Office circulars and resources) and criminal justice are used to 'challenge the view that prostitution is inevitable and here to stay [and] achieve an overall reduction in street prostitution' (Home Office 2006: 1). Current proposals for policy change are not geared towards managing the disruptive effects of prostitution, but disrupting the sex trade altogether. The reason for such a policy change is precisely because of governmental recognition of women's victimisation – or rather, because the conceptualisation of the problem of prostitution that government must now address is that women in prostitution are either wholly victimised (i.e. victims) or voluntarily engaged and therefore threats to community safety (i.e. offenders). Conceptualising the problem of prostitution in such a manner creates an imperative for action and the action that is recommended is a greater use of welfarist-based interventions not as an alternative to criminal justice sanctions, but backed by the full range of criminal justice sanctions.

Paying the Price and *A Coordinated Strategy* regularly repeat that the 'problems' that need tackling are: (i) the exploitation of women and children; (ii) trafficking of individual for commercial sexual exploitation; (iii) the ways in which debt and drug addiction trap individuals into prostitution; and (iv) the links between drugs markets, serious and organised crime and prostitution. Throughout both documents there are constant references to 'pimps', 'traffickers', 'dealers', 'sexual abusers', 'coercers' and a host of other hyper-masculine criminal men. Both documents also heavily draw on the explanation of involvement in prostitution that was put forward in relation to young people where poverty, constrained social and economic difficulties that women experience, and the ways in which women make choices to be involved in prostitution are rendered not important. To be clear, the problem of prostitution is now defined almost entirely in relation to the misdeeds of criminal men. And it is these criminal men's presence that contributes to the understanding of prostitution as causing an even wider community problem – that is, the very destruction of local communities.

> Prostitution undermines public order and creates a climate in which more serious crime can flourish. Street prostitution is often associated with local drug markets, bringing Class A drugs and gun culture to local communities. (Home Office 2004: 74)

Contemporary official policy draws on the stereotype of a prostitute-victim. In policy documents, doubt is cast about any expression of choice on the part of the women.

> Debt and drug addiction play a major part in driving people into prostitution as a survival activity. They are also significant factors, along with the threat of violence from pimps/partners, in making it difficult to leave. Those involved in prostitution can be particularly difficult to reach, claiming that prostitution is their choice and that they don't want to leave – through a combination of fear, the process of normalisation or in an effort to maintain their dignity. While preventative work at an early age is important we must also work to address the safety of the thousands already trapped by debt and drug addiction. (Home Office 2004: 55)

Such conceptions create the very conditions for increasing the levels of regulation and, indeed, criminalisation of women in prostitution. This occurs for two reasons: (i) the stereotype of the prostitute-victim is treated as though it is an adequate explanation; and (ii) by using an enforcement plus support approach to regulation, the current reforms relocate the centrality of criminal justice responses to women who do not leave prostitution voluntarily. I will explain each of these in turn.

In *Safeguarding Children in Prostitution*, *Paying the Price* and *A Coordinated Strategy*, individuals in prostitution are seen as victims because they do not voluntarily consent to sell sex. They are victims because something or someone else has forced or compelled them. Put another way, policy defines consent and voluntarism as the capacity to make a different choice than be involved in prostitution – or to choose not to work in prostitution. The key problem that policy now addresses is therefore to create the situation in which women make their own choice to leave prostitution.

Such a simple and naive understanding of the conditions in which women get involved in prostitution belie the economic and social realities discussed at the beginning of this chapter. They also contradict the ethnographic research that argues that women and young people do make choices, albeit not in conditions of their own choosing (Phoenix 2001; Saunders 2005). The experiences of these women plainly do not fit the model of explanation framing current policy directions. So, while many street-working women suffer some form of victimisation and exploitation, they are not all victims waiting to be saved by the police or other agencies. Many are just poor women struggling to survive.

The enforcement plus support approach that has now been adopted reinforces the centrality of criminal justice sanctions in the regulation of prostitution. This is a result of the very demarcation between victims and offenders that is at the heart of current policy. On this point, *Paying the Price* is clear. The criminal law can and should be used to 'rigorously clamp down on unacceptable behaviour [i.e. voluntarily engaging in prostitution] and criminality'. This is an approach in which, unless there is the presence of a 'pimp' or other such controlling man, the responsibility for involvement in prostitution is placed solely within poor choices made by the individual and in which the question of necessity never appears. Here, the full force of criminal justice is used to compel women to leave *without* any attention being paid to the socio-economic circumstances that created the impetus for prostitution. In other words, this final new layer of regulation generates greater and greater levels of intervention and control in women's lives while at the same time making them responsible (as in blameworthy) for their own poverty and their attempts to survive it.

The current offence of loitering or soliciting is a very low-level offence and, as such, the court will usually only consider imposing a fine. This is said to have very little deterrent effect and does not address the underlying causes of the offending behaviour. To rectify this situation, the Government intends to publish proposals for legislative reform to provide a penalty specifically tailored to the needs of men and women in prostitution. The intention will be for the courts to be able to order an appropriate package of intervention to address the causes of the offending behaviour where that behaviour is persistent. (Home Office 2006: 37)

In practice this means a variety of interventions which include voluntary self-referrals to outreach programmes, the use of civil Anti-Social Behaviour Orders and Intervention Orders by the police and local authorities compelling women into drug treatment or other treatment programmes (breach of either of which constitutes the possibility of a prison sentence of up to five years); pre-charge diversion in which individuals are referred to drug intervention programmes; conditional discharges; mandatory drug testing and compulsory attendance at drug intervention programmes following charging as well as the full range of ordinary criminal justice sanctions following repeated conviction. The aim is clear:

Under this staged approach those women (and men) who respond to informal referrals and seek help from support services to leave prostitution, and those who engage with the CJIT (Criminal Justice Integrated Team) workers to receive treatment and other support, *may* avoid further criminalisation. However, for those individuals who, for whatever reason, continue to be involved in street prostitution, the criminal justice system will respond with rehabilitative intervention to reduced re-offending and to protect local communities. (Home Office 2006: 39)

Under this new 'coordinated' regulation system, it is not merely and only the individual's prostituting activities that become the focus of intervention and sanction. Instead it is the totality of their lives and relationships. Their patterns of drug use, the appropriateness of their housing, their personal relationships with the men in their lives, their mental health, their educational and work status and so on all become the target of regulation.

It is this very net-widening in terms of both the interventions and the object of intervention that creates the conditions in which women who engage in prostitution will have their lives more intensely governed and regulated than they have hitherto experienced. And when their wider behaviour, actions, relationships and choices are judged and found wanting they become, by definition, appropriate subjects of even harsher criminal justice punishments. For, as stated before, the question of necessity has been excluded from policy as both an explanation for women's engagement in prostitution as well as an issue that should be addressed.

Conclusion

The multi-layered system of governing and regulating prostitution (and thereby the women in prostitution) that is now in place in the UK is a complex web of mixed intentions and mixed purposeful actions. As different aspects of prostitution are seen to take precedence for action over others, new forms of intervention spring up that do not function as alternatives to punishment, but rather are tacked on to existing and expanding punishments. In this way the centrality of punitive sanctions remains intact. What stays unaddressed in policy and practice is that it is precisely those women who are most vulnerable to victimisation and poverty who continue to bear the brunt of regulation and punishment – that is, women working from the streets. The approach of enforcement plus support with the express aim of reducing street prostitution ensures that these women will become an even smaller, more visible (to support agencies and police) and more controlled group of women – the totality of whose lives is now open to state-sponsored and sanctioned assessment and intervention. It is in this way that the regulation of prostitution ends up being an exercise in the control and governance of a small group of poor women, their relationships and their choices in the struggles to survive their own poverty.

Notes

1 At the time of writing, these proposals have yet to be fully implemented, although early indications are that they will be adopted wholesale.
2 The Wolfenden Report was implemented through the Street Offences Act 1959. However, the Sexual Offences Act 1956 also consolidated some

prostitution-related offences and made it illegal to control the activities of, live on the immoral earnings of or procure a prostitute. As will be seen later in the chapter, these provisions protecting women in prostitution are not policed at the same rate or level.

3 Mahood (1990) noted that in 1497 the Council in Aberdeen passed an Act that stated that all women in prostitution had to be branded so that members of the general population could identify them as possible carriers of syphilis.

References

Barnardo's (1998) *Whose Daughter Next? Children Abused Through Prostitution*, Ilford: Barnardos.

Carlen, P. (1996) *Jigsaw: A Political Criminology of Youth Homelessness*, Milton Keynes: Open University Press.

Church, S., Henderson, M., Barnard, M. and Hart, G. (2001) 'Violence by Clients Towards Female Prostitutes in Different Work Settings: Questionnaire Survey' *British Medical Journal*, 332: 524–5.

Council of Europe (2002). Recommendation Rec(2002)5 of the Committee of Ministers to member States on the protection of women against violence adopted on 30 April 2002 and Explanatory Memorandum. Strasbourg, France: Council of Europe.

Department of Health/Home Office (2000) *Safeguarding Children in Prostitution*, London: HMSO.

ECP (English Collective of Prostitutes) (1997) 'Campaigning for Legal Change' in G. Scambler and A. Scambler (eds) *Rethinking Prostitution*, London: Routledge.

Edwards, S. (1997) *Sex, Gender and the Legal Process*, London: Blackstone Press.

Equal Opportunities Commission (2003) *Women and Men in Britain: Pay and Income*, London: EOC.

Hill, M. and Tisdall, K. (1997) *Children and Society*, London: Longman.

Home Office (1957) *The Wolfenden Committee's Report on Homosexual Offences and Prostitution*, London: HMSO.

Home Office (2004) *Paying the Price: A Consultation Document*, London: The Stationery Office.

Home Office (2006) *A Coordinated Prostitution Strategy and a Summary of Responses to Paying the Price*, London: The Stationery Office.

Lee, M. and O'Brien, R. (1995) *The Game's Up: Redefining Child Prostitution*, London: The Children's Society.

Mahood, L. (1990) *The Magdalenes: Prostitution in the Nineteenth Century*, London: Routledge.

Matthews, R. (1986) 'Beyond Wolfenden', in R. Matthews and J. Young (eds) *Confronting Crime*, London: Sage.

Matthews, R. (2005) 'Policing Prostitution: Ten Years On', *British Journal of Criminology*, 45 (November): 877–95.

May, T., Edmunds, M. and Hough, M. (1999) *Street Business: The Links Between Sex and Drug Markets*, Police Research Series, Paper 118, London: Home Office.

McLeod, E. (1982) *Women Working: Prostitution Now*, London: Croom Helm.

Melrose, M., Barrett, D. and Brodie, I. (1999) *One Way Street? Retrospectives on Childhood Prostitution*, London: Children's Society.

O'Neill, M. (2001) *Prostitution and Feminism*, London: Polity Press.

Phoenix, J. (2001) *Making Sense of Prostitution*, London: Palgrave.

Phoenix, J. (2002) 'Youth Prostitution Policy Reforms: New Discourse, Same Old Story', in P. Carlen (ed.) *Women and Punishment: A Struggle for Justice*, Cullompton: Willan Publishing.

Phoenix, J. and Oerton, S. (2005) *Illicit and Illegal: Sex, Regulation and Social Control*, Cullompton: Willan Publishing.

Roberts, N. (1992) *Whores in History*, London: HarperCollins.

Saunders, T. (2005) *Sex Work: A Risky Business*, Cullompton: Willan Publishing.

Self, H. (2003) *Prostitution, Women and the Misuse of Law*, London: Frank Cass.

Smart, C. (1995) *Law, Crime and Sexuality: Essays in Feminism*, London: Sage.

Spongberg, M. (1997) *Feminising Venereal Disease*, London: Macmillan.

Ward, S., Day, S. and Weber, J. (1999) 'Risky Business: Health and Safety in the Sex Industry over a 9 Year Period', *Sexually Transmitted Infections* 75(5): 340–43.

Chapter 6

Stigmatised women: relatives of serious offenders and the broader impact of crime

Rachel Condry

This chapter draws upon research on a group of women whose lives were significantly affected by crime and its consequences.[1] Each of these women had a close kin relationship with someone accused or convicted of a serious crime. Second-wave feminism invited us to look upon women as victims and as offenders; a focus on offenders' families enables us to see yet further, illuminating the broader effects of crime and the criminal justice process on a greater number of women, and nowhere is this more pronounced than with the relatives of *serious* offenders. These relatives are affected by the heinous character of the crime, the public reaction, and the length of a prison sentence and other penalties subsequently imposed. The consequences of being a relative of a serious offender reach into every corner of their lives and structure their very identity and existence.

Feminist perspectives have shown the impact of crime and the criminal justice system on women offenders and women victims, and on women whose lives are connected to the criminal justice system through their working relationships – in the police (Brown and Heidensohn 2000; Heidensohn 1992; Silvestri 2003) or in prisons (Britton 2003; Farnworth 1992; Zimmer 1986) for example. We know less about the lives of women who are drawn in to these processes through their kin relationships as the wives, partners, mothers, daughters and sisters of offenders. Feminist perspectives in criminology and the debates they have stimulated have paved the way for some of the questions my research addresses: how gender relations structure the lives of women; how women view their own lives and what they do to manage difficult circumstances; and how stigma interacts with gender and how it can taint women's lives in very particular ways. Feminist perspectives drew our attention to ways in which women are stigmatised as 'doubly-deviant' criminal women, and as victims, particularly in the case of rape or intimate violence, and the damaging consequences of this stigmatisation. To this list we might add women who are stigmatised through their kin relationships – through shame brought upon the family – in this case the shame of serious offending.

My research involved ethnographic fieldwork over several years, including observation of a self-help organisation for the families of serious offenders; long, searching interviews with 32 relatives of serious offenders;[2] interviews with those working with offenders' families; and participant observation in a visitors' centre at a prison. It focused on how relatives made sense of their experiences, individually and collectively: how they described the difficulties they faced; whether they were blamed and shamed and in what manner; how they 'understood' the offence and the circumstances which had brought it about; and – for those that chose to support the offender – how they dealt with the contradiction inherent in doing this and yet not condoning his or her actions.

When the research began it soon became clear that this was a sphere in which women predominated. Almost all the active members of the self-help organisation were women; all but one of the participants who agreed to be interviewed were women, despite attempts to secure interviews with male family members; and as the research progressed it emerged that in most cases one female family member, usually a wife or mother, was taking primary responsibility for the offender and his or her needs and shouldering much of the burden of caring. We should not be surprised to find a higher number of wives taking the role of primary supporter – we know that in crime the sexual division of labour is distinctly marked and there are many more men convicted of crimes than women. In January 2006, for example, there were 4,229 women in prison in England and Wales out of a total prison population of 75,393 (Howard League 2006). We would expect, therefore, to see a higher number of women as primary supporters when the supporter is a spouse or partner.

However, it cannot be assumed that all offenders or prisoners are being supported by wives or partners. Surveys in a men's and a women's prison found that 51 per cent of male prisoners were visited by their parents, 46 per cent by their partners, 42 per cent by siblings and 36 per cent by children (Murray 2003a) while 56 per cent of female prisoners reporting visits received those visits from parents, 43 per cent from children, 39 per cent from siblings and only 28 per cent from partners (Murray 2003b). A discussion of the difficulties faced by offenders' families should therefore not be restricted to wives and partners (Mills 2004; Paylor and Smith 1994). Interviewees and fieldwork participants in this study included mothers, sisters, grandmothers, an aunt, and a daughter as well as wives and partners. Studies in the US have found prison visitors to be predominantly female: one described a visiting area at a male prison as 'a distinctly female space' with approximately 95 per cent of visitors being women (Comfort 2003); one found that twice as many mothers as fathers were prison visitors (Schafer 1994) and another that: 'Men in prison are visited by their wives and mothers and women in prison are visited by their mothers and sisters' (Girshick 1996: 24).

It is difficult to quantify the population of families of serious offenders because the category of 'serious crime' is a contested boundary (Francis *et al.* 2001). There are a range of components making a particular offence more or less serious, including the harm caused or risked by the offender's conduct, the offender's individual culpability and remoteness from the harm, and various factors of aggravation or mitigation (Ashworth 2005). There have been attempts to rank offences or allocate a category of high, medium or low seriousness, but this is far from straightforward and gives rise to complex debate about proportionality in sentencing which is beyond the scope of this chapter (see Ashworth 2005 for a detailed discussion). In practice in this study, the offences in question were violent or sexual or attracted a sentence of more than four years. None was a property crime, in the main they were non-instrumental and none was committed by an offender who was part of an organised or professional crime network (as far as their relative was aware). The individual offences included murder, manslaughter, serious wounding, rape, and sex offences against children. In addition, participants were self-defining as relatives of serious offenders and were found either through Aftermath, a now-defunct self-help organisation for relatives of serious offenders, or through a leaflet in a prison visitors' centre specifically asking for relatives of serious offenders who were willing to be interviewed.

A very approximate estimate of the number of relatives of serious offenders can be obtained by looking at the number of prisoners serving longer sentences: in 2004 there were 25,837 prisoners serving a sentence of more than four years but less than life and 5,594 serving a life sentence (Howard League 2006). There were therefore 31,431 prisoners serving sentences of more than four years. Extrapolating from this section of the prison population to the number of families involved can only give a very rough approximation. This might overestimate – we cannot assume that all those prisoners have the support of their family, and we know that with more grave offences and longer prison sentences this becomes less likely (NACRO 1994) – or underestimate because it excludes a number of serious offenders, such as those who are no longer serving a prison sentence but whose families are still affected by what has happened, or those who received a shorter sentence for an offence which would be deemed in the eyes of most as 'serious' and serious in its consequences for the family. One family in this study had their house attacked and their family torn apart by conflict following the conviction of the husband for sexual offences against children – the sentence he received, however, was only two years. But we can at least make a very approximate estimate of tens of thousands of families contending with difficulties of supporting a serious offender, and if the findings of my small ethnographic study reflect the bigger picture, tens of thousands of women shouldering much of that burden.

Surveying prisoners and their families to find out who visits is a useful place to start, but to explore the breadth and depth of the broader impact of crime on families of serious offenders it was necessary to spend time with the relatives themselves, talking about different aspects of their lives – what really happened in families, how life had changed, how support was negotiated – through long interviews (between two and five hours) that mostly took place in relatives' own homes. Interviews were interspersed with lunch and looking at photograph albums and newspaper cuttings. We explored in detail how the relatives themselves understood their experiences and how they described their daily lives. I had known many of the interviewees through fieldwork for many months and sometimes for years, and some commented that they would not otherwise have agreed to talk about personal and painful experiences – one mother said she would never have agreed to an interview had she not known me for 18 months beforehand.

I therefore had to rely on a slowly built sample of relatives selected by availability and opportunity. I was not able to select Aftermath members or prison visitors to provide a random sample, or to select participants on the basis of particular characteristics (other than all sharing a close kin relationship to a serious offender). Certain factors might therefore affect the degree to which the sample is representative. Compared to the general prison population the interviewees showed greater ethnic homogeneity[3] and a higher socio-economic level. Ethnic minorities are consistently over-represented in the general prison population; prison statistics 'suggest that around one and one-quarter per cent of the black population in England and Wales is in prison, about eight times that of the white population' (Bowling and Phillips 2002: 241). Work is emerging in the US that highlights the collateral consequences of mass imprisonment for relatives of prisoners, and how significant numbers of African-American women in particular are affected (e.g. see Comfort 2003; Mauer and Chesney-Lind 2002; Sokoloff 2003); the figures from England and Wales suggest there might be a similar disproportionate effect not reflected in my sample.

The relatives I met could be described as working or middle class, but most were not what might be described as 'socially excluded',[4] in contrast to both the general prison population and some of the families I observed at prison visitors' centres. According to the government's Social Exclusion Unit, many of those in the general prison population have experienced a lifetime of social exclusion with high levels of unemployment and drug use and a significant lack of basic reading, writing and numeracy skills (Social Exclusion Unit 2002: 6). Many participants were members of a self-help organisation which in itself raises questions about who joins self-help groups, and how the way they understood their predicament was shaped by the lens it provided. Conclusions drawn from a sample such as this must therefore be tentative and caution should be exercised in generalising to the wider population, although I did find parallels with a number of other studies of offenders' families and similar experiences were described in interviews with the managers of two prison visitors' centres who had daily contact with relatives of serious offenders.

Finding out

The women in this study described the day they found out about the offence as traumatic and life-changing – a knock at the door, a telephone call or a letter that turned their world upside down and was etched with clarity in their minds. Discovering the offence was the one event around which everything else was structured, and provided a new centre of gravity around which their lives revolved:

In every single aspect my life has been changed, you know. In effect, I feel I have a new life. That was my old life, this is my new life. It's just made me see everything in a different light, it kind of woke me up ... life began at 40 for me, March 1998, my world as I knew it, gone.
(*Gill, husband convicted of sex offences*)

For some, the shock of finding out manifested in physical symptoms – feeling sick, becoming ill, or unable to function in other ways. Some described reacting in uncharacteristic and surprising ways – one mother of a man arrested for rape described cleaning out all her kitchen cupboards when she was told of his arrest because she felt so defiled.

Relatives described feelings of grief and loss which they compared to bereavement. There were a number of losses described: of their relationship with the offender or of free contact with him or her following imprisonment; of their hopes and dreams for the offender and what his or her life might hold; of other family members – in some families conflict emerged over whether to support the offender, for example, resulting in rifts and severed relationships; loss of the victim, if within the family or close circle – obvious in homicide cases, but also a result of children being moved into care or contact ceasing with grandchildren; and finally, a less tangible but nevertheless devastating 'loss of the assumptive world' (Murray-Parkes 1975), of what they thought they knew and believed in. One participant, who was a supporter of a large number of other relatives, thought that relatives experienced post-traumatic stress disorder, such was the extent of their ordeal, suffering and feelings of helplessness.

Most relatives described this traumatic state as characteristic of the early stages – for many, life gradually improved as they found ways of coping, and many progressed to the point of being able to help others in similar situations. Relatives had to learn not only to cope with changes in their internal, psychological state, but also with dramatic changes in their everyday lives following discovery. I have discussed these changes in more detail elsewhere (Condry 2003; Condry forthcoming); my focus here is on three key ways in which the processes following this dramatic point were found to be gendered: the ways in which new responsibilities were managed within the family, the way in which secondary stigmatisation was rooted in familial shame and blame, and the use of self-help.

Increased responsibilities

When a serious offence is discovered, everyday family arrangements are thrown into disarray. In the families of those I interviewed, the traumatic impact forced a renegotiation of family responsibilities and life became more emphatically organised around the offender and his or her needs. New caring relationships were established, with one relative usually taking the lead in supporting the offender (and sometimes other family members) through the criminal justice process and imprisonment. In all the families in this study who were supporting an offender the primary supporter was a female relative and usually a wife or mother. In interviews and through fieldwork I repeatedly found women who had put their own needs to one side to meet the needs of the offender and other family members. Although it is difficult to assess the role of men in families without directly interviewing them, from the descriptions given by the women I interviewed and spoke to during fieldwork most men were not involved to anything like the same extent. These women sometimes had help with particular tasks from other family members and from friends, but were primary supporters in the sense that they were the first port of call, taking overall responsibility, and in most cases doing considerably more than anyone else.

Other studies have found that where there are choices to be made about caring, rather than a caring trajectory that is largely by default (such as caring for an ageing spouse) women are more likely than men to take it on. Decisions are made on the basis of kinship obligations which are strongly gendered in our society (Arber and Gilbert 1989; Finch 1989; Qureshi and Walker 1989). Finch (1989) has shown how kin relationships are renegotiated at points of disruption and suggests reasons why women are more likely to be responsible for caring for dependent family members and for running households and to play a more active role in family life than men: women have different access to resources, particularly sources of money; in the domestic division of labour men and women are given different responsibilities; and men's and women's lives are often organised differently so that women are more likely to be able to offer the time and domestic labour involved in caring for others. We know, for example, that women are much more likely to work part-time. This leads to a 'built-in tendency for caring responsibilities to fall on women' (Finch 1989: 53).

Caring for a relative is often narrowly perceived to mean physical care within the home but can encompass much more, particularly during times of adversity which bring additional problems that need to be managed. Horowitz makes a distinction between four broad categories of family care-giving activities: personal care and domestic tasks; emotional support; mediation with formal organisations; and financial assistance (Horowitz 1985). Brody adds another form of care, invariably provided by the family, of response and dependability in emergencies and other kinds of special need that do not occur on a daily basis (Brody 2004). These authors are writing about the care of the elderly; relatives of serious offenders do not usually provide physical care – and may have very little physical contact if the offender is imprisoned – but it is useful to conceptualise family care-giving in this way as it shows the breadth of possible kinds of caring.

Once an offender has been arrested, there is likely to be a need for practical support and emotional support throughout the criminal justice process. Practical support might include liaising with solicitors, dealing with the police during the investigation, attending court, fending off the media, and prison visiting. For mothers of offenders, organising one's life around the needs of an adult offspring might mean reverting to an earlier state of affairs. One interviewee, for example, organised her life around her son who was in his fifties and serving a prison sentence for sex offences, visiting him every two weeks, shopping for items he needed and also sending him money, writing regularly and generally being his first point of contact for any difficulties. She also cared for his son, her grandson, who was a young adult and who lived with her. Wives described organising their life around the needs of the offender, again visiting, shopping and sending in money, but also writing regularly and waiting in the home for phone calls from the offender in prison. One interviewee described how she would send a letter every day, which she would start writing before she went to bed and finish when she got up in the morning. This helped her to feel that she was sharing her life with her partner and that he was with her throughout the day.

Many women described being the emotional linchpin in the family and a source of emotional support for the offender and other relatives. Angela[5] described supporting her family when her husband was accused of child sex offences. She felt that she had to be strong and hide her own emotions from her adult sons who depended on her: '… everybody looks to Mum … "We'll be alright because me mum's alright"'. In the period of emotional upheaval following discovery, the main supporting relative may be leant on by the offender and by other relatives as they attempt to absorb what has happened. This is not to suggest, however, that all supporting relatives react to discovery with a show of strength. As we have seen, feelings of shock and trauma were described and many felt as if their world had fallen apart. Some relatives even had to seek psychiatric treatment at this point and many described their desperate need for support or their relief when they found it.

However, a significant number of the women in this study had considerable caring responsibilities and had to find ways to manage. Twenty-one interviewees described family responsibilities that occupied much of their time. Sixteen of them had adult offspring and described the support they gave them; ten had children under the age of 16, and six were single parents. Fourteen had grandchildren, and in some cases were their primary carers. In addition, supportive relationships were described with partners, nieces and nephews, and with elderly parents. The phrase 'women in the middle' has been used by Brody to describe women caught between multiple competing demands on their time and energy (husbands, children, parents and work) 'and often in the middle emotionally between elderly parents on the one hand and husbands and children on the other'. The negative consequences of this position have consistently been documented in research findings – on their own mental and physical health, family well-being, vocational activities and other aspects of their lives (Brody 2004). The women in this study were also 'women in the middle', caught between competing demands and often in the middle emotionally between the offender and other family members. Being so placed can take its toll and, in three families in this study, supporting mothers had become estranged from their other adult children through conflict over their dedication to supporting their offending offspring.

New responsibilities can revolve around dealing with the various stages of the criminal justice process. It is important to look at the whole criminal justice process, rather than just focus on the effects of imprisonment on the family; relatives are often very involved with each stage of the investigation and some cases can take years to process from discovery to sentencing. If a relative is held in custody from the point of arrest, a supporting relative can be a link to the outside world – a source of practical supplies, emotional support, and ability to bear news or relay messages. She may be in contact with the police at the point of arrest or during the investigation and might be interviewed or have her house searched. A number of relatives commented on having to clean up the mess after their house was searched at a time when they themselves were shocked and distressed. The offender might need different kinds of support as the police investigation develops and relatives might need to liaise with legal representatives who will also be an important source of information about likely outcomes.

The court experience and sentencing are usually the second most significant events after discovery of the offence. Many of the relatives I interviewed who attended court found it upsetting and frightening. They had to navigate the judicial system, often for the first time, and 'experience the trauma of facing the horrific gravity of the crime' (Aftermath 2000: 4). Some relatives were publicly identified for the first time and came into contact with the victim or the victim's associates; and others described their overriding concern for the welfare of the offender. Vivid accounts were given of listening to the verdict or sentence. Some relatives even collapsed.

Supporting a relative in prison or a special hospital imposed particular demands and relatives described many of the difficulties that appear in the prisoners' families literature: financial problems, emotional difficulties, stigma stemming from imprisonment, demands on time, the struggle to maintain a relationship with the prisoner and concerns about the impact on children (e.g. in the UK see Boswell and Wedge 2001; Codd 1998; Mills 2004; Morris 1965; Shaw 1992; and in the US see Comfort 2002; Fishman 1990; Girshick 1996; Hairston 1991). Participants often described devoting time to letter-writing, visiting, waiting for telephone calls and shopping for the prisoner, the needs of the prisoner becoming their primary occupation:

> My own life had to be shelved, we had to a) try and make [my son] realise there was a reason for living and b) just try and see him through this nasty mess and everything else had to just go by the board.
> (*Penny, son convicted of rape*)

Visiting a prisoner can be expensive, particularly if he or she is a long way from home. Although close relatives could claim transport costs from the Assisted Prison Visits Unit, the money had to be paid in advance, which some found difficult. For those on a low income, meeting the needs of a relative in prison was particularly difficult. Prisoners generally earn very low wages and depend on those outside to supplement their income so they can make purchases from the prison 'canteen', and to purchase items which they are allowed to have sent in. Participants on low incomes described 'going without' in order to meet these needs or to meet the costs of visiting – one fieldwork participant said she herself went without eating on visit days so she could spend the money she had on crisps and chocolate for her son.

Those I interviewed were preoccupied with worries about the prisoner, and mentioned concerns about his or her mental and physical health. In some cases there was a concern that the prisoner might attempt suicide. Some difficulties were specifically worse for participants because they were relatives of serious offenders and stemmed from the seriousness of the offence (which led to specific worries about the safety of the prisoner and, in some cases, difficulties when visiting, if the type of offence was known to other prisoners and their families); their lack of prior experience of the criminal justice system (most relatives in this study had had little or no experience,[6] were keen to separate themselves from 'criminal families' or repeat petty offenders and had to learn how to navigate the complexities of prison visiting), and the length of the prison sentence (some relatives might even be visiting prisons or special hospitals for the rest of their lives).

Stigmatisation and familial blame

Relatives of serious offenders are stigmatised and shamed and this stigma has its roots in ideas about familial blame and contamination. They have an uncertain status in relation to the offence and are caught on the cusp between victim and offender status; many claim secondary victim status, but simultaneously attract blame. Powerful discourses on family responsibilities permeate all areas of family life. The family is often represented as the guardian of morality and responsible for its members' failings; if they deviate, the family must have failed in its functions. This message has many sources. Historically, a white, middle-class nuclear family has been presented as the normative ideal in both American and UK academic discourse (Chambers 2001), politicians make morally crusading speeches about 'family values' and the media draw attention to failing families. Teenage pregnancies, lone mothers and truanting children are just some examples of failure from 'bad families' to which our attention is drawn.

Notions of familial responsibility are reflected in the relationship between the state and the family. There is a long history of the British government being concerned with family life and making assumptions about the role of the family in legislation. Since the 1970s there has been a greater stress on 'supporting the family', and families have been encouraged to look after their members, one theme being 'strong moral disapproval of people who apparently do not acknowledge that they have certain responsibilities to their relatives' (Finch 1989: 3). This disapproval is particularly strong in the case of parents of young offenders. Provision has been made in legislation to hold parents directly responsible for crimes committed by their children, with the parental 'bind over' in the Criminal Justice Act 1991 and the 'parenting order' introduced in the Crime and Disorder Act 1998, further widened in its use in the Anti-Social Behaviour Act 2003 and set to widen yet again with proposals made in 2006 under the government's 'Respect' agenda. In November 2000 the courts were given powers to send parents to prison for up to three months if they allowed their children to truant and a number of mothers have been imprisoned under these powers in recent high-profile cases. The continuing assumption in these parental responsibility laws is that parents of young offenders have not accepted responsibility and that they can be forced to do so with court orders and financial penalties (Arthur 2005).

Furthermore, expert and therapeutic analyses repeatedly locate explanations for offending behaviour within the family. Studies show family factors to be important predictors of offending. Reviewing these studies, Farrington suggests that the important factors are criminal and antisocial parents; large family size; child-rearing methods (poor supervision, poor discipline, coldness and rejection, low parental involvement with the child); abuse (sexual and physical) or neglect; and parental conflict and disrupted families (Farrington 2002: 670). Studies of sex offenders point to factors in family background such as poor parental relationships in the case of incest male-object perpetrators (Gebhard *et al.* 1965) or problems with mothers in the case of incest offenders (though apparently not other paedophiles) (Paitich and Langevin 1976), even though 'evidence on this matter is very spotty and inconclusive' (Finkelhor *et al.* 1986). Dobash *et al.* (2001) found that just over a third of men currently serving prison terms for homicide offences came from broken homes, and a quarter had a father who was violent to their mother, though as Levi and Maguire point out, these statistics show that a 'surprisingly large percentage do not appear to come from a severely dysfunctional family or personal background' (2002: 815).

Expert knowledge that locates explanations for offending within the family filters through and informs the everyday understandings of lay people; most people in society would be aware of seeking explanations for offending behaviour within childhood experiences and family background. Expert knowledge in turn condenses common-sense reasoning and relatives are confronted with such knowledge as they, or the offender, interact with professionals. Offenders might interact with psychiatrists, doctors, probation officers, social workers, and take part in anger management or sex offender treatment programmes, all of which can have underlying messages about the source of offending behaviour. Relatives in this study felt they were constantly faced with the belief that serious offenders were 'made' by their families.

So how might familial blame be gendered? The roles of 'mother' and 'wife' are constructed around responsibility for the well-being of other family members and mothers and wives may be particularly blamed when things go wrong. Historically, motherhood and mothering have been subject to particular regulation, often targeted at working-class mothers. Informal networks were undermined as a source of knowledge as experts such as health visitors and midwives were trained to instruct mothers. In the modern era, there are numerous experts, often in disagreement, vying for the right to define 'good mothering'. Bowlby's theory of maternal deprivation (Bowlby 1981) was very influential from the 1940s and 1950s onwards, pointing to adverse consequences if the bond between mother and child and the constant presence of the mother were in any way threatened (Chambers 2001: 52–3). Neo-Freudian thought was prominent in the 1940s and 1950s, with the emphasis on looking at the family of origin in order to understand the individual (Ladd-Taylor and Umansky 1998). The legacy of these perspectives persists: good mothers create emotionally secure children and adults, and either explicitly or implicitly, bad mothers create a catalogue of different problems.

Mother-blaming has a long history. Until relatively recently psychiatric discourse blamed autism on mothers rejecting their children; schizophrenia was blamed on maternal rejection; and anorexia on troubled mother–daughter relationships. Homosexuality was blamed on overprotective or independent-minded mothers from the 1890s to the 1950s; and juvenile delinquency on working mothers (Ladd-Taylor and Umansky 1998). An analysis of 125 articles written by mental health professionals in scholarly journals found that mothers were blamed for 72 different kinds of problems in their offspring (Caplan and Hall-McCorquodale 1985) and in many of the articles the writers 'stretched ludicrously far in order to avoid blaming anyone other than the mother' (Caplan and Caplan 1994: 70). In the mental illness literature before the 1960s families were seen as causal agents; poor socialisation and communication with parents were blamed, though again mothers in particular were seen to be at fault (Caplan and Hall-McCorquodale 1985; Cohler *et al.* 1991; Cook 1988; Cook *et al.* 1997). A subsequent generation of research has questioned whether poor communication and the other symptoms observed in these families might not actually have been caused by the offspring's mental illness rather than the other way around (Cook *et al.* 1997).

Notions of motherhood are constructed around both the biological bearing of children and the social construction of mothers as idealised nurturers (Davies and Krane 1996). Mothers of serious offenders in this study felt blamed and also experienced a sense of responsibility and guilt based on both nature and nurture. They often spoke of their horror that someone born of their body had committed such a terrible act, questioned their role in the upbringing of the offender, and asked whether or not some aspect of the way in which the offender was raised could have contributed to his or her actions. Motherhood is central to how women are defined by others and to their self-perceptions (Phoenix *et al.* 1991), and in being defined through motherhood these mothers came to think that they were defined through their offending sons and that they were deemed responsible, having brought them into the world, for their very existence.

Though marriage and other intimate relationships have undergone significant changes in recent years (e.g. see Beck and Beck-Gernsheim 1995; Giddens 1992), discourses based upon traditional models of marriage and intimacy remain powerful. For example, Cheale (1999) has suggested that the promotion of new family forms centres on the growth of individual freedoms and erodes the sense of duty that binds families together in caring for each other. Chambers points that the undercurrent here is that it is *women* who are deemed disruptive for demanding freedoms which for men are taken for granted and that female emancipation continues to be blamed for the breakdown in modern family values (Chambers 2001: 129). Women as wives have particular 'duties' and are imbued with particular responsibilities for maintaining family values and promoting 'good families', and blamed for not fulfilling them when things go wrong.

Studies of the wives of men who sexually offend against children have found that they are often blamed, particularly in the case of father–daughter incest. The father is not held totally accountable, and the mother is centrally implicated, blamed as collusive, or seen as orchestrating the abuse through her inadequacies or emotional absence (Davies and Krane 1996). Assumptions such as these have been shown to feature in the accounts of some child protection professionals such as social workers, police officers and nurses (Kelley 1990) and in the child sexual abuse literature, which 'carries a legacy of at least twenty-five years of blaming non-offending mothers either partially or fully for the sexual abuse of their children' (Humphreys 1994: 50). In my own study, the victim of Frances's husband's crime was their teenage foster daughter. She says she had not known of the offence until her husband was charged:

> My CPN [Community Psychiatric Nurse] had arranged to come round and see me, well, the day, the day that [my husband] went down to the police station he was charged, she came to see me a couple of hours after he was due at the police station and she got in touch with one of the doctors at the hospital who came out to see me the next day, and his first words to me were, 'Did you know it was going on and did you condone it?' And I thought if somebody of a professional nature has said that, how many other people were saying that? And whether some people thought that I knew it was going on I don't know, but I have lost a hell of a lot of friends.
> (*Frances, husband convicted of sex offences*)

Relatives in this research experienced secondary stigma and shaming in their interactions with others which was conveyed in many ways: friendships were ended, acquaintances crossed the road to avoid conversation, and they were subject to gossip, verbal abuse and, in a few cases, physical attack. One fieldwork participant even had slogans painted on her house. Relatives of serious offenders are subject to shame and are perceived to be contaminated and blame-worthy along several dimensions: for mere association; because of an alleged genetic connection which provokes primitive ideas of bad blood; for sins of omission, not knowing about or failing to prevent the offence; sins of commission, such as collusion, covering up or direct involvement; and for continuation of their stigma when they offer the offender their support (Condry 2003; Condry forthcoming). They must contend with the daily experience of ascertaining whether their status is known, and make decisions about whether to disclose or conceal information in ongoing interactions (May 2000).

The experience of stigmatisation and shaming may be even more powerful for those left on the outside when a relative is imprisoned. In prison, coping with daily life may take precedence over concerns about stigmatisation and prisoners can exist in an environment where offences are not discussed and their past actions not challenged. They may also be among other offenders where their offending is in some sense 'normalised'.[7] The wives, mothers and other close kin have to continue everyday life, often in communities where their tainted status is known. They have to live with daily examples of shaming and it is they, rather than an imprisoned offender, who must face whispering as they pass in the street, gossiping in the post office or open comments, as Stephanie described:

> **S**: It was only when I went into the village where my mum lived that people started taunting me, 'you murderer's wife'.
> **R**: Just walking down the road? People you knew or people that just knew who you were?
> **S**: People I'd grown up with. My friends that I thought were friends, school friends, didn't even speak to me.
> **R**: Really? Right. So did you still go to the village?
> **S**: Yeah, I never stopped because my mum was there and that was my main priority. But as time went on people forgot, or they just didn't say anything to me, but even now I go to the village and I can see, they look at you, you know, as if to say 'oh, we know who you are'. Yeah, they do know who I am.
> **R**: And how does that make you feel now?
> **S**: Why am I still being punished? It's as though I've done a life sentence as well, which I honestly think I've done more of a life sentence than he has. Because he's in prison he's doing the sentence, *but it's me what gets the flak out here*.
> (*Stephanie, husband convicted of homicide offence, emphasis added*)

This state of affairs can continue for many years and in some cases for life.

Self-help and gender

Many of the relatives who participated in this research were members of Aftermath, a national self-help organisation for the families of serious offenders set up in 1988, and the site of much of the fieldwork in this study (see Howarth and Rock 2000 for a detailed analysis of the organisation). Aftermath folded in April 2005, having helped well over 1,300 families. The organisation found it difficult to gain recognition and legitimacy and relied on funding from charitable sources which was often not sufficient, itself a revealing indication of the moral and social marginality of its membership. It almost reached the point of closure several times due to financial crises, and finally did so in April 2005. Aftermath was the only national organisation run by and for families of serious offenders. It supported its members through self-help meetings known as 'lunches' run in several areas, telephone support and counselling, an annual residential weekend and a newsletter. All Aftermath's supporters and counsellors were relatives of serious offenders.

It was striking that almost all the active Aftermath members were women. Women made up all but one of the members who offered formal support to other members and around 90 per cent of those attending functions. They were often wives and mothers but also other female relatives such as grandmothers and sisters. Men attending would either be ex-offenders or would be 'accompanied' men, usually with their wives, but sometimes with other female family members. During more than three years of fieldwork I only met two male relatives of offenders who had come alone to Aftermath gatherings. On several occasions, men would be attending reluctantly or just to support their wives. At a weekend gathering, one man came with his wife but did not attend the formal sessions while she attended them all. At another meeting, a man waiting for his wife sat in his car, reading his paper throughout the session.

I asked a small group of Aftermath members why they thought most members were women, eliciting some interesting reasons including the restricted, stereotypical image of men as 'tough' and reserved, qualities which they thought were transmitted through social conditioning, peer pressure and other sources such as the media; the 'different kind of bonding' that they thought women experienced; assumptions about women's verbal ability and greater capacity for sympathy; and the straightforward practical reason that in many families the offender is the male partner who might be in prison. They thought men would be less likely to approach an organisation like Aftermath for help and support as men are more likely to keep their feelings hidden, not want to admit help is needed and are less likely to choose to be in an environment focusing on emotional support. Harriet suggested the bond between mother and child might explain the greater number of mothers in Aftermath:

> Never for one minute did I think, 'well, if he's done it I don't want anything to do with him'. He came from my body; I couldn't turn on him whatever he'd done. And I think this is

why, when you say, 'why are there more women in Aftermath?', because they carried the child, they gave birth to the child, they knew the child from nine months before the father did, and I think many fathers ... haven't bonded in the way that the mother has.
(*Harriet, son accused of sex offences*)

It is helpful to seek more broadly applicable explanations because such a gender imbalance is not unique to Aftermath. Studies have shown that members of self-help groups are characteristically drawn from similar populations: female, white, middle class and with a higher level of education (Gidron *et al.* 1990; Heller *et al.* 1997; Lieberman and Snowdon 1994; Norton *et al.* 1993; Videka-Sherman 1982). A similar gender imbalance has also been found in readers of self-help literature (Simonds 1992).

In trying to understand why the majority of members are female, it is useful to think about what self-help could offer women who were the primary supporters of offenders. Aftermath members repeatedly emphasised the importance of meeting other relatives of serious offenders: to share stories and experiences, for mutual support and friendship, and to share practical information and ways of coping with their predicament. They thought that other relatives of serious offenders understood how they felt and could empathise in a way that non-relatives could not:

Because there's people [in Aftermath] in the same boat. They know exactly what's hitting your heart, what you're thinking, what you're feeling, how you feel and it's just amazing to have somebody there that knows exactly.
(*Pauline, son convicted of homicide offence*)

Through self-help, group members can gain knowledge and learn strategies to help with their predicament. This might be the outcome of counselling processes, or conveyed between members who have, as they say, 'been there'. Aftermath also offered practical support and information about prison visiting or court hearings. Those relatives that had had no past experience of the criminal justice system had to go through a process of 'socialisation', of learning what to do and how to do it. The professional and 'experiential' knowledge (Borkman 1990) gleaned through Aftermath was invaluable in making this possible.

Groups such as Aftermath help members to manage stigma and repair damaged identities. It was important to relatives to know that they were not the only families in their situation and to find other people (and often other caring wives and mothers) who shared their circumstances and were 'normal':

> I felt everybody could look at me and see we've got a prisoner in the family, and yeah, you do, you just feel awful, you think nobody else has got one. It's only when I went, and that is the good thing about it, when I went to Aftermath and you find there are perfectly normal respectable people out there.
> (*Mary, daughter convicted of violent offence*)

Aftermath provided a way of understanding their problem, constructing relatives of serious offenders as 'the other victims of crime' (see Howarth and Rock 2000) and therefore minimising their culpability, and further boosting members' sense of self and identity through the confidence and sense of belonging engendered by membership. Another study of women in self-help groups for prisoners' partners found that they maintained a positive identity through helping others (Codd 2002); this may be a reason why women stay in these groups when the level of support they themselves need diminishes, but is less likely to be the explanation for why most women join.

The predominance of women in Aftermath might partially be explained, therefore, by female relatives seeking support in managing new responsibilities and in managing a stigma partly based on the gendered construction of kin relationships. If female family members, and particularly wives and mothers, take on the greater load of support both in emotional and practical terms, support might be sought from groups such as Aftermath to help in managing this load. If women's identities are more closely constructed through their kin relationships, they may be more subject to blame and shame for the deviation of a family member, and they may feel a greater need to seek help as a result when something goes wrong. It is likely that women feel more comfortable asking for emotional support and discussing sensitive familial issues and there is a sense in which the family, kinship and related problems are seen as women's domain and women's responsibility, and a normative expectation that it is for women to sort them out. Men remained somewhat hidden in this process. One interviewee was a father who clearly cared deeply about his son and had given him considerable support, although his wife was the more active Aftermath member and had set up our interview. I had conversations with other men during fieldwork, but in most cases they were involved with their wife or other female relative. It is evident that some fathers, husbands, brothers and sons do support offenders. Further research would be useful to understand more about their experiences, perhaps reaching them through prison visitors' centres.

In doing this research, I was struck by the continued relevance of some of the concerns of earlier feminist scholars: concerns with the invisibility in the criminological literature of women affected by crime; concerns with rigid constructions of femininity and of kin relationships and the consequences that follow; and concerns with women's caring responsibilities and their hidden work in the private sphere. The women in my study did not passively accept the personal and structural constraints imposed by their circumstances, but rather actively tried to shape their lives and find creative solutions to the difficulties they encountered. I heard stories of resilience, of women forging relationships with other women, and finding friendship and strength through mutual support in some of the most difficult of circumstances.

The women's stories often reflected progress and a sense of moving forward from an initial point of devastation, with much of that progress driven by the women themselves, many of whom took pride in the strength of family bonds and their determination to support despite censure. A study of mothers in prison in America suggested that 'mothering is simultaneously a positive source of pleasure and identity formation and a vector for the social control of women' (Ferraro and Moe 2003). Correspondingly the women in this study constructed their sense of self positively around their kin relationships while those kin relationships, both in daily reality and in social construction, were simultaneously a source of social control. Their lives were structured by gender, with women in the family taking primary responsibility for managing both the emotional impact and the strain of worrying about and supporting the offender. Within those constraints women were carving the contours of their own lives. Gender perspectives can sensitise us to important questions about the structural processes shaping people's lives and stimulate connections and a conversation between those asking similar questions; focusing on how individuals describe their own experiences brings to the fore the intimate details of how those lives are understood and lived.

Acknowledgements

Thanks are due to the relatives of serious offenders who participated in this study and to Frances Heidensohn, Nicola Lacey and Paul Rock for their comments on an earlier version of this chapter.

Notes

1 The research was funded by the ESRC (award no: R0042983451).
2 Twenty-four interviewees were relatives of male offenders and eight relatives of female offenders. Ten were wives or partners, 17 were mothers, one grandmother, one sister, one aunt and one daughter. Eleven offenders were accused or convicted of homicide offences (murder and manslaughter), ten of sexual offences against children, three of rape, seven of serious violent offences, and one of a serious drugs offence. Five relatives were not supporting the offender, all of whom were former wives or partners.
3 Thirty classifying themselves as 'white UK', four of whom classified the offender as 'mixed race', and only two classifying themselves as 'black UK'.
4 The government has defined social exclusion as 'a shorthand term for what can happen when people or areas suffer from a combination of linked problems such as unemployment, poor skills, low incomes, unfair discrimination, poor housing, high crime, bad health and family breakdown' (Social Exclusion Unit 2004). Those I interviewed had individual problems to contend with, but these were not of the same magnitude or severity as many of the visitors I observed in prison visitors' centres.
5 All participants' names are pseudonyms to preserve anonymity.
6 Two-thirds of interviewees did not report previous offending. This is lower than we might expect. A recent study found that 32 per cent of murderers and 36 per cent of serious sexual offenders had no previous convictions (Soothill *et al.* 2002). The lower rates reported might be a factor of my sample, relatives might not have been willing to speak about past offending, or they might not have been aware. As Howarth and Rock point out, much offending is committed by males in public places and may not be reported to women; women who are in a position of dependence may not be able to afford to know too much; and even if they do ask questions they may not receive a reply (Howarth and Rock 2000: 65).
7 Although some offences, such as sex offences against children, may well lead to a prisoner being stigmatised with potential serious consequences, and some prison regimes go to great lengths to challenge offending behaviour.

References

Aftermath (2000) *Aftermath Annual Review*, Sheffield: Aftermath.

Arber, S. and Gilbert, N. (1989) 'Transitions in Caring: Gender, Life Course and Care of the Elderly', in B. Bytheway, T. Keil, P. Allatt and A. Bryman (eds) *Becoming and Being Old: Sociological Approaches to Later Life*. London: Sage.

Arthur, R. (2005) 'Punishing Parents for the Crimes of their Children', *Howard Journal of Criminal Justice*, 44(3): 233–53.

Ashworth, A. (2005) *Sentencing and Criminal Justice*, 4th edn, Cambridge: Cambridge University Press.

Beck, U. and Beck-Gernsheim, E. (1995) *The Normal Chaos of Love*, Cambridge: Polity Press.

Borkman, T. J. (1990) 'Experiential, Professional and Lay Frames of Reference' in T. J. Powell (ed.) *Working with Self-Help*, Silver Spring, MD: National Association of Social Workers.

Boswell, G. and Wedge, P. (2001) *Imprisoned Fathers and their Children*, London: Jessica Kingsley.

Bowlby, J. (1981) *Attachment and Loss, Volume III, Loss: Sadness and Depression*, Harmondsworth: Penguin.

Bowling, B. and Phillips, C. (2002) *Racism, Crime and Justice*, Harlow: Longman.

Britton, D. M. (2003) *At Work in the Iron Cage: The Prison as Gendered Organization*, New York: New York University Press.

Brody, E. M. (2004) *Women in the Middle: Their Parent Care Years*, 2nd edn, New York: Springer.

Brown, J. and Heidensohn, F. (2000) *Gender and Policing*, Basingstoke: Macmillan/Palgrave.

Caplan, P. and Hall-McCorquodale, I. (1985) 'Mother Blaming in Major Clinical Journals', *American Journal of Orthopsychiatry*, 55: 345–53.

Caplan, P. J. and Caplan, J. B. (1994) *Thinking Critically About Research on Sex and Gender*, New York: HarperCollins College Publishers.

Chambers, D. (2001) *Representing the Family*, London: Sage.

Cheale, D. (1999) 'The One and the Many: Modernity and Postmodernity' in G. Allan (ed.) *The Sociology of the Family: A Reader*, Oxford: Basil Blackwell.

Codd, H. (1998) 'Prisoners' Families: The 'Forgotten Victims', *Probation Journal*, 45(3): 148–54.

Codd, H. (2002) '"The Ties that Bind": Feminist Perspectives on Self-Help Groups for Prisoners' Partners', *The Howard Journal* 41: 334–47.

Cohler, B. J., Pickett, S. A. and Cook, J. A. (1991) 'The Psychiatric Patient Grows Older: Issues in Family Care', in E. Light and B. Lebowitz (eds) *The Elderly with Chronic Mental Illness*, New York: Springer.

Comfort, M. (2002) '"Papa's house": The Prison as Domestic and Social Satellite', *Ethnography*, 3(4): 467–99

Comfort, M. (2003) 'In the Tube at San Quentin: The "Secondary Prisonization" of Women Visiting Inmates', *Journal of Contemporary Ethnography* 32: 77–107.

Condry, R. (2003) *After the Offence: The Construction of Crime and its Consequences by Families of Serious Offenders*, PhD thesis, University of London.

Condry, R. (forthcoming) *Families Shamed: The Consequences of Crime for Relatives of Serious Offenders*, Cullompton: Willan Publishing.

Cook, J. A. (1988) 'Who "Mothers" the Chronically Mentally Ill?', *Family Relations*, 37: 42–9.

Cook, J. A., Pickett, S. A. and Cohler, B. J. (1997) 'Families of Adults with Severe Mental Illness – The Next Generation of Research', *American Journal of Orthopsychiatry* 67: 172–6.

Davies, L. and Krane, J. (1996) 'Shaking the Legacy of Mother Blaming: No Easy Task for Child Welfare', *Journal of Progressive Human Services*, 7(2): 3–22.

Dobash, R. E., Dobash, R. D., Cavanagh, K. and Lewis, R. (2001) *Homicide in Britain*, Research Bulletin No. 1, University of Manchester.

Farnworth, L. (1992) 'Women Doing a Man's Job: Female Prison Officers Working in a Male Prison', *Australian and New Zealand Journal of Criminology*, 25: 278–96.

Farrington, D. P. (2002) 'Developmental Criminology and Risk-Focused Prevention', in M. Maguire, R. Morgan and R. Reiner (eds) *The Oxford Handbook of Criminology*, Oxford: Oxford University Press.

Ferraro, K. J. and Moe, A. M. (2003) 'Mothering, Crime and Incarceration', *Journal of Contemporary Ethnography*, 32(1): 9–40.

Finch, J. (1989) *Family Obligations and Social Change*, Cambridge: Polity Press.

Finkelhor, D., Araji, S., Baron, L., Doyle Peters, S. and Wyatt, G. E. (1986) *A Sourcebook on Child Sexual Abuse*, Thousand Oaks, CA.: Sage.

Fishman, L. T. (1990) *Women at the Wall: A Study of Prisoners' Wives Doing Time on the Outside*, Albany: State University of New York Press.

Francis, B., Soothill, K. and Dittrich, R. (2001) 'A New Approach for Ranking "Serious" Offences: The Use of Paired-Comparisons Methodology', *British Journal of Criminology*, 41: 726–37.

Gebhard, P., Gagnon, J., Pomeroy, W. and Christenson, C. (1965) *Sex Offenders: An Analysis of Types*, New York: Harper & Row.

Giddens, A. (1992) *The Transformation of Intimacy: Sexuality, Love and Eroticism in Modern Societies*, Cambridge: Polity Press.

Gidron, B., Guterman, N. B. and Hartman, H. (1990) 'Stress and Coping Patterns of Participants and Non-participants in Self-help Groups for Parents of the Mentally Ill', *Community Mental Health Journal*, 26: 483–96.

Girshick, L. B. (1996) *Soledad Women: Wives of Prisoners Speak Out*, Westport, CT: Praeger.

Hairston, C. F. (1991) 'Family Ties During Imprisonment: Important to Whom and For What?', *Journal of Sociology and Social Welfare*, 18: 87–104.

Heidensohn, F. M. (1992) *Women in Control? The Role of Women in Law Enforcement*, Oxford: Oxford University Press.

Heller, T., Roccoforte, J., Hsieh, M. A., Cook, J. A and Picket, S. A. (1997) 'Benefits of Support Groups for Families of Adults with Severe Mental Illness', *American Journal of Orthopsychiatry*, 67: 187–98.

Horowitz, A. (1985) 'Family Caregiving to the Frail Elderly', in C. Eisdorfer, M. P. Lawton and G. L. Maddox (eds) *Annual Review of Gerontology and Geriatrics*, 5, New York: Springer.

Howard League (2006) *Prison Information Bulletin*, January, available online at http://www.howardleague.org/fileadmin/howard_league/user/pdf/Prison_information_bulletin1_01.pdf.

Howarth, G. and Rock, P. (2000) 'Aftermath and the Construction of Victimisation: "The Other Victims of Crime"', *The Howard Journal*, 39: 58–78.

Humphreys, C. (1994) 'Counteracting Mother-Blaming Among Child Sexual Abuse Service Providers: An Experiential Workshop', *Journal of Feminist Family Therapy*, 6(1): 49–65.

Kelley, S. J. (1990) 'Responibility and Management Strategies in Child Sex Abuse: A Comparison of Child Protective Workers, Nurses and Police Officers', *Child Welfare*, 69(1): 43–51.

Ladd-Taylor, M. and Umansky, L. (1998) *Bad Mothers: The Politics of Blame in Twentieth-Century America*, New York: New York University Press.

Levi, M. and Maguire, M. (2002) 'Violent Crime', in M. Maguire, R. Morgan and R. Reiner (eds) *The Oxford Handbook of Criminology*, Oxford: Oxford University Press.

Lieberman, M. A. and Snowdon, L. R. (1994) 'Problems in Assessing Prevalence and Membership Characteristics of Self-Help Group Participants', in T. J. Powell (ed.) *Understanding the Self-Help Organization: Frameworks and Findings*. Thousand Oaks, CA: Sage.

Mauer, M. and Chesney-Lind, M. (eds) (2002) *Invisible Punishment: The Collateral Consequences of Mass Imprisonment*, New York: The New Press.

May, H. (2000) '"Murderers' Relatives" Managing Stigma, Negotiating Identity', *Journal of Contemporary Ethnography*, 29: 198–221.

Mills, A. (2004) '"Great Expectations?": A Review of the Role of Prisoners' Families in England and Wales', Vol. 7, Selected papers from the 2004 British Society of Criminology Conference, Portsmouth, July, available online at http://www.britsoccrim.org/v7.htm

Morris, P. (1965) *Prisoners and their Families*, London: George Allen and Unwin.

Murray, J. (2003a) *Visits and Family Ties Amongst Men at HMP Camphill*, London: Action for Prisoners' Families.

Murray, J. (2003b) *Visits and Family Ties Amongst Women at HMP Cookham Wood*, London: Action for Prisoners' Families.

Murray-Parkes, C. (1975) 'What Becomes of Redundant World Models? A Contribution to the Study of Adaptation to Change', *British Journal of Medical Psychology*, 48: 131–7.

NACRO (1994) *Opening the Doors: Prisoners' Families*, London: National Association for the Care and Resettlement of Offenders.

Norton, S., Wandersman, A. and Goldman, C. R. (1993) 'Perceived Costs and Benefits of Membership in a Self-Help Group: Comparisons of Members and Nonmembers of the Alliance for the Mentally Ill', *Community Mental Health Journal*, 29: 143–60.

Paitich, D. and Langevin, R. (1976) 'The Clarke Parent-Child Relations Questionnaire: A Clinically Useful Test for Adults', *Journal of Consulting and Clinical Psychology*, 44: 428–36.

Paylor, I. and Smith, D. (1994) 'Who are Prisoners' Families?', *Journal of Social Welfare and Family Law*, 2: 131–44.

Phoenix, A., Woollett, A. and Lloyd, E. (1991) 'Motherhood: Meanings, Practices and Ideologies', London: Sage.

Qureshi, H. and Walker, A. (1989) *The Caring Relationship*, London: Macmillan.

Richards, M., McWilliams, B., Allcock, L., Enterkin, P., Owens, P. and Woodrow, J. (1994) 'The Family Ties of English Prisoners: The Results of the Cambridge Project on Imprisonment and Family Ties, Occasional Paper No. 2, Cambridge: Centre for Family Research.

Schafer, N. E. (1994) 'Exploring the Link Between Visits and Parole Success: A Survey of Prison Visitors', *International Journal of Offender Therapy and Comparative Criminology*, 38.

Shaw, R. (ed.) (1992) *Prisoners' Children: What are the Issues?*, London: Routledge.

Silvestri, M. (2003) *Women in Charge: Policing, Gender and Leadership*. Cullompton: Willan Publishing.

Simonds, W. (1992) *Women and Self-Help Culture: Reading Between the Lines*, New Brunswick, NJ: Rutgers University Press.

Social Exclusion Unit (2002) *Reducing Re-Offending by Ex-Prisoners*, London: Office of the Deputy Prime Minister.

Social Exclusion Unit (2004) *Tackling Social Exclusion: Taking Stock and Looking to the Future – Emerging Findings*, London: Office of the Deputy Prime Minister.

Sokoloff, N. J. (2003) 'The Impact of the Prison Industrial Complex on African American Women', *SOULS: A Critical Journal of Black Politics, Culture and Society*, 5(4): 31–46.

Soothill, K., Francis, B., Ackerley, E. and Fligelstone, R. (2002) *Murder and Serious Sexual Assault: What Criminal Histories Can Reveal About Future Serious Offending*, Police Research Series Paper 144. London: Home Office.

Videka-Sherman, L. (1982) 'Effects of Participation in a Self-help Group for Bereaved Parents: Compassionate Friends', *Prevention in Human Services* 1: 69–77.

Zimmer, L. (1986) *Women Guarding Men*, Chicago: University of Chicago Press.

Part Two: Gender and the Criminal Justice System

Introduction

Frances Heidensohn

Among the many important debates generated by late twentieth-century feminist criminologists, two stand out. First are those studies concerned with equity versus chivalry. 'Chivalry' had been introduced by a much older generation of criminologists (Pollak 1950; Mannheim 1965) to explain lower levels of recorded crime by females. Broadly, they argued that all aspects of law enforcement and criminal justice systems operated a benign and protective regime in relation to women and girls, so that they were criminalised less and punished far more moderately than their male counterparts. Feminists not only challenged these ideas (they were not usually the subject of empirical testing) (Smart 1977; Heidensohn 1985) but they proposed an alternative interpretation: that women, or some particular groups of women, were treated as 'doubly deviant'. These equity studies, as they came to be called, covered courts (Eaton 1986), sentencing (Daly 1994) and for the most part did not discover chivalrous treatment.

In this section, Kate Steward tackles chivalry, among other questions, in her comparative study of remand decisions in several London magistrates' courts. She does find some evidence of chivalry and of women being perceived as being 'doubly deviant', but not of being doubly damned. Remand decisions are a topic that has scarcely been covered, despite decades of gender studies, and Steward's work is important for this alone. She also used participant observation of the courts, as well as interviews with many criminal justice personnel to explore their attitudes and assumptions. The other three studies here add to the range of work on women in prison and especially to the debates about penal policies for female offenders.

These debates are well established and draw on historical as well as criminological scholarship. The consistent theme of this work has been that women experience prison (and other punishments) in different ways from men: they are more damaged, since they are more vulnerable, and in any case the system is harsher towards them (Carlen and Worrall 2004). Another stream of research has explored the various experimental regimes imposed on female offenders over the modern era. For the most part, these studies have argued that such innovations, however well intentioned, end in failure (Rafter 1992, Zedner 1991; see Heidensohn and Gelsthorpe 2007).

These authors in this section consider, develop and contradict these arguments. Nicola Hutson and Carrie Anne Myers examine the experiences of young women in prison, employing their subjects' own voices. In interesting counterpoint to several other chapters in this book, they show that the 'girls' had absorbed the current individualised and personally specific vocabulary of penal policy for women. They sought solutions to their problems through counselling and therapy, some of them even becoming 'counselling evangelists'. Barbara Mason and Stephanie Hayman present markedly different accounts of the development of special penal policies for adult women. Mason's study of the Dóchas Centre in Dublin is the first such analysis of an Irish establishment. She found that this was one woman-centred prison that did succeed in achieving its aims of gender-specific and appropriate treatment. She attributes this to political support and sustained leadership. Hayman looked outside the UK for her example, in this case to Canada, where the project to replace the federal prison for women has already been widely noted and studied.

Her conclusions are the polar opposite of Mason's. Despite participation by feminist activists and aboriginal women in the project's Task Force, these prisons are more punitive than the one they replaced. Hayman traces this outcome to factors in both the policy process and its implementation. The two case studies provide unique comparative potential since they involve analyses of policy documents and deliberations as well as observations of the respective outcomes and add to the growing debates led by Carlen (2002) and Snider (2003).

References

Carlen, P. (ed.) (2002) *Women and Punishment*, Cullompton: Willan Publishing.

Carlen, P. and Worrall, A. (eds) (2004) *Analysing Women's Imprisonment*, Cullompton: Willan Publishing.

Daly, K. (1994) *Gender Crime and Punishment*, New Haven, CT: Yale University Press.

Eaton, M. (1986) *Justice for Women?*, Milton Keynes: Open University Press.

Heidensohn, F. (1985) *Women and Crime*, Basingstoke: Macmillan.

Heidensohn, F. and Gelsthorpe, L. (2007) 'Gender and Crime', in Maguire *et al.* (eds) *The Oxford Handbook of Criminology*, 4th edn, Oxford: Oxford University Press.

Mannheim, H. (1965) *Comparative Criminology*, London: Routledge.

Pollak, O. (1950) *The Criminality of Women*, New York: Barnes/Perpetua.

Rafter, N. (1992) *Partial Justice: Women in State Prisons 1800–1935*, Boston, MA: North Eastern University Press.

Smart, C. (1977) *Women, Crime and Criminology*, London: Routledge.

Snider, L. (2003) 'Constituting the Punishable Woman: Atavistic Man Incarcerates Postmodern Woman', *British Journal of Criminology*, 2: 354–78.

Zedner, L. (1991) *Women, Crime and Custody in Victorian England*, Oxford: Clarendon Press.

Chapter 7

Gender considerations in remand decision-making

Kate Steward

We saw that the numbers of women remanded in custody have been increasing, that they made up a quarter of the female prison population, and yet only 30 per cent eventually receive a custodial sentence. Considering the distress and disruption caused by imprisonment for the women and the difficulties which this creates for the management of prison regimes, this would appear to be an obvious first place to seek a reduction in the female prison population. *Yet we know all too little about how and why courts use remand*. (Wedderburn 2000: 51 emphasis added)

Decision-making about women in the remand system is a curiously under-researched and under-theorised area, particularly given that the recent growth in the female custodial remand population is proportionately far greater than the increase in the male custodial remand population. To explore how and why courts use remand for women, this chapter draws on an empirical study of magistrates' decision-making in remand hearings involving women 'at risk' of a custodial remand.

The data demonstrate that while the majority of remand decisions are based primarily on offence seriousness, without consideration of the defendant's gender, in 'cusp' cases magistrates employed a far more individualised decision-making strategy when resolving whether or not to remand in custody. In these cases gender became more significant: defendants were observed being morally (re)constructed as women who 'deserved' bail, with their defence lawyers often employing explicitly gendered narratives to this end.

The research on which this chapter is based was a primarily qualitative study of magistrates' decision-making in five courts in three metropolitan areas. Verbatim accounts of 103 remand hearings (untried defendants and convicted unsentenced defendants being remanded for reports) were analysed along with 41 semi-structured interviews with lay magistrates, Crown Prosecution Service (CPS) officers, defence lawyers, and women residing in a bail hostel. As magistrates rarely verbalised their decision-making rationales in court, ideal-typical case vignettes were constructed from observations and used in interview to explore how magistrates and other criminal justice professionals approached, categorised and processed cases. As the study focused on the use of custodial remand, only cases where women were at risk of being remanded in custody were observed; the police decision to hold a female defendant in custody overnight was used as a proxy indicator of this risk. This was, of course, an imperfect indicator of risk as women may be held overnight for reasons other than concerns about bail risk, for instance if the woman is incapacitated by alcohol or drugs or if her identity cannot be confirmed.

The remand decision throws into relief one of the most fundamental conflicts in the criminal process: balancing the rights of the individual not to be imprisoned prior to conviction and/or sentence against the requirement to protect the public from crime. It appears that this balance may be shifting for some defendants as prison service data show marked increases in the frequency with which women are being remanded in custody, often for relatively minor offences. Between 1992 and 2002 there was a 196 per cent increase in receptions on custodial remand, compared to a 52 per cent increase for men (WORP 2004). Analysis of the increase in the use of custodial sentences for female offenders suggests that women are not committing more serious offences, but that sentencing has become more severe in recent years: custody is increasingly used in place of non-custodial sentencing (Hedderman 2004). Similar dynamics may account for the marked growth in the female custodial remand population.

This chapter focuses on furthering our understanding of women's treatment by, and experience of, the criminal justice system by looking at how and why remand decisions are reached, and the relative importance of gender in these decisions. It demonstrates that some of the traditional feminist criminology questions are still relevant to the analysis of women, crime and criminal justice (for comprehensive summaries of these questions see, for example, Gelsthorpe 1997; Heidensohn 1987; Heidensohn and Silvestri 1995).

One of the main feminist critiques of mainstream criminology has been the 'invisibility' of women: the absence of a consideration of gender in criminological theories and research until the late twentieth century (Heidensohn 1968, 1987). While there has been some gender-specific work done on remand decision-making, it has been on a very small scale (Eaton 1987) or has focused on women's experiences of being held on custodial remand (Casale 1989). The question of gender in the wider remand literature tends to be limited to identifying whether or not women are treated more 'leniently' than men (Brown *et al.* 2004; Doherty and East 1985; Hucklesby 1994, 1996; Home Office 2003). While some findings suggest that women are treated more leniently (Jones 1985; Kellough and Wortley 2002), the majority finding is that women's significantly lower risk of custodial remand is explained by their less serious offences/offending patterns and bail records.

Women have long been observed to be understood and responded to by criminal justice personnel according to dominant social narratives of female domesticity and sexuality (Allen 1987a, 1987b; Carlen 1983; Daly 1994; Eaton 1984, 1987; Worrall 1990). One of the central concerns of this chapter is to document the ways in which women are conceptualised and constructed in the remand system, demonstrating that in some cases this does impact on decision outcomes.

However, the importance of gender as an explanatory factor in decision outcomes should not be overstated. First, as will be seen, in the majority of cases remand decisions were based on offence seriousness alone, unrelated to extra-legal factors such as gender or race. Second, although the data from this study did not support such an analysis, ideally gender should not be considered in isolation: to fully understand remand outcomes we should be exploring the intersection of gender with other extra-legal factors. Comparative work illustrates that we cannot meaningfully compare women's treatment in the criminal justice system en masse to men's; different groups of men and women are treated differently depending on a range of other variables such as race, class and offence type (Hedderman and Hough 1994; Kellough and Wortley 2002).

The first section of this chapter explores the centrality of offence seriousness and the absence of gender considerations in magistrates' decision-making rationales in remand hearings concerning serious and petty offences. The second section looks at the individualised decision-making employed in 'cusp' cases (those cases that cannot be easily categorised by the seriousness of the offence) where gender considerations were evident.

The legal framework

It has been noted that remand law allows court personnel a great deal of discretion in their decision-making (Doherty and East 1985; Lydiate 1987; Zander 1967). Although there have been subsequent amendments, the Bail Act 1976 remains as the primary piece of remand law. Under this Act, untried defendants and convicted unsentenced defendants (being remanded for reports to be written) have a right to bail unless one of the exceptions to this right applies: the primary ones are that there are substantial grounds for believing they will abscond, offend on bail, or interfere with the course of justice. In assessing whether an exception applies, magistrates can consider a wide range of grounds encompassing both the offence and the circumstances of the person charged with the offence. There is a dualism in the approach to bail decisions in this legislation as there is a tension between the rights of the individual not to be imprisoned and the rights of the public not to be offended against. The research attempted to explore these tensions and how they were resolved in the routine practices of actors in magistrates' courts, with a particular focus on the role of gender in remand decision-making.

Questions about the necessity of custodial remands are often raised based on the relatively petty offences for which many women are remanded in custody; for example, 41 per cent of remand receptions of females in 2002 were for theft and handling.[1] Further, the majority of women (59 per cent in 2002) remanded in custody do not go on to receive a custodial sentence. If these offences and offenders are not considered serious enough to warrant a custodial sentence, why is it necessary to hold them on custodial remand prior to trial and/or sentence? Why do magistrates' courts remand so many individuals in custody when the offences charged are relatively minor? There is an important debate to be had about the need to reform bail law, for instance, whether it is equitable to remand someone in custody for petty offences that will, in all likelihood, not attract a custodial sentence. This chapter, however, focuses on how the current legal framework is implemented in magistrates' courts.

The effect of a custodial remand

Research illustrates the damaging consequences of a custodial remand on what is evidently a particularly vulnerable group with extensive adverse life experiences and disadvantageous personal characteristics, including parental separation, histories of sexual and physical abuse, time in local authority care, disrupted education, low household income, poor employment histories, homelessness, mental and physical health problems, and drug and alcohol misuse (see Eaton 1993; Edgar 2004; Loucks 2004; Wedderburn 2000). A custodial remand 'threatens housing, work and, particularly for women, contact with their children' (HMIP 2000: 24).

Although female remand prisoners only constituted 22 per cent of the female prison population in 2002, they made up 65 per cent of female receptions. Their characteristics, such as drug misuse, mental health problems, self-harm and suicide risk, as well as social and educational needs, can also make them a potentially difficult group for prison staff to manage (HMIP 2000).

Gender and the use of custodial remand

While there has been some analysis of the remand system, where women's custodial remands are mentioned in research, the discussion is typically cursory. As 92.6 per cent of the custodial remand population in England and Wales is male, this focus is understandable. However, analysis of the remand population as a whole obscures the distinctive characteristics of and trends in the female custodial remand population.

The evidence that does exist suggests that women are not discriminated against in magistrates' remand decisions and may, in fact, be treated more leniently.

> Females are less likely than males to be remanded in custody during proceedings at magistrates' courts (24% of females compared with 42% of males). However, research has shown that taking into account offending history and type of offence, the defendant's sex seems to have only a marginal effect on remand decisions. (Home Office 2003: 15)

It is the nature of the 'marginal effect' that gender has on remand decisions which is the primary concern of this chapter: it could be

129

that *all* remand decisions are 'marginally' influenced by the gender of the defendant, or perhaps in the majority of cases gender does not enter into the decision-making rationale at all but it has a profound impact in a few (types of) cases. When and to what extent is analysis of defendants' gender helpful in elucidating patterns of remand decision-making?

Decision-making rationales: offence seriousness

Previous research on remand has found offence seriousness to be strongly correlated to remand outcomes (Doherty and East 1985; Hucklesby 1994; Jones 1985; King 1971). This research also found that in the vast majority of cases, offence seriousness is the primary consideration, making the resolution of a case 'self-evident' (female CPS): petty offences invariably resulted in bail and serious offences in custodial remand. In these cases, decisions were based on offence-related criteria and character assessments rarely influenced outcomes. There were some cases that could not be easily categorised in terms of offence seriousness: 'cusp' cases. Cusp cases will be further discussed below but, in sum, in these cases decision outcomes rested primarily on moral assessments of the deservingness of the individual defendant rather than simply on the category of offence.

It is argued here that magistrates employed a bifurcated approach to remand decision-making when offence seriousness was the primary criterion for reaching a decision. There was significant differentiation in the ways magistrates approached and applied bail law to serious and non-serious offences. This dual approach was witnessed in observations and explored in the vignettes.

Despite strong contrary indications to granting bail (i.e. previous failures to appear and offending on bail), magistrates were extremely reluctant to remand women in custody for non-serious offences. In interview, the universally stated reason for this was that if the offence was not serious enough to warrant a custodial sentence, it should not attract a remand in custody. In this context, 'non-serious' offences are defined as nuisance offences (such as criminal damage, allowing yourself to be carried in a stolen car) and lesser property offences (such as handling stolen goods and shoplifting).

Anticipating sentencing, magistrates argued that they would not consider a custodial remand in light of a probable non-custodial disposal.

> At the end of the day if she's convicted then it's very unlikely that she'll go to prison and therefore remanding her in custody is not equitable.
> (*Male magistrate*)

The anticipated length of a remand compared to the probable sentence length was a very important consideration for many magistrates who felt they had a responsibility not to punish defendants excessively.

Further, the trivial nature of these offences meant that magistrates chose to ignore obvious bail risks when making decisions.

> I mean it's worrying, I have to say, and one would be running a risk by giving her bail but I am willing to risk another shop losing another couple of jackets.
> (*Female magistrate*)

> With that sort of record but with crimes against the person, he [*sic*] would be a definite remand in custody but for this one, it's extremely unlikely.
> (*Female magistrate*)

> There's a good chance she'll offend on bail, in fact I know near as damn it that she will. But I'm not going to remand her in custody.
> (*Male magistrate*)

In such cases, consideration of the harm done to the defendant by a remand in custody supersedes the potential harm to the public, and defendants are invariably bailed. The overwhelming majority of non-serious offences were bailed but it was possible for such cases to become 'cusp' cases and thus be at risk of a custodial remand if the offending was exceptionally prolific and the defendant was considered to be blatantly defying the court (see below).

Magistrates employed a very different approach to making remand decisions on serious offences. In this context, 'serious offences' are defined as any offences where violence or the threat of violence is used; domestic burglary; and offences involving large sums of money. Defendants charged with serious offences were only very rarely bailed by magistrates; the seriousness of the offence overrode other considerations. In court observations, the relationship between offence seriousness and custodial remands was evident:

- Seven charges of robbery: all were remanded in custody.
- Six charges of domestic burglary: four were remanded in custody and in the remaining two there were queries about whether 'burglary' was an inappropriate charge which should be reduced to, for example, 'unlawful entry'.
- Two charges of arson: both were remanded in custody.
- Two charges of living off immoral earnings: both were remanded in custody. They involved allegations of human trafficking for the purposes of prostitution, violent intimidation of victims/witnesses, and very large sums of money.

Although the nature and gravity of the offence is not one of the exceptions to the right to bail under the Bail Act 1976, Hucklesby (1994) observed that the seriousness of the offence had, in fact, become a *de facto* exception to the right to bail. This reason for refusing bail was also observed to be accepted unchallenged in courts in this research.

In contrast to the rationales of bail risk assessments for non-serious offences, with serious offences magistrates were not prepared to take any chances with reoffending. Even those magistrates who were not convinced of the guilt or bail risk of defendants were unwilling to grant bail because of the seriousness of offences. Discussing one self-evidently weak charge of domestic burglary (that was withdrawn the following week by the CPS because of a lack of evidence) a magistrate stated:

> This is a marginal one but I think my reaction is more that it would be better to keep her in custody because of the seriousness of the offence.
> (*Female magistrate*)

Court observations demonstrated that with serious offences, bail was refused because of a fear of the consequences *if* the defendant offended and not because of a probability, or even possibility, that she *would* offend. This was true even when the objections to bail were not substantial or even substantiated. Custody appeared almost inescapable for serious offences, regardless of mitigating factors. Referring to the weak case of domestic burglary cited above, a female magistrate explained how simple the decision rationale was:

> The fact that the people were upstairs means it is a serious offence. That is probably over-weighing everything else.

Evidently, in the majority of cases the seriousness of the offence charged was the most significant consideration in remand hearings. Offence seriousness framed how magistrates approached cases and was the primary determinant of case resolution, usually irrespective of other issues, including gender. Hucklesby was struck by the fact that magistrates still often granted bail even when defendants had breached their bail:

> 72 per cent of defendants who were charged with a bail offence were still granted bail which is surprising considering the historical and legal significance of failing to appear and suggests that the majority of defendants charged with a bail offence are trusted to appear at a later date. (Hucklesby 1994: 210)

In the context of the decision-making approaches outlined above, these figures are not surprising. It is posited that the majority of the 72 per cent were not actually trusted to reappear but were re-granted bail because their original offence was not serious enough to warrant a remand in custody despite the evident bail risk.

However, some defendants fail to appear or offend on bail with such regularity that, even though their offences are not serious, their contempt for court proceedings eventually results in their re-categorisation as cusp cases, which exposes them to the risk of being remanded in custody. It is to cusp cases that the discussion now turns.

Decision-making rationales: cusp cases

Cusp cases are those that do not fall easily into the bifurcated pattern of decision-making outlined above: they are on the borderline between conditional bail and custodial remand. Different types of cusp cases were observed: first, where the offence initially appeared serious but when the details were presented in court there was reason not to remand in custody because the nature of the offence did not automatically warrant it. This finding reflects more general comparisons between male and female offending: that broad offence categories can mask the typically less serious nature of women's offences (Daly 1994). The second group were those offences that were not serious in their character but were aggravated by the prolific nature of the offending. Commonly observed examples were shoplifting and attempted deception using stolen credit or debit cards. The level and frequency of offending had to be very significant for magistrates to debate whether to use custodial remand for a non-serious offence. It is the use of custodial remand in these cases that explains the high proportion of females remanded for minor acquisitive offences.

Cusp cases resolution was not primarily organised around the seriousness of the offence – decision-making was much more individualised and the particular characteristics and needs of the defendants were paramount. This is in the tradition of the positivist approach to criminal justice decision-making which is concerned with the reasons why individuals offend, and what interventions, if any, could and should be employed in particular cases. In this research, cusp case remand decisions were seen to be highly individualised and 'evidence' was selected and interpreted depending on the moral assessment of a defendant. A favourable impression meant that 'other potentially condemning data can now be re-assembled so that it becomes more difficult to ascribe unfavourable meanings to them' (Hawkins 1983: 110).

Female defendants at risk of custodial remands were found to be a very rare group in the magistrates' courts. The individualised approach that was observed to be taken with women who could not be easily categorised and processed on the basis of offence seriousness alone may partly be accounted for by the rarity of women in contested remand hearings. It is argued that decision-makers had not had the opportunity to develop concepts of 'normal cases' (Sudnow 1965) with this group of female defendants.

> It's predominantly men that we see and the question of bail is usually much more straightforward than with women because of the offences they've committed.
> (*Male magistrate*)

It was found that where 'perceptual shorthand' (Skolnick 1966) was used by decision-makers to classify, and thus appropriately process, female defendants, it was often framed more in terms of their gender than their criminality. Perhaps in the absence of a 'normal' female defendant in contested cases, magistrates relied more on whether a defendant was a 'normal' woman (Shapland 1987).

It is argued that magistrates' gender expectations meant that they responded to women's mitigation in cusp cases because they were less inclined to perceive women as entrenched and culpable offenders. While there is evidence that this perception is based in the reality of female offending patterns (Burman 2004; Daly 1994; Hedderman and Hough 1994; Hedderman and Gelsthorpe 1997; Home Office 2003), some magistrates admitted that it was gender roles, rather than gendered offending patterns, that shaped their bail decisions. For example, magistrates said that they were reluctant to remand in custody women with dependants, for the sake of the dependants, but that they viewed men who claimed to be carers with suspicion, as men who were 'trying it on' to secure bail. Gender role expectations shaped magistrates' perceptions of male and female defendants.

Many magistrates were deeply committed to the idea of 'doing something to help' and were prepared to take chances and release 'risky' defendants because of their perceived needs. There was, however, a sharp moral distinction made between those women who magistrates felt were genuine and would benefit from help, and those who were seen to be 'playing the system', cynically making pleas for help or pretending to be candidates for rehabilitation in order to secure bail. Evidence of the importance of gender in reaching this moral division between the 'troubled' and the 'troublesome' (Hedderman and Gelsthorpe 1997) women, those who deserved help and those who did not, is presented in more detail below.

Mitigation[2] techniques: (re)constructing women's characters

In cusp cases, the distinction between who should be bailed and who should not was not simply made on the basis of previous records of offending, though that did represent an obstacle to be overcome. Women could indeed have offending histories that indicated they were poor bail risks but this was not sufficient to explain the pattern of decision-making. Although the nature and frequency of a woman's offending was found to be one of the most important factors in whether or not she was perceived as someone who could or should be bailed, it was not insurmountable if her defence representative was able to convince the court to make a positive moral assessment of her. Cases were observed where women with long records of offending and failing to attend court were granted bail. Conversely, some women with relatively minor offending histories were remanded in custody. In these cases it appeared that the moral assessments that magistrates made about the individual defendants profoundly influenced the remand outcome.

This section explores the ways in which defence representatives often sought to portray their clients as 'reformable' women (Daly

1994) in need of protection and support (Allen 1987a, 1987b; Hedderman and Gelsthorpe 1997; Home Office 1974) in order to provoke a sympathetic reaction from magistrates and to secure bail. It will be seen that gender is a theme that runs through many of these narratives – it is evident in how the women were constructed as women and as offenders.

I She's ready to change now

Of the 27 cusp cases observed (18 women remanded in custody and nine conditionally bailed), nine women were presented by their defence lawyer as having recently experienced a significant event that had prompted them to change old patterns of behaviour. The catalysts for this preparedness to change included the shock of a recent custodial sentence (particularly if it was their first experience of imprisonment); children being taken into care and the defendant realising she could not regain custody of them until she was drug-free; recent detoxification which the defendant wanted to maintain; and a health scare necessitating a drug-free life. These women were all presented as being at a turning point in their lives and the courts were encouraged to recognise and support their efforts to change. 'Change', if perceived to be genuine, has been identified as an important issue in successful parole applications too (Hawkins 1983). The examples below provide an illustration of how this technique could secure bail even in very difficult cases.

Example

A 22-year-old woman appeared on overnight custody on a charge of shoplifting. She had a very extensive history of offending and a poor bail record. It was acknowledged that she had been repeatedly remanded in custody and sentenced to custody before. Her defence representative said:

> She pleads guilty at the earliest opportunity and accepts that her offending makes prison likely but she wants to ask for a remand for reports. She realises it is a risk as she may be remanded in custody but she is trying to make changes in her life ... She wants the chance to get reports not so much to give you details of her life and conditions but to prove that she can keep appointments and show willing.

The male district judge granted conditional bail and addressed the defendant, saying:

The time has come to make some effort to make some changes and if you're prepared to do so, we'll take that risk.

2 She's a good person, really

Of the 27 cases, 12 offered information on the general 'goodness' of the woman, which served to challenge perceptions of her simply as an offender and prove she was not beyond redemption. In these cases, worth was signified most commonly by accounts of what a good mother she was (five cases) but was also evidenced by one or more of the following: the fact that her three children all had the same father; there was no social services involvement in her children's lives; she was an intelligent and educated woman; she had previously held down a good job; and she was a carer for the disabled/aged. A common adjunct to this script was that innocents (those the women cared for) would suffer if she were not bailed.

Example

A 23-year-old woman appeared at Old Market Street charged with handling stolen goods and attempted deception. Bail was opposed on the grounds that at the time of committing the offence, she was on bail to another magistrates' court and Old Market Street for similar offences. There was also concern about failure to surrender and a risk of further offences being committed on bail. She had eight convictions for 13 offences and four cautions, all for similar offences. In her bail application, her defence representative said:

> She has been a user and that has been the reason for most of her offending. She does have some successful parts to her life too though, most notably a six-year-old son with whom she has a very good relationship. Her mother informs me that she is a good mother and that she cares for her son well. She takes him to school every day. This is a lapse, she has slipped up.

The defendant was released on bail with a condition of reporting to the police station.

3 She's more a victim than an offender

Of the 27 cases, 13 offered accounts of debilitating difficulties in women's lives. These included illness (six cases); homelessness; and abuse as a child (see below for abuse from male partners). These defendants were presented as women struggling to cope with their problems, perhaps not fully culpable because of circumstance and certainly deserving of some protection and support.

Example

A 25-year-old woman appeared at Old Market Street charged with criminal damage. She had damaged some internal walls of the hostel she was living in. She had become angered when the staff asked her to leave after finding a man in her room, against hostel rules. Her defence representative told the court:

> She accepts that she caused the damage. You have heard that she was asked to leave the hostel. The man in her room had followed her in from the street and followed her to her room. She tried to get him to leave but couldn't make him. Staff wouldn't listen to her explanation and this frustrated and angered her ... She was married with children aged seven and nine. Her husband physically abused her. A later boyfriend also abused her and this is why she is in a hostel. She has had five miscarriages in the last few years and is signed off on a pension because of this. She asks the court for help finding accommodation as she cannot return to this hostel.

4 She's free of him now

The removal of a corrupting man from the woman's life was cited in nine cases. This could be included in the 'ready to change' category but is separated out because 'change' is predicated on an acceptance of past guilt and an opportunity for redemption. In this category the woman was presented as not being fully culpable (particularly when the man was violent) and now the man had gone, she could be trusted to return to her natural law-abiding self. She was led astray and/or pressurised but now that influence has gone.

Example

A 22-year-old woman appeared at Inswick Corner and pleaded not guilty to a charge of theft from a person. It was regarded as a serious offence as money had been snatched from a woman at a cashpoint, and the victim had been assaulted by the defendant's alleged co-defendant. In his bail application, the defence representative argued:

She has a boyfriend and a drug habit and the two are entwined. She buys her drugs from her boyfriend and owes him money. He is very possessive of her. He doesn't know her home address so if you grant her bail she therefore has an opportunity to break away from him, and thus hopefully from her habit ... The reason for much of her offending is drugs. She has broken away from her boyfriend who is the root cause of her habit.

The defendant was bailed with conditions of residence at her family's home address, daily reporting at a police station, and an exclusion from the city.

5 She's an honest offender

In bail, unlike sentencing, extensive records of offending can actually sometimes be an advantage. In four cases, offending history was used to provide evidence that the defendant would not abscond or offend. A record without failures to appear could provide proof that the woman could be trusted to attend. Additionally, a prolific record with a recent hiatus could be cited as proof that the defendant had changed and was now law abiding and/or free of a drug habit. Past misdemeanours were offered as evidence that these women could be trusted to co-operate and behave.

Example

A 34-year-old woman appeared before a male district judge at Connorton Road charged with a failure to appear in court proceedings, one charge of theft of credit cards and five charges of deception (using stolen credit cards to obtain goods), values ranging from £30 to £112. She pleaded guilty to all charges. Her defence representative said:

It is difficult to apply for bail given her record but these matters pre-date her last court appearance. She instructs me she has now turned a corner. She was in a violent relationship which is now over and clearly she has problems. Her last prison sentence got her clean and there have been no offences committed since she was released three weeks ago. She points out that she usually offends within two days of being released. She asks the court to appreciate that she has turned a corner now.

The defendant was bailed with conditions of residence, reporting to a police station three times a week and a night-time curfew.

6 She's got the support of others

In five of the remand in custody cases women were said to have support in the community. The argument was that the bench may not judge her to be trustworthy but there were others who would take responsibility for her. Importantly, 'support' was only successful in securing bail at the second application when it was allied to 'control', such as a husband on whom, the court was told, she was financially dependent; a father who would offer residence and would make her work in his shop; a brother-in-law who was sitting in the back of the court ready to escort her out of the city to return home. The offers of support from mothers did not result in bail being granted at second bail applications. The number of cases is too small to make any meaningful generalisations from but they are suggestive of Eaton's (1984) findings that courts respond to traditional models of family structures: male relatives are seen to offer 'control', an essential adjunct to 'support' when bail is being considered. Carlen (1983) also found that courts were more likely to impose formal controls if the defendant was perceived to be beyond the informal controls of familial structures.

Example
  A 20-year-old woman appeared at Castleford Road on a charge of theft to the value of £153; the goods were recovered. She had been remanded in custody for one week previously. The defence representative said that his client could leave the city, to get away from her drug-taking lifestyle, and return to live in her family home. He said the defendant's brother-in-law was in court to take her back: 'He's assured me he'll escort her through the front door.' The defendant was bailed with conditions of residence and reporting to a police station.

Not all of the above scripts that defence representatives used were conspicuously gendered. However, the themes of the women's needs, informal controls, familial responsibilities, and victimisation repeat through the majority of them. Previous research shows that magistrates are predisposed to understand female defendants and their actions in terms of the women's needs. This research showed that if women and their defence representatives could also successfully persuade magistrates to give the defendant a positive character assessment, custodial remands could be avoided. Narratives that appealed to gender stereotypes were used by defence representatives to minimise perceptions of women as 'troublesome' and encourage perceptions of them as 'troubled'. Evidence of women's fulfilment of normative gender roles was presented by defence representatives to demonstrate their good character, to define the woman as someone who was deserving of help: 'I find that one common presupposition is the domestic division of labor and the vaunted "good family woman"' (Daly 1994: 197).

The findings reflect Eaton's (1986) and Carlen's (1983) claims that courts operate on, and perpetuate, gendered conceptions of men's and women's roles in the criminal justice system and in wider society. While Daly (1994) agrees that images of 'good family women' are used in courts to some women's advantage, she disputes the contention that the existence of such attitudes and their use in mitigation is necessarily detrimental to those women who do not satisfy these criteria.

> I am not persuaded that surrounding women with familial and maternal imagery restricts the range of possibilities for womanhood (excluding, for example, single women, those not in heterosexual couplings, and those without children). This argument may be right in the abstract, but it is less so in actual court practices – at least in United States courts, with which I am familiar. When there are good family women, their labor for others is affirmed. But women who are not considered to be good family women are not penalized for this status ... We should expect to find gendered presuppositions in courtroom discourse and actions, but we should explore whether such presuppositions harm or adversely affect some women ... We should not assume that they harm all (or even most) women in all courts. (Daly 1994: 197)

The data from the present research broadly support Daly's position. Of course magistrates and others may have brought unspoken prejudices to the remand court, but while defence representatives did, at times, use gender role fulfilment in mitigation, the CPS were never observed referring to women's gender role misdemeanours in their objections to bail. 'Good family women' were observed in the courts in this study to be characterised more positively, and thus were more likely to be bailed, but there was little evidence that women whose characters were more negatively perceived were treated any more harshly than men. There was little identifiable evidence that women in this study were being doubly damned for being doubly deviant (Carlen 1983; Carlen and Worrall 1987), but there was evidence that successful mitigation was often framed in terms of gender roles, for both women and men; defence representatives were also occasionally observed to successfully use men's gender roles to encourage magistrates to grant bail. For example, if a male defendant had a job, magistrates would try harder to keep him out of custody because of the strong links between steady employment and reduced offending, and to ensure his family did not suffer economic privations by losing the family's income.

Conclusion

This chapter has explored the extent to which gender influenced magistrates' remand decision-making. Although the data from this research did not support such an analysis, it would be interesting to explore whether the gender of the magistrates, and other court personnel, affected remand outcomes (Worrall 1987). There was anecdotal evidence that some of the older male magistrates had paternal attitudes towards the younger female defendants.

> The system is skewed towards women receiving bail rather than custody. It's skewed partly because a lot of us old-fashioned men, that's how we were brought up, so the mindset is that you will start off by looking at a female defendant as a person less likely to commit an offence.
> (*Male magistrate*)

Such 'chivalrous' views may have translated into more lenient remand decisions by magistrates with certain personal characteristics, but this needs to be properly explored in future research.

This research suggests that the gender effect in remand decision-making does not operate across all cases alike. In the overwhelming majority of cases, it is offence seriousness alone that determines remand outcomes, regardless of the personal characteristics of the defendant. However, in those cases that fall on the cusp, more complex decision-making approaches are (necessarily) employed. It is in these cases that a defendant's gender can become relevant to understanding remand outcomes, as it is one of the extra-legal cues (which may also include ethnicity, nationality, age and class) that inform magistrates' perceptions of the individual defendant and whether or not they 'deserve' to be bailed.

Magistrates' perceptions of female defendants' characters were found to be significantly structured around normative gender roles. Women were typically perceived to be more 'troubled' than men, which encouraged magistrates to use the remand decision in cusp cases as an opportunity to help and support defendants. Gender role fulfilment was found, consequently, to be a resource that defence representatives used to (re)construct their clients as women who (now) deserved bail. Although this was found to benefit those women who could demonstrate these favourable characteristics, those 'troublesome' women whose defence representatives failed to reconstruct their characters in the eyes of the magistrates were not afforded the same latitude.

While there was little evidence that women who were defined as troublesome were treated more harshly than men were, it is suggested that some women were less likely to receive the (sometimes dubious) 'benefit' of being perceived as troubled because of their personal characteristics such as race and class. The skill of the defence representative was instrumental in defining magistrates' perceptions of women's characters but some women may be less successfully (re)constructed because of their 'social distance' from magistrates: their personal characteristics contrasted with magistrates' own.

The social distance between defendants and the magistracy has implications for the extent to which magistrates' concerns about bail are justified. Similar to Fitzmaurice and Pease's 'false consensus bias' (1986), magistrates equated defendants' views and motivations with their own and 'understood' bail issues accordingly. Hedderman and Gelsthorpe found magistrates were 'often flummoxed ... [and] ... clearly confused' (1997: 47) by family structures that did not reflect their own. Consequently, in those cases where it was considered relevant, magistrates perceived fewer reassuring structures of informal social controls in 'unconventional' family structures compared to those that reflected magistrates' own.

The greater the social distance between defendants and the magistracy, the less familiar, and therefore less accessible, the defendants' motivations and lifestyle were and the greater the chances of magistrates having unjustified bail concerns. An obvious and necessary area for future research is if and how (different groups of) magistrates' moral assessments of women varied with extra-legal factors and personal characteristics such as defendants' demeanour, race, nationality, class and age.

Notes

1 All figures in this chapter relate to England and Wales. Unless otherwise stated, all figures in this chapter are from Home Office (2003) *Statistics on Women and the Criminal Justice System* and Home Office (2002) *Prison Statistics England and Wales 2002*.
2 Within the criminal justice context, the term 'mitigation' usually refers to defence statements in the sentencing process. It is used here to describe the arguments put forward by defence representatives which aimed to counter or lessen the strength of CPS arguments in favour of custodial remand.

References

Allen, H. (1987a) 'Rendering Them Harmless: The Professional Portrayal of Women Charged with Serious Violent Crimes', in P. Carlen and A. Worrall (eds) *Gender, Crime and Justice*, Milton Keynes: Open University Press.

Allen, H. (1987b) 'The Logic of Gender in Psychiatric Reports to the Courts', in D. C. Pennington and S. Lloyd-Bostock (eds) *The Psychology of Sentencing*, Oxford: Centre for Socio-Legal Studies.

Brown, K., Duff, P. and Leverick, F. (2004) *A Preliminary Analysis of the Bail/Custody Decision in Relation to Female Accused*, Edinburgh: Scottish Executive Social Research.

Burman, M. (2004) 'Breaking the Mould: Patterns of Female Offending', in G. McIvor (ed.) *Women who Offend*, London: Jessica Kingsley.

Carlen, P. (1983) *Women's Imprisonment*, London: Routledge.

Carlen, P. and Worrall, A. (eds) (1987) *Gender, Crime and Justice*, Milton Keynes: Open University Press.

Casale, S. (1989) *Women Inside: The Experience of Women Remand Prisoners in Holloway*, London: Civil Liberties Trust.

Daly, K. (1994) *Gender, Crime and Punishment*, New Haven, CT: Yale University Press.

Doherty, M. and East, R. (1985) 'Bail Decisions in Magistrates' Courts', *British Journal of Criminology*, 25(3): 251–66.

Eaton, M. (1984) *Familial Ideology and Summary Justice: Women Defendants Before a Suburban Magistrates Court*, Sociology, LSE.

Eaton, M. (1986) *Justice for Women?*, Milton Keynes: Open University Press.

Eaton, M. (1987) 'The Question of Bail: Magistrates' Responses to Applications for Bail on Behalf of Men and Women Defendants', in P. Carlen and A. Worrall (eds) *Gender, Crime and Justice*, Milton Keynes: Open University Press.

Eaton, M. (1993) *Women After Prison*, Buckingham: Open University Press.

Edgar, K. (2004) *Lacking Conviction: The Rise of the Women's Remand Population*, Prison Reform Trust.

Fitzmaurice, C. and Pease, K. (1986) *The Psychology of Judicial Sentencing*, Manchester: Manchester University Press.

Gelsthorpe, L. (1997) 'Feminism and Criminology', in M. Maguire, R. Morgan and R. Reiner (eds) *The Oxford Handbook of Criminology*, 2nd edn, Oxford: Clarendon Press.

Hawkins, K. (1983) 'Assessing Evil: Decision Behaviour and Parole Board Justice', *British Journal of Criminology* 23(2): 101–27.

Hedderman, C. (2004) 'Why are More Women being Sentenced to Custody?', in G. McIvor (ed.) *Women Who Offend*, London: Jessica Kingsley.

Hedderman, C. and Gelsthorpe, L. (eds) (1997) *Understanding the Sentencing of Women*, London: Home Office.

Hedderman, C. and Hough, M. (1994) *Does the Criminal Justice System Treat Men and Women Differently?*, London: Home Office.

Heidensohn, F. (1968) 'The Deviance of Women: A Critique and an Enquiry', *British Journal of Sociology* 19(2): 160–75.

Heidensohn, F. (1987) 'Women and Crime: Questions for Criminology', in P. Carlen and A. Worrall (eds) *Gender, Crime and Justice*, Milton Keynes: Open University Press.

Heidensohn, F. and Silvestri, M. (1995) *Women and Crime*, 2nd edn, Basingstoke: Macmillan.

HMIP (2000) *Unjust Deserts: A Thematic Review by HM Chief Inspector of Prisons of the Treatment and Conditions for Unsentenced Prisoners in England and Wales*, London: Home Office.

Home Office (1974) *Bail Procedures in Magistrates' Courts. Report of the Working Party*, London: HMSO.

Home Office (2002) *Prison Statistics England and Wales 2002*, Cm 5996, London: Home Office.

Home Office (2003) *Statistics on Women and the Criminal Justice System* London: Home Office.

Hucklesby, A. (1994) *Bail or Jail? The Magistrates' Decision*, University of Glamorgan/Prifysgol Morgannwg.

Hucklesby, A. (1996) 'Bail or Jail? The Practical Operation of the Bail Act 1976', *Journal of Law and Society* 23(2): 213–33.

Jones, P. (1985) 'Remand Decisions at Magistrates' Courts', in D. Moxon (ed.) *Managing Criminal Justice*, London: HMSO.

Kellough, G. and Wortley, S. (2002) 'Remand for Plea', *British Journal of Criminology*, 42: 186–210.

King, M. (1971) *Bail or Custody?*, Nottingham: The Cobden Trust.

Loucks, N. (2004) 'Women in Prison', in G. McIvor (ed.) *Women Who Offend*, London: Jessica Kingsley.

Lydiate, P. (1987) 'Bail Proceedings in Magistrates' Courts: Basic Procedures', *Justice of the Peace*, 151: 164–7.

Shapland, J. (1987) 'Who Controls Sentencing? Influences on the Sentencer', in D. C. Pennington and S. Lloyd-Bostock (eds) *The Psychology of Sentencing*, Oxford: Centre for Socio-Legal Studies.

Skolnick, J. (1966) *Justice Without Trial: Law Enforcement in Democratic Society*, New York: Wiley.

Sudnow, D. (1965) 'Normal Crimes: Sociological Features of the Penal Code in a Public Defender Office', *Social Problems*,12: 255–76.

Wedderburn, D. (2000) *Justice for Women: The Need for Reform*, London: Prison Reform Trust.

WORP (2004) *Women's Offending Reduction Programme Action Plan*, London: Home Office.

Worrall, A. (1987) 'Sisters in Law? Women Defendants and Women Magistrates', in P. Carlen and A. Worrall (eds) *Gender, Crime and Justice*, Milton Keynes: Open University Press.

Worrall, A. (1990) *Offending Women: Female Lawbreakers and the Criminal Justice System*, London: Routledge.

Zander, M. (1967) 'Bail: A Re-appraisal', *Criminal Law Review*, 25–39: 100–11; 129–43.

Chapter 8

'Bad Girls' or 'Mad Girls' – the coping mechanism of female young offenders

Nicola Hutson and Carrie Anne Myers

Introduction

Feminist criminologists have documented their concern about the treatment of female offenders within the penal system. Indeed a number of researchers have highlighted the fact that women have a propensity to be defined as in need of medical or psychological treatment rather than as purely criminal (Morris 1987; Carlen and Worrall 1987; Dobash *et al.* 1986). These observations are over 20 years old but do they still hold true?

Historically, the construct of gender has been ignored when exploring criminal behaviour, and this could be due to a dissonance between our perception of women as carers and as criminals – capable of perpetrating acts of violence and disarray (Chesney-Lind and Pasko 2004). Refreshingly, more recently there has been a movement towards looking at women in prison as a group in their own right, and this movement has been driven by feminist criminology.

Looking at young women prisoners as individuals is an illuminating task, which throws up some perplexing but persistent truths. They are an under-represented group, and there is little documentation of their experiences in the literature to date. We draw on existing feminist criminological literature for comparison. Although from the outset this may not seem accurate, we will demonstrate that the issues documented are identical, and the experiences of women as a group are the same, regardless of age.

Using qualitative methodology we will argue that the 'medicalisation' of female offenders continues to be practised. We will show the coping mechanisms that the girls use, which often revolve around issues of self-harm and suicide, and will present the 'real' from the 'fake' self-harmers. We will demonstrate the escalating problem of eating disorders as a means of exerting control and fighting against the pressures of day-to-day life in an institution. Finally, we will document the 'real' needs that the women have, as expressed by themselves, and show how the provisions on offer often fail to address the problems the girls experience.

Researching women in custody

The aim of working with female young offenders was to embed ourselves in their social worlds for a short period of time, and understand the impact of their experiences on the 'here and now' of their life in custody. Given this remit, we agreed from the beginning that a reductionist quantitative approach frequently used in criminology (Britton 2004) would limit our findings. Furthermore, avoiding positivistic methods is in line with a feminist approach, so that we could comprehend women's experiences in their own terms. As Worrall (1990: 3) highlighted, taking a qualitative approach allowed us to account for the women's experiences without reducing them. Many of the girls we interviewed had consistently existed on the socio-economic margins of life. Indeed, as research on female offenders accumulates, it becomes apparent that they are usually victims themselves and have often suffered physical and emotional abuse. Consequently, a qualitative approach is more sympathetic to these issues.

However, while a feminist perspective is useful, we also advise that this should be embedded within a wider sociological approach if we are going to truly unpack and understand the experiences that these young girls have in prison. We will argue that women's crime, and their response to it, is sociologically embedded in their prior experience. It is no coincidence that the highest rates of crime and delinquency have often been found in those areas exhibiting high rates of multiple other social problems, such as single-parent families, unemployment, joblessness, multiple-family dwellings, welfare cases and low levels of education (Chesney-Lind and Shelden 1998).

Ultimately, the women's life history prior to incarceration should be viewed as an integral part of their treatment and rehabilitation while in prison. In reality, this is often ignored. Through practising the 'blurred boundaries' thesis we will argue that women's offending is intimately linked to their previous victimisation (Britton 2004), and while the number of young women in custody may be small, this does not mean they have 'small' problems (Chesney-Lind and Pasko 2004).

Young women as criminals – the importance of life history

Life histories had an important impact on how the young women 'handled' their incarceration. Many had experienced previous mental health problems, and these were often exacerbated by their incarceration. Many attributed their reason for being in prison to the myriad factors that made up their past, and the context that had produced them. The majority of girls that we interviewed felt that their childhood experiences had had a direct influence on their current situation:

> I believe it comes from when you are a child, I mean something that happened a long time ago … that happened in childhood. I think, from the parents. Maybe you've been abused or … seen a lot of abusing going on in the family, and that's what stirs it all up … seeing all that has an influence, man.

More substantiated life histories were also mentioned, beyond the girls' own situation. The role and significance of extended family continued to influence the young women's behaviour and experience:

> My mum has been … she had years of abuse, and torture and stuff like that … pure nastiness … she can't deal with it man … Now she ain't in that relationship but she ain't having nothing like that done to her no more … I think she feels like she ain't normal no more cos it aint happening to her … and it's hard for her to sort out things in her head … she's not good at coping with anything .. I dunno … she's not right in the head … And it's not her fault …

Others alluded to the ways in which the stress they had experienced both before and during their prison sentence manifested. As one interviewee concluded, 'everyone's been through something … all the girls in here have a story about their life'.

The mental health of female young offenders

It is a universal truth that women are much more likely to have treatment for mental health problems than their male counterparts. As Allen (1987) observed, 'The female is not the "special" but the normal form of the psychiatric patient.' However, these observations become more pronounced among the female prison population. The Office for National Statistics (1998) conducted a Survey of Psychiatric Morbidity among prisoners in England and Wales and found that the proportion of females who had received help or treatment for a mental health problem in the 12 months before entering prison was 40 per cent – almost double the proportion of male prisoners (Home Office 2003).

The Prison Reform Trust (2000) found that two-thirds of women in prison suffered from numerous mental health problems, and more than half were suffering from a personality disorder. Home Office data (2003) supports these findings, although to a slightly lesser extent, with statistics showing that 37 per cent of sentenced female prisoners had previously attempted suicide (Singleton *et al.* 1998). Furthermore, over 40 per cent of sentenced women said that they had harmed themselves intentionally and or attempted suicide (Home Office 2003). Data on young offenders committing suicide or acts of self-harm is difficult to find. However, we do know that between 2000 and 2003, 64 young people have committed suicide while in prison (source: www.mind.org.uk).

Medicine, like law, views itself as 'gender neutral' (Worrall 1990), but the evidence contradicts this. Furthermore, despite changes in rhetoric over the last 20 years, developments in the treatment of women prisoners continue to be nominal and tokenistic. It appears to be the case that the arguments presented by Genders and Player in 1987 still stand. There continues to be a mismatch between the treatment and control of women in prison and the day-to-day experiences of women prisoners (Genders and Player 1987).

Taking the pain away – the medicalisation of female young offenders

Perhaps one of the most shocking revelations was the admission by the girls that they had all been offered medication for depression, sleeping problems, anxiety and a wide range of other psychological conditions. One female documented how this process began in the court room:

> I got a long sentence and when I went to court, like they said to me, 'Do you want anti-depressants and sleeping tablets?' and stuff like that, and I said, 'I haven't got a problem with my sleeping and I'm not depressed or nothing I'm alright with it', cos I knew what kind of sentence I was going to get. But they just wanted to give it to me cos they said, 'But it will help you'. I said, 'But I don't need the help so why are you trying to push tablets on me?'

The practice of prescribing psychotropic drugs to inmates who were not diagnosed as 'sick' but viewed as suffering from 'normal' difficulties associated with imprisonment was a consistent theme. The girls were fully aware that medication was not the solution to their problem:

> I've really noticed here, a lot of people feel really down, and they'll go to the doctor and the doctor will just put them straight on medication, now obviously those issues they should really be speaking to someone about it.

And often felt forced by the prison system into taking drugs to alleviate their problems:

> The first time I went to the doctor he just said to me, 'I can give you some medication', and I said to him, 'I don't want medication because you can get addicted from it', yeah. You say, 'I feel depressed' and they're like, 'alright, have some Prozac'.

It is likely that the rationale for over-prescribing among the prison staff was an attempt to alleviate some of the negativity of a prison sentence, and soften the experience with medication. Nonetheless, the young women were aware that this was often not the best way to meet their needs. Many felt that medicalisation resulted in the 'bad stuff' building up, and being 'released' inappropriately:

> How I think of it in prison, is a lot of people, if they're upset and things like that they don't get to deal with it, they get given

anti-depressants, so it's just blocking everything. So then when anything, like, when the [anti-]depressants start to wear off, everything's just bursting out of them at once so then they start to cut up.

Unsuitable and excessive prescribing to young women with normal levels of stress seemed to be a common practice, both before and during their prison sentence. Consistent with previous research, it appeared that the system felt the need to compensate for the burden of putting young women into a man's world (i.e. a prison) with drugs.

Furthermore, over-prescribing was accompanied by poor prescribing habits. Some young women expressed a desire to receive medication to help them cope with their prison sentence and the prison responded accordingly. However, some rather careless prescribing habits were highlighted by the girls, who felt that they lacked control over their own medication. One woman spoke of receiving a change in medication, without the required medication instructions:

They changed my medication, cos I felt I couldn't cope when I first come in and they gave me Prozac and I felt that it weren't working, so I asked for something else, so they gave me Seroxat but I had to ask them for the leaflet for the symptoms and side effects and stuff, cos they ain't gonna tell you, they're just going to give it to you.

Another issue that arose was the recognition that some young women were 'working the system'. For some, their need for medication was obviously a reaction against their current situation, rather than the result of any endogenous psychiatric requirement. Some of the young women reported getting medication under false pretences in an attempt to numb the pain of being in prison:

People work the system and go on like they're mad just to get medication to go to sleep at night, you know what I mean? And I don't think that's right cos that's damaging yourself, addicted to tablets, you know what I mean, hooked on this medication and there's nothing wrong with you, you know what I mean?

They also recognised the difficulties this situation presented for the prison staff. If young women were 'faking' their medical requirements, how could the prison service prescribe effectively? The dilemma of recognising who had real needs and who was 'faking' was acknowledged:

People just play the system and just go on like they're mad and we see it, but they [the staff] have to believe you cos they ain't got no other choice but to believe you.

However, the overall ethos over whether to offer the young women medication or not always seemed to fall on the side of prescribing. Medication offered a 'quick fix' solution to the girls' problems during their incarceration, and meant the prison service was not obliged to deal with the real issues that the young women faced. This was noted during many interviews, and the need for alternative forms of treatment to meet mental health needs was a commonly cited request:

I've got loads of people in my family who've got schizophrenia and it's hard that is. I think you need more help. Not ... keep drugging them up on medication, they need more psychiatrists, more special people from 'the out' coming in every now and again to speak to them.

Input into their lives from people from 'the out' was considered by the girls to be an essential part of their recovery. Through involving outsiders in their treatment and rehabilitation, they felt that their situation could be improved. People from 'the out' were considered the 'recovery elixir', as through them the young women could re-engage with the outside world, and exert some control over their lives and their own sanity. These findings were consistent with the work of Genders and Player (1987) who pointed out that underlying any benevolent wish on the part of medical staff to reduce levels of pain experienced by women in prison, is the idea that the nature of the relief provided denies the women responsibility for their problems, confirms their dependence on outside sources of support, and denies their capability of being able to look after themselves.

Releasing the pain – self-harm as a coping mechanism

Finding ways to exert control and maintain their sense of 'self' (Liebling 1992; Genders and Player 1995) and identity within the 'total institution' (Goffman 1961) of the prison was a common preoccupation for the girls.

Many of the young women employed self-harm as a coping strategy and a way of relieving their mental anguish. Many of the girls we interviewed employed self-harm as a coping mechanism, as both a means of exerting some control over their life, and a method of physically alleviating some of their mental suffering.

Self-harmers were regarded by both inmates and prison staff in a negative light, and 'self-harming' behaviour was generally not popular with other prisoners or the staff. There was a definite stigma attached to 'cutting up'. Girls who used this tool as a coping strategy were often derided by their fellow inmates. Their motivation was also questioned, and a number of the young women felt that the self-harmers were rewarded for their actions:

> They've come in with their skin clean and that, no scars or nothing and then they start slashing their wrists cos like everybody else is doing it. And other people that are getting attention for doing it, I mean they give self-harmers colouring books and stuff, you know what I mean? They give them stuff for doing it, so people are doing it just to get stuff, you know what I mean? I know people that do it just to get stuff and I think it's stupid. It is, it's stupid, cos you're marking your skin, scarring your precious skin, you know what I mean and it's gonna be there for life, you know what I mean?

This concern also manifested in discussions about how self-harmers were treated by the system. Many of the girls felt that self-harmers were often ignored or unsupported, with few preventative measures being taken to avoid them self-harming again:

> In prison people cutting their arms and stuff like that ... I dunno, they don't treat 'em very good cos they still give 'em razors ... to keep in their cells.

Furthermore, the inadequacies of the prison system for dealing with self-harming were observed by the girls:

> No, that's the thing, they should have put her in Healthcare [the self-harmer], she's got it real bad, and she does it, and she tried hanging herself the other day, and they still got her in her

room and that … dunno, she should be in Healthcare on watch
all the time, suicide watch ya know …

However, the women who were actively self-harming, while
aware of the stigma attached to their actions, felt there was a lack
of understanding about what they were going through and the
psychology of why they did it. There was a divide within the prison
between those that did understand, and self-harmed, and those that
did not:

> I used to cut my arms, and when I first come on the wing here
> and everyone saw it, they'd say 'I hate people who cut their
> arms'. They just don't understand why people do it … but
> people who do it understand, and them's the only people that
> do understand, people who's getting it.

It seemed that the issue of self-harm operated at two levels. The
prisoners were aware of the chasm between the young women who
used self-harm as a tool to get what they wanted, and those that
genuinely used it as a mechanism for releasing their mental torment
and exerting control over their environment. The difference between
the real self-harmers and the 'fakers' was abundantly clear to the
prisoners, in terms of which parts of the body were selected to
be 'cut up'. Some girls used their cuts as a trophy, and a physical
manifestation of their mental pain. Others (often with existing pre-
custodial psychiatric disorders), went to great lengths to hide their
pain, by cutting up 'hidden' parts of their body:

> The thing with self-harming, say like if I was to cut myself here
> [slashes arm] then they'll [the officers] know but if I was to cut
> myself here or here [slashes groin and leg] they [the officers]
> don't know things like that. And people do do it secretly.

The girls were very aware of the self-denial that often accompanied
self-harm as a coping mechanism. Many of the girls normalised self-
harm, and were confused about what self-harm said about their
mental state:

> There's this one girl, and she don't think she's mental, cos she
> cuts her wrists and that, but other people would look at it and
> say you're obviously mental for cutting your wrists in the first

place, but people look at things differently though, don't they ... but like most people in here have had a bad life, so it's different, different issues and that ... but most people don't think they're nuts ... like I don't think I have mental health problems, but then I do have mental health problems I'm just not nuts!

However, 'mental' or otherwise, self-harmers were commonly derided by other inmates, who failed to understand why they 'cut up'. A subgroup emerged among the young women who all self-harmed, and were sympathetic to one another's situations. They almost seemed to encourage self-harm as a legitimate coping mechanism:

They [the girls] take the piss out of self-harm. I cut up, you know. It's cos we can't show, our ... we can't talk about our feelings. We do it in another way. Everyone's got different opinions about other people.

Exploring other ways of coping – taking control

Taking control of their lives through avoiding the medication was another theme in these girls' lives, although finding a replacement for the drugs in prison was not always easy. Getting on with it, through talking about it, and then moving on, were considered the best responses, although this was not always an easy path to take:

Everybody's got stress. Everyone in here's been through something; you know what I mean? All the girls have, all the girls have a story about their life. And it's just talking about it. That's all it boils down to really, they need to speak about it and get on top of it, cos it's letting the problem get on top of them and that's not healthy. That is not healthy for them.

Being aware that there were certain times during the prison day when coping was more difficult than at other times was an important part of staying strong. Long periods of uninterrupted 'lock down' were not considered conducive to good emotional health. Time alone in the 'pad', thinking, was something that was dreaded by many:

Everyone's alright in the day, it's lock down, you're behind your door at night that's when you think, that's when you've got the time to think, and it can be bad, man.

Hiding the pain through relying on alcohol and drugs had been a common coping mechanism for many prior to incarceration, and some of the girls commented on how their prison sentence had helped them break this cycle, and supported them in getting off alcohol and drugs. The in-prison addiction programmes tended to be viewed very favourably by the young women, and they were grateful for the counselling and support that they received:

> I didn't start drinking till I was 15 but like before that I was properly depressed ... but I didn't know I was depressed ... I was drinking but I did a lot of bad stuff on drink but then the next day cos I'd realise I'd done bad stuff I'd go out and have another drink cos I didn't want the guilt to bring me down and I'd just carry on and carry on and carry on ... there's only so much happens to make me have a wake-up call and realise no, this is not right ... and they've helped me get off that in here, and I'm really grateful for that.

Alongside medical routes the girls would control their situation through diet. Food was used as a weapon by a number of girls. Many reported that the prison food was awful and the diet was not conducive to the maintenance of a 'good figure' or a 'healthy diet':

> On the out you don't really eat as much fattening food and when you get here, you get chips, mayonnaise and things like that so you put on weight. Cos I've been here only since January and I've already put on a stone. So like people say like 'I'm not gonna eat', they'll take like laxatives to get rid of it, things like that.

Alongside disgust at their diet, the girls reported that the prison regime itself did not help the girls to remain fit and healthy:

> The food here, there's a lot more like grease and things like that, so then even if you're trying to cut down, you're still like putting it on. And it's like the gym's only in the mornings. It's like we get up, eat, go to education, lunchtime we eat again, then it's education again, then we eat again, then we're back in our cells. So like even if we cut down on our food, by the time we get back to our cells we're just stuck there, my boyfriend is in prison and they have like evening gym as well. So I think they've got more access to gym than we do.

The girls described how fellow inmates would develop eating disorders while they were in the prison:

> I know somebody that doesn't eat and it's not the fact that it's the food, it's the fact that she's got problems and she just never feels hungry and once you go without food for like three or four days and you just don't eat nothing but fruit, for three days, then you don't wanna eat nothing after that cos your stomach's closed up. And then every time you try and eat, you'll like bring it up. Then you're sick, you know what I mean. You're wasting away. And it's not healthy and you have to stay strong in a place like this. You have to stay strong. Cos if you're sick and you waste away then you're no good.

Once again the girls reported a misunderstanding between the needs of the inmates and the actions of the prison staff, this time in relation to refusing to eat:

> I think it's OK but there are people who don't eat here. Cos they don't really care. They [prison officers] don't say like, 'Oh come on have your lunch', they just leave them. Like if they're [prisoners] not eating they [prison officers] should like at least bring some food back for them and leave some on the table just in case they will like eat it and that. But people here, the staff here they don't understand what we're going through. They say they do but they don't.

In connection, the young women noted that it was only the inmates who knew the true extent of the eating disorders among the girls and this was only discovered after a girl had been sick:

> But the officers they can't really pick up on that [bulimia], it's only like us. Like you'll go in a toilet and someone's been sick and you're like, 'Oh why didn't you clean the toilet?' or something like that and that's the only way you'll find out. But by then they [the officers] don't know who it is. It gets hidden.

The girls had developed many different ways to cope with incarceration and a number of these avenues were obscured from the prison authorities. We asked about official means and methods that helped the girls deal with their problems.

'Official' routes to cope with prison

Alongside the medication provided by the doctors, there was a resident psychiatrist and opportunities for the girls to receive therapeutic interventions. Indeed, some of the women felt that a programme of counselling was their only hope for getting off the anti-depressant medication that they were prescribed in prison. Some girls took the initiative themselves, and insisted that they received some form of counselling. They realised that, in the long term, taking the medication would not solve the deep-rooted psychological issues that haunted them:

> I went back to the doctor and said I want to speak to someone, I need to speak to someone because taking this medication [anti-depressants] may save me for a year and after that year's up the stuff that's going on in my head will still be going on. When you come here people just go on it, they've never been depressed before in their life, but they are like I feel, really low, I can't sleep you know … it's not about 'Do you want to talk to someone, you should talk to someone'.

The positive perception of counselling as a coping mechanism was fuelled by those who had 'come out the other side' and completed a successful programme of counselling, feeling better and stronger. This created a number of 'counselling evangelists' in the prison, who spread the good news of how counselling had helped them to cope with their emotional trauma:

> There's like two of my friends, suffer really bad from depression and stuff, and cos I've been there like, got help, and gone to a counsellor, I've spoken to them about it, and said you can get help, go to a counsellor and trust me, if you're ready you'll be able to do it, and they've gone along that path and they've got better.

The officers were commended for supporting the young women through counselling. It was obvious that the staff recognised that many of the problems experienced by the girls were endemic to their social situation outside prison. However, many of the young women recognised that some of the problems that they were presented with in prison could be alleviated by staff intervention, but this required the girls to be proactive, take the initiative and ask for help:

> When I'm down I'd probably go to my counsellor … yeah, I've got a counsellor, I go to counselling meetings … or I get on quite well with some of the officers and I trust some of the officers and I'd go to my personal officer, because it's important to have a relationship with the officers.

The young women also held stringent views on how counselling could be most effective. The need for one-on-one support was constantly referred to, with group work considered a poor second. Many of the girls had not received much personal attention in their lives, and the need for individual support in prison was likely to be a reflection of this. Furthermore, there was a lack of trust among the inmates, making group work unlikely to succeed:

> I think it [counselling] should be given individually, because, if you are in a group, let's say a group of 10, say, right, people in the groups, they start mucking about, cos their mates are there, the audience is there, you can't be bothered listening, you're not going to admit some of your issues as your friends are there, whereas when you are on a one to one, or like, two people and an inmate or something, then it's different as you know this ain't gonna go any further, whereas in here … if you are in a group of 10 there may be someone in that group you don't trust, so you ain't gonna open up, you'll think maybe she's gonna go round and tell someone about it.

Talking to an officer was also viewed as a good practical measure to take, in order to deal with practical issues. Emotional issues were not considered suitable for this forum:

> Certain things like, when I'm leaving prison I'll go and talk to an officer, obviously they're older and they've got more of the know-how, but talk about deep problems, I don't think I'd talk to anyone else about them.

The impact of culture and life history played an important role in influencing how the girls responded to their emotional requirements in prison.

> In my culture we have to be too strong, and we don't see counsellors, but when I came to this country I realised that there are issues that I need to deal with and things I need to

talk about. So I spoke to a counsellor, I asked for some help and those things, so personally for me, yeah, it would be useful.

Informal counselling through 'friends' in prison was not something that the young women generally relied upon, as prison friendships were often based on a lack of trust, and fear of recrimination. The importance of being able to talk to someone from 'the out' was a theme that consistently emerged:

> I don't say nothing to no one … I think lots of people just get stressed and smash up their cells and that, and other people talk to their mates, but it's not very often, you haven't really got mates in here. I didn't know anyone when I came in here and I've only been in here a little while, so I can't really call anyone my mates … I have got friends and that, but not anyone I feel I could talk to about stuff, and that… I usually just let it out, like, the other day I had a meeting with my probation officer and I kept her there for about two hours! Chatting … told her all about my life and everything, got it all out. And I haven't talked to anyone about my problems, not my counsellor nor nothing, so that was good … Yeah, I came out much happier.

Confidence in the selected individual one confided in was fundamental in the process of accepting help. The inmate had to make sure that the person was empathetic without being patronising, and this was crucial for subsequent recovery. Counselling had to be the right sort, from the right person, in order to be effective:

> The people that you are going to go and talk to, they need to take it seriously rather than she just thinks she's mentally ill or whatever … cos sometimes people that you are supposed to go and talk to … they don't really care, so unless it works both ways, then it can't work.

Presenting problems in the right way was also vital to effective treatment:

> I think lots of people think … like you don't even understand yourself. So when people are saying, you've got a problem you don't even think … I haven't got a problem, I just feel low about myself and I want help. You're telling me I've got a problem? Do you know what I mean, putting it in those terms is quite

harsh I think ... And to let people know it's ok to go and see a psychiatrist, and they don't think you're mad, it's alright to talk, and listen and see if they can help you, not that it's a bad thing to do ... and you're not mad or nothing.

Inadequacies of support and help were often referenced, particularly the limited availability of the psychiatrist:

The psychiatrist is a nightmare to see, you can't see her whenever you want to. And if you are on her list to see her, you see her every three weeks. Say you put in like a note to say you wanna see the psychiatrist now, three months later you're still waiting. You're on a waiting list, they should have more people in the prison doing it.

The difficulty of recognising the benefits that counselling could have for one's mental state was also a consideration. Many of the young women had approached counselling reluctantly, only to become a 'convert' and champion of its benefit on successful completion:

But the thing is when you're depressed or whatever you don't really want to talk to anybody ... do you really want them to know what you're feeling or what's going on in your head, it's afterwards, or when you start to recover that you think, yeah well, maybe I'd like to talk to someone.

Nonetheless, the girls unanimously agreed that the therapeutic and psychiatric provisions available in prison were very much in demand, yet sadly, low in supply.

Conclusion

The findings of this research suggest that the experiences of incarcerated female young offenders has changed little since the work carried out by feminist criminologists over 20 years ago. The medicalisation issue that was highlighted as a cause for concern over two decades ago is still overtly practised within the female young offender population.

Within the domain of criminology, girls and their delinquent problems have been ignored for a long time. As highlighted, the need to take into account previous experiences prior to incarceration is vital if the young women are to be cared for appropriately during their custody. Girls in institutions still appear to be the 'forgotten few' (Bergsmann 1989). Nonetheless, the alarming rates at which the girls practise coping mechanisms by way of medicalisation, self-harm and eating disorders clearly demonstrate a need to develop ways to help female young offenders during their time within prison.

By giving the young women 'a voice' in the research we have demonstrated that there is still a lot to be achieved in terms of improving the conditions and experience of the penal system for female young offenders. The girls' responses resonated with important messages, and highlighted how the current penal system disregards the compelling needs of young women in prison.

Current information and practices available to young women to help them 'cope' with prison are not adequate and do not address their needs. Consistent with the findings of Genders and Player (1987) we have found that the idea of girls being 'mad' rather than 'bad' still prevails. However, future research needs to unpack the issues of medicalisation. Some young women come into prison with pre-existent, diagnosed mental health problems. During this research it emerged that for many girls, issuing drugs and medication to them was a systemic 'quick fix' that temporarily alleviated the problems they faced but did nothing to 'solve' them. The wider, sociological, pre-custodial conditions of their life histories were rarely considered during their incarceration.

Feminist criminologists advocated that different treatments considered appropriate for females should be explored as women are biologically, psychologically and socially different from men (Genders and Player 1987). However, as we have seen, such initiatives have yet to filter into the female young offender population.

The girls reported their desire for counselling and therapeutic practices delivered by people from 'the out'. They documented their concern at the poor diet and lack of exercise necessary to maintain a healthy weight level. Furthermore, the reality of self-harming was evident and the need to address the separate needs of the 'real' self-harmers and the attention-seeking 'fakers' was paramount. All of these areas require further consideration and investigation, as well as the implementation of appropriate policies.

Female young offenders clearly have a number of issues that need to be addressed in order to improve conditions for them. Perhaps future research can add to their cause, and help give them a voice. A role for contemporary criminological feminist scholars should be to pick up the baton handed to them by their 'founding mothers' and continue to add to existing criminological research in order to highlight the plight of women and girls within the criminal justice system.

References

Allen, H. (1987) *Justice Unbalanced: Gender, Psychiatry and Judicial Decisions*, Milton Keynes: Open University Press.

Bergsmann, I. R. (1989) 'The Forgotten Few: Juvenile Female Offenders', *Federal Probation*, 12: 73–8

Britton, D. M. (2004) 'Feminism in Criminology: Engendering the Outlaw', in P. J. Schram and B. Koons-Witt (eds), *Gendered (In)Justice: Theory and Practice in Feminist Criminology*, Long Grove, IL: Waveland Press: 49–67.

Carlen, P. and Worrall, A. (eds) (1987) *Gender, Crime and Justice*, Milton Keynes: Open University Press.

Chesney-Lind, M. and Pasko, L. (eds) (2004) *Girls, Women, and Crime*, Thousand Oaks, CA: Sage.

Chesney-Lind, M. and Shelden, R. (1998) *Girls, Delinquency and Juvenile Justice*, 2nd edn, Belmont, CA: West/Wadsworth.

Dobash, R. E., Dobash, R. P. and Gutteridge, S. (1986) *The Imprisonment of Women*, New York: Routledge.

Genders, E. and Player, E. (1987) 'Women in Prison: The Treatment, the Control and the Experience', in P. Carlen and A. Worrall (eds) *Gender, Crime and Justice*, Milton Keynes: Open University Press.

Genders, E. and Player, E. (1995) *Grendon: A Study of a Therapeutic Prison*, Oxford: Clarendon Press.

Goffman, E. (1961) *Asylums*, New York: Anchor Books.

Home Office (2003) *Statistics on Women and the Criminal Justice System: A Home Office publication under Section 95 of the Criminal Justice Act 1991*, London: The Stationery Office.

Liebling, A. (1992) *Suicides in Prison*, London: Routledge.

Morris, A. (1987) *Women, Crime and Criminal Justice*, Oxford: Blackwell.

Prison Reform Trust (2000) *Justice for Women: The Need for Reform*, London: Prison Reform Trust.

Singleton, N., Meltzer, H. and Gatward, R. (1998) *Psychiatric Morbidity Among Prisoners: Summary Report*, London: Office for National Statistics.

Singleton, N., Meltzer, H., Gatward, R., Coid, J. and Deasy, D. (1998) *Psychiatric Morbidity Among Prisoners in England and Wales*, London: Office for National Studies.

Worrall, A. (1990) *Offending Women: Female Lawbreakers and the Criminal Justice System*, London: Routledge.

Chapter 9

A gendered Irish experiment: grounds for optimism?

Barbara Mason

Introduction

The enduring theme from the literature on female offending is that their rate of offending is much lower compared to men and the nature of their offences is generally less serious (Heidensohn 1997; Blomberg and Lucken 2000; Gelsthorpe and Morris 2002). Nevertheless, in more traditional criminology, offending women were likely to be demonised as witches or harlots, pathologised as victims of their own biology or infantilised as inadequate or mentally unstable (Carlen *et al.* 1985; Walklate 1995). With the rise of the feminist movement of the 1970s explanations became centred on women as victims – their behaviour being the result of physical, sexual and emotional abuse, sexism, racism or classism (Snider 2003). However, more radical feminists considered that this notion posed a danger of viewing offending women as passive, accepting and lacking agency rather than seeing their behaviour as an empowering device to reassert their own personal identities through resistance (Walklate 1995; Bosworth 1999).

In the UK the authorities responded to these changing explanations of female criminality by implementing gender-specific penal reforms. In the 1970s and 1980s Holloway (in England) and Cornton Vale (in Scotland) introduced new regimes which emphasised treatment rather than punishment. It was hoped that by concentrating on medical, psychiatric and abuse problems within a more relaxed and homely setting, the women's perceived needs could be addressed. In a similar vein, the underlying philosophy of five new Canadian prisons opened in the 1990s was influenced by feminist input based on women's need for personal empowerment, meaningful choices, respect and dignity, a supportive environment and shared responsibility (Hannah-Moffat and Shaw 2000; Hayman 2006).

However, the outcomes from these gender-centred developments never fulfilled their original aspirations. In the Foucauldian power knowledge sense, far from addressing the special needs of female offenders they resulted in greater levels of surveillance and control. For detailed accounts of how the ideals of the initiators were gradually eroded, see Rock (1996) on Holloway Carlen (1983) and Dobash *et al.* (1986) on Cornton Vale and Hannah-Moffat (2001) and Hayman (2006) on the new prisons in Canada.

More recent feminist discourse has focused on the increased levels of incarceration that have occurred in the last decade. Carlen argues that what she describes as 'carceral clawback' is predicated on the notion that because many female prisons now incorporate programmes aimed at psychological readjustment, training in parenting, drugs rehabilitation and general education, they provide a legitimising rationale for locking up not only serious offenders but also those convicted of minor crimes (Carlen 2002). Snider suggests that by emphasising gender difference, feminist criminologists whose intention was to legitimate less punishment have, under the guise of 'special needs', legitimated more problematic, high-surveillance, therapeutic regimes. She also argues that whereas some feminist criminologists advocate the continuance of more 'effective' gender-specific programmes, Foucauldian academics see the 'failure' of these programmes as an example of women reasserting agency through resistance (Snider 2003). In the Canadian context, the empowering ideals envisioned by the feminist reformers were reinterpreted by Corrections Canada to make the offender responsible for her own rehabilitation despite her choices being censored and predetermined by the wider penal structure (Hannah-Moffat 2002).

These arguments provide a very pessimist outlook for female incarceration and would appear to support the conclusion that 'penal history is littered with unfulfilled promises, abandoned hopes and discarded institutions' (McConville 1998). However, failure is neither inevitable nor total. I plan to show that a small gendered experiment in Ireland produced a rather different outcome and provides an encouraging example of how sustained commitment to an ideal can offer some level of success in an otherwise rather bleak picture of female incarceration at the beginning of the twenty-first century.

Innovation in Ireland

On 29th September 1999 the first new prison for women in almost 200 years was officially opened in Dublin. Called the Dóchas Centre (dóchas is the Irish word for hope), it marked the beginning of an innovative penological development aimed at female offenders. There was no specific evidence that the initiators had been influenced by feminist thinking or the academic discourse discussed above. However, not unlike earlier developments, the idea of the new prison was to encourage the women to take greater responsibility for their own lives and help prepare them for reintegration back into society.

Although relatively small in size (built for 80 prisoners), the Dóchas Centre represented a penological microcosm that included both sentenced and remand prisoners and covered the complete spectrum of ages, offence types, sentence lengths and backgrounds. Up to this time, women's treatment in prison in Ireland had followed the general pattern common in many other jurisdictions: because of their smaller numbers, they were marginalised within the penal system and subjected to prison accommodation, regimes and controls dominated by the needs of men. The new prison in Dublin was intended to break that mould.

This chapter covers part of a broader ethnographic study that took place within the new prison during the first 30 months of occupation. Through a series of visits, the evolution of the experiment was tracked from the initial weeks of turmoil and uncertainty created by the move, through a gradual period of adjustment to a state of equilibrium. The method employed included long periods of observation followed by interviews, both formal and informal, with prisoners and staff. Concentrating mainly on the prisoners, the chapter reveals that despite initial setbacks many of the ideals underlying the original aspirations remained intact.

The Irish context

Background

Ireland gained independence from the United Kingdom in the early 1920s. For the following 50 years it had one of the lowest imprisonment rates in Europe. The near absence of crime reflected a society that was devoutly Catholic and conservative, with a strong sense of community and respect for authority (Brewer, *et al.* 1997).

This particularly applied to women. In the late 1920s the number of females committed to prison was around 1,000 per year and falling. By the late 1970s it had reduced to around 150, mainly for offences of drunkenness, larceny, prostitution and begging (MacBride 1982). In holy Catholic Ireland, [President] DeValera's 'comely maidens' were strictly controlled within the family, within the school and by the Church and were unlikely to defy 'authority' by engaging in criminal activity (Beale 1986; Carey 2000).

In the first half of the century, women prisoners were housed in the original female penitentiary at Mountjoy in Dublin, which had opened in 1858. In 1956, with the steady decline in numbers, this building was changed to accommodate juvenile males and renamed St Patrick's Institution. The females were relegated to the basement and the ground floor of one wing (B wing) where they were held in substandard conditions – marginalised, forgotten, invisible.

In the 1980s things began to change. For the first time, young female heroin addicts began to arrive into the prison. The numbers more than doubled. The physical conditions deteriorated – some cells, with no integral sanitation, were now shared by four or even five women. The position was untenable. Eventually the decision was made to renovate St Patrick's and the women were moved, temporarily, to D wing to occupy three floors. In this new wing there were about 50 cells, each with a toilet, and although not ideal as the women still had to eat in their cells, it was an improvement on where they had come from. However, the renovation of B wing was seen as a disaster by those responsible for the female prisoners.

> It was awful, just typical, as they would revamp it for a man in prison. Everything in prison is designed towards male prisoners because the majority of the prisoners are men.
> (*Governor*)

The situation had gone from bad to worse and at the same time the numbers continued to rise.

An experiment conceived

In 1992, Máire Geoghegan Quinn became the first female Minister of Justice in Ireland. She visited Mountjoy and Governor Lonergan, who was responsible for both males and females, ensured that she would visit the women's prison and see the conditions for herself. She immediately sanctioned the establishment of a multi-disciplinary working group to design and develop a new purpose-built prison. Their first task was to canvass the views of prisoners and prison officers to identify what they considered were their needs. Using their feedback and input from other relevant sources a 22-page strategy document was developed, which emphasised the importance of addressing the particular needs of women in prison. It stated:

> In many respects they are categorically different from those of men. Because there are so few women in prison there is the likelihood they will be thought of in the same way as men when regimes, programmes, buildings etc. are being planned and decided about. The emphasis was on adopting a women's prison perspective from the outset. The approach to be eschewed was to deal with the matter by asking what extras would be needed for a women's prison regime. The implication of stressing a woman's perspective in regime planning are expected to include increased emphasis on maintaining contact with family and children; dealing with the distress of being in prison and the need to talk with someone; increased emphasis on healthy living, diet, exercise and relaxation; providing for a high percentage of short sentences; reduced emphasis on custody provisions; emphasis on preparing people for situations other than employment after their release; emphasis on maintaining links between the prison and agencies who can provide continuing support after release.

The working group underlined their aspirations by publishing a vision statement against which achievement could be monitored:

- We are a community which embraces people's respect and dignity.
- We encourage personal growth and development in a caring and safe environment.
- We are committed to addressing the needs of each person in a healing and holistic way.
- We actively promote close interaction with the wider community.

It was interesting to note that this statement avoided any mention of punishment and concentrated on the idea of addressing *individual* needs rather than aspiring to provide generic solutions. To support these aims the architectural requirement was 'to create living accommodation arranged in a number of self-contained houses to reflect, as far as possible, an urban domestic environment', consistent with living arrangements on the outside. However, during the

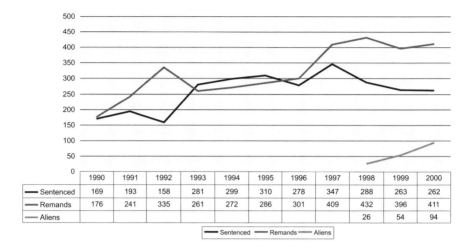

Figure 9.1 Female committals to Mountjoy 1990–2000

development/build period, the numbers and composition of the committals was changing and this had an adverse effect on the speed with which the aims could be addressed.

A changing population

During the 1990s committals to Mountjoy increased considerably particularly remands and in 1998 'aliens' began to appear (see Figure 9.1). Aliens were mainly foreign nationals stopped at ports of entry who were held in the prison pending their deportation. There were 26 aliens in 1998, increasing to 94 by 2000. Of the sentenced population the vast majority were aged between 21 and 39, although there was a significant minority aged 17 to 20. Women with sentences of over three years, though still small in absolute terms, increased in the second half of the decade. Many of these were likely to be foreign nationals convicted of drug importation. However, sentences of less than three months were still the most common, representing anywhere between 47 per cent and 62 per cent during that time.

As in many other prisons, drug addiction and psychological problems were major issues. Although no up-to-date official data was available, anecdotal evidence and observation suggested that drug use affected nearly 80 per cent of the women.

That is the main reason a lot of them are here [in prison]. The drugs is the major thing. They would be in for different charges. They would be in for shoplifting, for robbing, for soliciting, assault but what is at the back of it all is drugs – heroin. It has a lot to answer for. There are a few in here for alcohol, they won't touch drugs, it is just drink. Most of them – is all drug related – from what I can tell.
(*Officer*)

This statement was supported by the results of a number of studies, which concluded that between 60 and 83 per cent of female prisoners could be categorised as drug users (Carmody and McEvoy 1996; Allwright *et al*. 1999; Hannon, *et al*. 2000).

The categorisation of psychological problems was less clear cut. It was based on an initial assessment by a nurses at the time of reception and/or a subsequent assessment by the medical staff or officers based on behaviour. Such categorisation could not avoid some level of fallibility. Labels like 'disordered', 'unstable' and 'disruptive' involved subjective judgements that often discounted the effects of imprisonment on a woman's sense of self and manifested itself in unacceptable behaviour (Bosworth 1999; Matthews 1999). A study undertaken in Mountjoy in 1994 found that 49 out of 100 women had had psychiatric treatment in the past, with one in four requiring hospital admission (Carmody and McEvoy 1996). In a later study of the prison population, all mental health indicators were higher for females than for males: 75 per cent of females as against 48 per cent of males were identified as having a need for psychiatric intervention (Hannon *et al*. 2000). These findings were similar to results from England and Scotland (Maden *et al*. 1994; Loucks 1997) and supported anecdotal evidence from several members of staff.

Birth of a new world

The reality of the new design

The design of the Dóchas Centre contrasted dramatically with the traditional radial design of the old prison. It did not look like a prison from either the outside or the inside. There was no high external wall, no barred windows or barbed wire and no visible outside indication that this new complex was actually a prison. The red brick boundary walls of the buildings were the prison boundary walls. The heavy metal entrance door (not visible from the street) and the CCTV cameras provided the only hint that this was a 'secure' building. It was divided into three main sections: two accommodation areas colloquially known as the 'big yard' and the 'small yard', and a section containing an outdoor sports area bounded on two sides by the school, gym and workshops and on the third by the block that incorporated the laundry, reception, staff rooms and offices.

The 'big yard' was a garden around which five of the houses, the dining/visitors' building and one side of the health care unit were situated. The houses, with one exception, were named after trees – Laurel, Hazel, Elm and Cedar – and were designed on similar lines. Phoenix, the fifth house, provided private bed-sitter accommodation and was intended for long-term prisoners who in the months leading up to their release usually went out to work. The 'small yard' was similar but contained only two houses, Rowan and Maple, and the other side of the health care unit. All houses had individual rooms with ensuite facilities (there was no 'spy hole' in these ensuites), a fully equipped kitchen and a comfortable lounge area commonly called the 'rec'. The office for the staff was off the 'rec'. The main kitchen served two brightly decorated, well-furnished communal dining rooms, one of which doubled as a visiting room. The purpose-built health care unit was well equipped and had bedrooms for women who were sick and two padded rooms where women who were a danger either to themselves or to others could be regularly monitored.

The rationale for the two yards had been to facilitate the separation of the drug-users from the drug-free and remands from those who were sentenced. However, due to the composition of the committals this proved impracticable. Three months after the move a form of privilege system was introduced. The idea was to provide an incentive for the more volatile drug-users to stabilise on a methadone programme and to encourage good behaviour. Women would start in the small yard and then earn the privilege of moving to the big yard – first to the less privileged houses and eventually to the more privileged. The main difference was the level of supervision and the lock-back times, as Table 9.1 indicates.

The aim of the design brief, to avoid the appearance of an institution, was achieved. The architect who led the project concluded:

Table 9.1 Differences in privileges between houses

	House	Lock-back time	'Category'	No. of rooms
Big Yard	Phoenix	Unlocked	Unsupervised	7/8
	Cedar	Unlocked	Unsupervised	18
	Elm	10.00 pm	Semi-supervised	12
	Hazel	7.30 pm	Supervised	12
	Laurel	7.30 pm	Supervised	10
Small Yard	Rowan	7.30 pm	Supervised	10
	Maple	7.30 pm	Supervised	10

The primary measure of success was that the original guiding concepts of the project, namely humane, rehabilitative, non-institutional detention, were preserved, despite continuous pressure from within and without the client organisation. An innovative major public facility, having numerous stakeholders of conflicting interests, was completed to the substantial satisfaction of all of the stakeholders.

The more important question was how the occupants would cope with their new environment.

Initial turmoil

The official opening of the Dóchas Centre occurred in September 1999, creating an expectation of imminent departure from the old premises. However, the physical move did not occur until Christmas week, leaving both prisoners and staff in limbo for three months. The timing was inauspicious. Christmas is an emotional period particularly if one is separated from family and friends, but this was exacerbated as it was the last Christmas of the twentieth century.

Preparations were inadequate and the impact of the move underestimated. Many of the prisoners were angry, disoriented and bewildered. They were faced with a change from the routine and familiar, which was predictable and secure, to a new era of uncertainty in uncharted surroundings. A number of constraints had also been imposed. The women were confined to their own houses and access to and from the yards was controlled by a locked gate which could only be opened by an officer. Very quickly the architectural ideal of providing greater freedom of movement was in danger of being undermined by what the women saw as increased restrictions.

The size and layout provided a greater challenge to the staff. From being detailed to work on one of three floors of one wing, they were now spread across several buildings, and in many cases were out of sight and hearing of colleagues. Their biggest concern was personal safety. There were too many blind spots in the houses and no cameras in the kitchens, recreation rooms or stairwells. Although there was an emergency alarm in staff office in the house, they had not been issued with personal alarms and considered their radios an inadequate means of calling for help. Because their office was situated off the recreation room on the first floor, it was impossible to monitor who was coming in and going out of the house. House officers felt particularly isolated as they could spend many hours in a house without encountering another officer. Not only were they disenchanted with their new environment, they also felt ignored by their management.

However, unlike the Holloway move so vividly described by Rock, where the social order within its walls continued to be problematic (1996: chapter 8), the atmosphere of disruption and instability that pervaded the Dóchas Centre in the immediate aftermath of the move gradually diminished. Within three to four months the majority of prisoners were beginning to adjust to their new physical conditions. They learned to adapt to the limitations of the locked gates, and new arrivals who had not experienced the old prison were not aware of the perceived reduction in freedom experienced by their colleagues. Efforts were also made to address the concerns of the officers. The issue of isolation gradually diminished as they became more familiar with their new environment and adopted alternative stratagems to overcome the problem. Attempts were made to address the safety issue by detailing two officers to work together in the houses that required supervision and improved management communications provided an opportunity for other worries to be discussed and solutions sought.

Regime change

One of the main problems in the early weeks had been a lack of structure to the day. Gradually a more systematic routine was introduced. The women were not compelled to adhere to it as the regime was predicated on exercising personal choice – for example, they could decide what time they got up out of bed, whether they went to school, whether to go to the dining room for their meals and what time they went to bed. Involvement in the school and other programmes was encouraged though not mandated. Irrespective of whether they took advantage of the opportunities on offer, the school and other programmes provided the major element of stability that had been missing in the early days of the move.

The school ran a varied and comprehensive programme that covered formal state-recognised education courses: cookery for the National Certificate in Food and Cookery; computer training for all levels including the European Computer Driving Licence (ECDL), a pan-European qualification; art, photography and video production; music, woodwork, French, life and social skills; hairdressing qualifications; and physical education skills that would benefit those who wanted to pursue a career in the leisure industry. As part of their development, women with artistic or other talents were encouraged to exhibit and sell their paintings at outside exhibitions, to participate in literary competitions, or to run courses like dancing, kick-boxing or jewellery-making during the summer months when school was closed.

According to the literature on female prisons, this degree of choice was unusual (Carlen 1983; Bosworth 1999). In an article on general prison education in England and Wales, Lustgarten described how the move to increased managerialism and the subcontracting of services led to a crass dictum of 'bums on seats' that made the underlying premise quite clear:

> The new dogma represented a subtle reaffirmation of expected social and class roles; instead of qualifying people in readily assimilable and marketable skills like IT and web design, with salaries that might compete with a criminal income, we gave them lowest common denominator qualifications that, on their own, are not likely to override the stigma of criminalisation for prospective employers. (Lustgarten 2001)

With the variety of opportunities, many of them geared to prospective employment, the Dóchas Centre was not following that trend. The head of education pointed out: 'our emphasis wouldn't be on numbers. Our emphasis would be on the quality of the stuff we are doing with the women who are interested in education'.

In an attempt to address individual needs a programme called Connect was introduced during 2000. Connect is a European-funded project that aims to help offenders in prison to make well-informed choices about their future and use their time in prison to prepare for their return to the community, specifically to the labour market. It was run by specially trained prison officers who worked with groups of between five and eight prisoners. The programme encouraged the women to identify their specific needs, be they educational, vocational, social, psychological, or other personal requirements. It also covered a variety of topics, from confidence-building and self-assertiveness to how to manage time and leisure and how to recognise healthy living. For women who did not require such intensive work, Connect helped with individual personal planning for the future. Follow-up support was available from the officers even after the women had been released.

Welcoming the outside world

In order to promote closer interaction with the outside world, visits to the prison were encouraged. They included various guests – for example, Mary Robinson, the ex-President of Ireland, and the well-known author Maeve Binchy. Outside agencies visited to give practical help in the area of jobs, training, housing, counselling and other support. Group visits were encouraged throughout the year to enable people from the outside to gain some level of understanding of what went on inside.

Whereas individual visitors were generally welcomed, the constant stream of group visits, particularly school groups, was often considered an unacceptable intrusion. The women complained that they were being treated like animals in a zoo. For some whose children were not aware of their incarceration, there was a permanent worry about recognition and disclosure. Goffman argued that whereas such information may safely be shared with other adults within the family, children could be seriously damaged by such knowledge (Goffman 1963). Others, whose cases had been well publicised, felt particularly vulnerable to intrusive scrutiny and were forced to go into hiding during the course of such visits to avoid providing vicarious pleasure to the curious.

The combination of education, development programmes, various initiatives and outside visits helped provide both a welcome diversion and, more importantly, a focus and a structure to the day that helped the women to cope with the vicissitudes of incarceration. However, the new regime, which involved living in houses, had some unexpected consequences.

Adjusting to living in houses

Resolving disputes

The women spent many hours within the confines of the houses particularly during inclement weather, which meant that they were restricted to the company of the other occupants. They had to learn to adapt to their idiosyncrasies, to compromise and to continuously negotiate the challenges of sharing a confined space with a frequently changing population. Because they had responsibility for the running of the house they were expected to resolve conflicts when disputes arose. This applied particularly to domestic chores. It was up to the women themselves to devise a system that ensured that the communal areas were kept clean and tidy and that communal stocks of tea, sugar, milk and bread were replenished on a daily basis. This proved problematic.

The issue of domestic chores was a cause of dissent in all the houses at some stage. On reflection, it was not surprising. Domestic chores are seldom viewed as a desirable task. Within most families it is frequently a cause of tension, requiring intervention by parents. In other forms of community living, such as religious orders, the problem is overcome by virtue of the vows of obedience. In institutions like boarding schools, military establishments and traditional prisons, domestic arrangements are likely to be mandated. In settings of a more social nature, where groups live together on a temporary basis, say for holidays, without a strong element of co-operation disputes or resentment over domestic arrangements are almost inevitable. Even for the kibbutz movement in Israel, where community living was characterised by mutual support and co-operation, sharing domestic chores posed a problem (Spiro 1956; Blasi 1986).

Women's lower level of offending have led to assumptions about their being more conformist and more prepared to adhere to rules (Naffine 1987; Heidensohn 1996). This may be true in society in general but within the specific milieu of a prison, it is questionable. A common theme in prison literature was the extent of women's non-compliance with the rules (Carlen 1983; Faith 1993; Kruttschnitt *et al*. 2000). There could be many complex reasons for this phenomenon but the issue of avoidance of house chores might be illustrative of a weak sense of conformity within the specific setting of a prison. On the other hand, emphasis on domesticity need not necessarily be viewed as perpetuating a gendered model of female imprisonment

(Carlen 1983; Bosworth 1999). It could be seen as a small but practical application of the philosophy of encouraging women to take responsibility and, more importantly, of learning to resolve issues among themselves. In the Dóchas Centre the diversity of the population and the high turnover of occupants militated against a permanent solution to the issue of chores. However, it was not the only problem. Another unexpected difficulty that developed over time involved foreign nationals.

Accepting foreign nationals

Ireland had traditionally been a country of sustained emigration until the economic success of the 1990s. The arrival of increased numbers of foreign nationals was a new and controversial phenomenon within Irish society. Although the number was comparatively small, media representation used the flood metaphor to describe them. They were portrayed as acquiring income by illegitimate means, exploiting the welfare system and engaging in begging (Curry 2000).

The increase in foreign nationals was reflected in the prisons. In 1995 the number of female foreign nationals committed to Mountjoy was three. By the year 2000 it had increased to 36, plus 94 aliens. Initially there did not appear to be a particular problem in the Dóchas. However, with the increase in numbers and the introduction of the privilege system of house allocation, their presence began to cause resentment. Cedar, the most privileged house (often called the 24-hour house) was the cause of the most controversy. Women were moved there for being drug-free and unlikely to cause any trouble. Foreign nationals in particular fell into this category (they constituted between 20 and 25 per cent of the total inmates at any one time during the study period). They were likely to be 'drug mules' but not drug addicts, serving sentences from four to ten years. They also tended to be slightly older and were usually model prisoners. Although Irish women also moved to Cedar, foreign nationals were in the majority – between 60 and 70 per cent. This was a cause of particular resentment from the indigenous population. The following are typical examples of the sentiments expressed:

> They offer the 24-hour house to very few of my own, the likes of me. They are all foreign. I am not a racist or anything. They say that you have to work your way around – these girls didn't work their way around, they just walked into it. I think it is very

unfair. It is resented by a lot of the girls. Because it disheartens you. You are told that you work your way into them and you do and you work and you clean for them [the staff] and you do this for them, and then you don't even see these people [the foreign nationals] – they haven't gone through the system or gone around and next you see them walking out of the 24-hour house. I think that is wrong.
(*Prisoner*)

Don't get me wrong, I say I am racist but I think Cedar gets a lot more than we do. Anything going in this prison, they get it. I know they are from a foreign country and this that and the other but what is thrown in our faces is – 'Ah they are not on drugs'. That is always what is put down to us. It kind of pisses me off. It is making people who are not racist turn into being racist.
(*Prisoner*)

Although racism was not a major feature of life in the Dóchas Centre the force with which some of the Irish women expressed their views, coupled with other indicators, suggested it was not too far beneath the surface.

Getting on

Despite the difficulties, overall the women appeared to succeed in getting on even if only on a superficial level. It was likely that because they were forced to share a house with people not of their choosing they decided they might as well make the best of it. Whatever the reason, they appeared to get on surprisingly well. Evidence could be seen in many acts of kindness and support – for example, sharing cigarettes, lending one another clothes, comforting and encouraging one another if upset. This contrasted with Carlen's account of relationships in the houses in Cornton Vale where social intercourse with fellow prisoners was constrained and made tense by the constant presence of officers (Carlen 1983). In the Dóchas Centre there was not the constant presence of prison officers, nor was there any overt intrusive surveillance. On the contrary, it was the absence of officers from the kitchens and the recreation rooms that was noticeable. However, the new regime created a number of other challenges that had the potential to undermine the original aspirations.

Ongoing challenges

Regime 'laxity'

The subject of discipline is a recurring theme in the literature on prisons in general but on women's prisons in particular. It is argued that women are subjected to a wider range of petty restrictions than their counterparts in male establishments (Dobash *et al.* 1986; Zedner 1998; Kruttschnitt *et al.* 2000). Carlen (1998) quoted a senior Home Office official: 'There is a negative culture in women's prisons and much of it is very punitive' and a male governor of a female prison: 'I was shocked when I came here at the severity of female staff towards prisoners, much severer than male staff on male prisoners, much less tolerant'. The Dóchas Centre presented a different picture.

The whole ethos of the new prison was to engage with the women and to help them take responsibility for their own lives. Managing by the rule book was the antithesis of this concept. However, officers complained about what they considered the lack of discipline and the leniency with which the women were treated when they were put on disciplinary report. The following view was typical.

> There is a lot more leniency down here than there would have been up in the old prison where the regime would have been a bit stricter. You get away with it a lot more down here but if you do something bad enough down here, then you will get punished for it. It can be frustrating a lot of the time because you are writing a report on something and you don't see a result or you don't see somebody getting the slap on the wrist and they think they can do it again then. Or you end up thinking what is the point of writing the report if you are not going to do something about it.
> (*Officer*)

However, evidence from the discipline report book suggested a remarkable consistency in the volume of breaches of discipline between the old and new prison: 1999 (the old prison) showed a total of 377 breaches (0.53 per prisoner) and 2000 (the new prison) indicated 336 (0.44 per prisoner). Despite a higher number of occupants in 2000, the number of disciplinary reports actually decreased. As with any statistics, care must be taken with the interpretation of the data. Official numbers on discipline breaches reflect the end-product of staff decisions and do not take into account the discretion of the officers in the application of the rules (Sparks *et al*. 1996). The prisoners themselves when questioned did not consider that discipline was a major feature of their daily lives. However, the perceived laxity of the regime gave rise to a number of security breaches that could have had serious implications.

Security breaches

The first security breach occurred when a prisoner who had been serving a long sentence absconded when out on a training programme. She was recaptured within 12 hours. The director general of the Prison Service pointed out: 'Any outing of this kind has a degree of risk but a prison system without this degree of risk would have little or no rehabilitation function and society would be the loser in the long term' (*Irish Times*, 1 August 2000). In the second case, four women, who were accompanied by three officers, were visiting a hairdressing salon as part of a course. They absconded. The feature in the *Irish Independent* dated 23 May 2002: began 'Jail staff were faced with a "hair today, gone tomorrow" dilemma when four inmates on day release escaped from their escort today.' In this case the governor faced criticism from within the Prison Service for underestimating the level of risk. However, three of the absconders returned of their own volition within a few days and the fourth, a little later.

More serious breaches involved two escapes from the prison itself. A woman carrying her child walked out with her family after a visit. She was quickly recaptured. As one officer commented:

> Security isn't a major issue here. I know one woman walked out. The fact that she held a baby in her arms that obstructed an officer's vision of her and she mingled with people. It was very simple. But you can't compensate for everything. If you want to have freedom of movement these things are going to happen – you are going to encounter that. It didn't get the media headlines. There was only a small paragraph in the evening paper.
> (*Officer*)

The second escape posed a greater potential threat. Two young women gained unauthorised access to Phoenix (the pre-release house), broke a window and ran away. One was quickly recaptured but the other evaded the authorities for much longer.

The accumulation of security breaches could have undermined the whole philosophy of the new prison and derailed the experiment. According to Governor Lonergan, this did not happen because

> it [women absconding or escaping] hasn't as high a political consequence as if prisoners from Portlaoise escaped [a high security men's prison in midlands Ireland]. That would be seen as a weakness of state security and a political embarrassment. I suppose that is one of the plusses we have established from conditioning over a number of years, that there is an acceptance that the Dóchas Centre is not a top security prison. [This is a reference to opportunities taken to publicise what the Dóchas Centre was trying to achieve via talks and discussions on television and radio.] I have always said to the public, it is not the worst thing in the world – where are they [the women] going; they are not going to kill anybody; they are not any risk at all, certainly not as much a risk as many people walking in O'Connell St [the main street in central Dublin] just now. My own experience is they have nowhere to go and they all come back. And they are all back in a few days and some of them come back themselves which is an amazing thing.

In the event these incidents were accepted as risks that were the inevitable consequence of a regime predicated on the notion of personal autonomy.

Conclusion

The gendered penal developments in England, Scotland and Canada mentioned at the beginning of this chapter demonstrated that despite the benevolent intentions of the initiators many factors both within and outside the control of the institutions led to a dilution and distortion of the original ideals. In the case of the Dóchas Centre, this study concluded that despite the unpromising start and ongoing challenges, the aspirations underlying the vision statement remained intact. There are a number of reasons for this. Unlike in other jurisdictions, the same leaders were in place at the initiation of the development and still *in situ* throughout the study period. This ensured ongoing commitment to the original ideals and a determination to overcome setbacks. They were also willing to experiment, adapt in the light of practicalities and take risks where necessary. The small scale of the prison facilitated innovation and minimised the level of political and media interference. Irish cultural attributes of sociability and informality, together with more comfortable living arrangements, contributed to the creation and maintenance of a spirit of community.

The new architecture played an important role in creating a degree of normalcy and in providing accommodation that supported the aspirational aims of respect for the individual. This judgement is subject to the caveat that living in houses created its own tensions and was not an overall panacea for the pains of imprisonment. The regime encouraged the women to take personal responsibility by providing a level of choice that appeared to exceed that which is available in many other female prisons. Programmes were implemented that were directed at the specific needs of individuals rather than treating the women as a homogeneous group although it is important to reiterate that the needs of all women were not and could not be met. Involvement by the outside world was encouraged and included not only active and practical support from various agencies but also more informal involvement by volunteers and members of the public. These were generally, although not universally, welcomed by the women.

The more fundamental question remains – does the Dóchas Centre work? Recidivism is the traditional measurement of success of penal reform programmes. However, there are no official data published on recidivism for Irish prisoners. Without statistical evidence, the effect of the Dóchas Centre can only be considered using less tangible and more subjective indicators. Measured against the objectives of realising the vision statement, considerable progress has been made. The responses from the women themselves indicated a general level of satisfaction. Many took advantage of the variety of educational opportunities on offer, which helped not only in the area of personal development and preparation for the job market on release, but also acted as a coping mechanism to help them do their time. Living in houses added a degree of normalcy. It demanded a level of self-discipline and responsibility that was likely to be more akin to the demands of living in the wider community, and in that sense could be seen as a reasonable preparation for life after release. On the other hand, life on the outside was likely to present a variety of problems that no amount of preparation could totally alleviate, for example, lack of accommodation, lack of money or being forced to return to the area where they would be most tempted to reoffend. See O'Loingsigh (2004) for a recent discussion on the experience of both male and female Dublin prisoners after release.

A number of individual validations are worth mentioning. Three repeat offenders who were self-confessed drug addicts and started their rehabilitation in the Dóchas Centre managed to overcome their addiction and start a new life. They returned on a regular basis to speak on the subject to those still inside. Other released women were helping in treatment centres and another was working on a project aimed at helping reintegrate prisoners back into the community. A long-term prisoner wrote to the head of education at Dóchas after her release to say that she had a job and her own accommodation. She explained: 'I could never have achieved any of this without the support, opportunity and kindness shown to me by the staff in the Dóchas Centre and in the school.' The mother of a South African who visited while her daughter was incarcerated afterwards wrote to the Governor:

> My mind and heart were bursting with gratitude. I left knowing that T [her daughter] was in the most professional and caring hands. With sincere and grateful thanks from T's family, her children her sisters and brothers and of course, especially from me, her mother.

These examples by definition are selective and partial but support the general thrust of the empirical findings that the Dóchas Centre was fulfilling many of its original aspirations.

It is too early in the life of this new prison to assess whether the ideals expressed in the vision statement will survive. Over the course of the study, the regime continued to evolve. As Governor Lonergan remarked:

> I think we have achieved some of our Vision. We have put in place something that is different. With some minor exceptions, it has been trouble-free generally. I think it has made a lot of progress. But it hasn't achieved anything like its potential yet. It is like a marathon – we probably have two or three miles run and we are still up there with the pace. But we still have 20 miles to go and I suppose, when we have 20 miles done, there will be more to do.

> But the end product is, can they [the women] be reintegrated into society – with the whole support system they need when they go out? Without an infrastructure in the community, without support and enthusiasm in the community, then you

are never going to achieve the sort of levels you require. You can do what you like in-house in a way. Unless you have a longer term strategy of bringing back into the community and reintegrating into jobs, into housing, into family structures – that sort of stuff, you are at nothing.

Sadly, the future outlook for the Dóchas Centre is not encouraging. The Irish Prison Service has begun to introduce more stringent financial controls which have already seen the demise of the Connect programme. A much more worrying move was headlined in the *Irish Times* dated 11 February 2004 (many months after this study was completed) – 'Mountjoy women's prison may also be closed'. The article goes on to explain that at a recent government cabinet meeting, the decision had been taken to sell the site of the Mountjoy complex to a developer and rebuild the prison/s on a green field site. This follows years of criticism of the appalling conditions in the men's prison which have been condemned both nationally and internationally. It is ironic that once again, the fate of the female prisoners may be in danger of being overshadowed by the needs of the men. On a more optimistic note, it is also possible that the positive lessons learned from the Dóchas Centre experiment will act as an example to the Irish Prison Service and their counterparts in other jurisdictions, of what can be achieved with commitment and dedication and will provide a more enlightened model for future prison development in the twenty-first century for both males and females.

References

Allwright, D. S. *et al.* (1999) *Hepatitis B, Hepatitis C and HIV in Irish Prisoners: Prevalence and Risk*, Dublin: Department of Community Health and General Practice, Trinity College.

Beale, J. (1986) *Women in Ireland: Voices of Change*, Basingstoke: Macmillan.

Blasi, J. (1986) *The Communal Experience of the Kibbutz*, New Brunswick: Transaction Books.

Blomberg, T. and Lucken, K. (2000) *American Penology: A History of Control*, New York: Aldine de Gruyter.

Bosworth, M. (1999) *Engendering Resistance: Agency and Power in Women's Prisons*, Aldershot: Dartmouth.

Brewer, J., Lockhart, B. and Rodgers, P.(1997) *Crime in Ireland 1945–95: Here be Dragons*, Oxford, Clarendon Press.

Carey, T. (2000) *Mountjoy: The Story of a Prison*, Cork: Collins Press.

Carlen, P. (1983) *Women's Imprisonment: A Study in Social Control*, London: Routledge and Kegan Paul.

Carlen, P. (1998) *Sledgehammer: Women's Imprisonment at the Millennium*, Basingstoke: Macmillan.

Carlen, P. (2002) 'Controlling Measures: The Repackaging of Common Sense Opposition to Women's Imprisonment in England and Canada', *Criminal Justice*, 2(2): 155–72.

Carlen, P. *et al.* (1985) 'Introduction–Criminal Women: Myths, Metaphors and Misogyny', in P. Carlen (ed.) *Criminal Women*. London: Polity Press.

Carmody, P. and McEvoy, M. (1996) *A Study of Irish Female Prisoners*, Dublin: The Stationery Office.

Curry, P. (2000) '"She Never Let Them In": Popular Reaction to Refugees Arriving in Dublin', in M. MacLachlan and M. O'Connell (eds) *Cultivating Pluralism: Psychological, Social and Cultural Perspectives on a Changing Ireland*, Dublin: Oak Tree Press: 137–52.

Dobash, R., Dobash, R. and Gutteridge, S. (1986) *The Imprisonment of Women*, Oxford: Blackwell.

Faith, K. (1993) *Unruly Women: The Politics of Confinement and Resistance*, Vancouver: Press Gang Publishers.

Gelsthorpe, L. and Morris, A. (2002) 'Women's Imprisonment in England and Wales: A Penal Paradox', *Criminal Justice* 2(3): 277–301.

Goffman, E. (1963) *Stigma: Notes on the Management of Spoiled Identity*, London: Penguin.

Hannah-Moffat, K. (2001) *Punishment in Disguise: Penal Governance and Federal Imprisonment of Women in Canada*, Toronto: University of Toronto Press.

Hannah-Moffat, K. (2002) 'Creating Choices: Reflecting on Choices', in P. Carlen (ed.) *Women and Punishment: The Struggle for Justice*, Cullompton: Willan Publishing: 199–219.

Hannah-Moffat, K. and Shaw, M. (2000) 'Introduction: Prisons for Women – Theory, Reform and Ideals', in K. Hannah-Moffat and M. Shaw (eds) *An Ideal Prison? Critical Essays on Women's Imprisonment in Canada*, Halifax, Nova Scotia: Fernwood Publishing: 11–27.

Hannon, D. F. *et al.* (2000) *General Healthcare Study of the Irish Prison Population*, Galway: Dept of Health Promotion, NUI Galway.

Hayman, S. (2006) *Imprisoning Our Sisters: The New Federal Women's Prisons in Canada*, Montreal: McGill-Queen's University Press.

Heidensohn, F. (1996) *Women and Crime*, 2nd edn, Basingstoke: Macmillan.

Heidensohn, F. (1997) 'Gender and Crime', in M. Maguire *et al.* (eds) *The Oxford Handbook of Criminology*, 2nd edn, Oxford, Clarendon Press: 761–98.

Kruttschnitt, C., Gartner, R. and Miller, A. (2000) 'Doing Her Own Time: Women's Responses to Prison in the Context of the Old and the New Penology', *Criminology*, 38(3): 681–717.

Loucks, N. (1997) *Research into Drugs and Alcohol, Violence and Bullying, Suicide and Self-injury and Backgrounds of Abuse at HMP Cornton Vale*, Scottish Prison Service.

Lustgarten, A. (2001) *'Notes from the Underground'*, *Prison Report*, Summer (no. 55): 21–2.

MacBride, S. (1982) 'Report of the Commission of Enquiry into the Irish Penal System', in S. MacBride, *Crime and Punishment*, Dublin: Ward River Press: 9–112.

Maden, A., Swinton, M. and Gunn, A.(1994) 'A Criminological and Psychiatric Survey of Women Serving a Prison Sentence', *British Journal of Criminology* 34(2): 172–89.

Matthews, R. (1999) *Doing Time: An Introduction to the Sociology of Imprisonment*, London, Macmillan.

McConville, S. (1998) 'The Victorian Prison: England 1865–1965'. in N. Morris and D. Rothman (eds) *The Oxford History of the Prison: The Practice of Punishment in Western Society*, Oxford: Oxford University Press: 117–50.

Naffine, N. (1987) *Female Crime: The Construction of Women in Criminology*, Sydney: Allen and Unwin.

O'Loingsigh, G. (2004) *Getting Out, Staying Out: The Experience of Prisoners on Release*. Dublin: Community Technical Aid.

Rock, P. (1996) *Reconstructing a Women's Prison: The Holloway Development Project 1968–1988*, Oxford: Oxford University Press.

Snider, L. (2003) 'Constituting the Punishable Woman: Atavistic Man Incarcerates Postmodern Woman', *British Journal of Criminology* 43(2): 354–78.

Sparks, R., Bottoms, A. And Hay, W. (1996) *Prisons and Problems of Order*, Oxford: Clarendon Press.

Spiro, M. (1956) *Kibbutz: Venture in Utopia*, Harvard: Harvard University Press.

Walklate, S. (1995) *Gender and Crime: An Introduction*, Hemel Hempstead: Prentice Hall.

Zedner, L. (1998) 'Wayward Sisters: The Prison for Women', in N. Morris and D. Rothman (eds) *The Oxford History of the Prison*, Oxford: Oxford University Press: 295–324.

Chapter 10

Reforming the prison: a Canadian tale

Stephanie Hayman

The history of women's imprisonment has generally been subsumed within the larger history of male prisoners. It is still unusual for women prisoners to be the entire focus of historical studies and there remains a tendency to relegate their story to a discrete chapter within a publication, rather than seeing that record as an integral part of any history of incarceration. While there are honourable exceptions to this pattern in Europe (see Dobash *et al.* 1986; Zedner 1991), much of the most commonly cited historical literature, focusing entirely on women, derives from North America (see Rafter 1985; Freedman 1981). Until relatively recently (see Hannah-Moffat 2001) the larger geographic component of North America – Canada – was not considered a likely source of such information, largely because, historically, the country has had relatively few prisons for women. Canada's sole women's federal penitentiary,[1] the Prison for Women, was never seen as an exemplar, yet its history, and the reasons for its final closure, offers present-day prison reformers an instructive lesson. Indeed, this story reflects what Cohen warns against: that the 'well-intentioned plans of reformers (conscience) are systematically transformed by the obdurate nature of social reality', leaving reforms channelled 'in directions diametrically opposed to the original vision' (1985: 92).

What this Canadian story also highlights is the way in which feminist interventions in the criminal justice arena have contributed to more oppressive regimes for women prisoners, even if the women involved have not necessarily been entirely responsible for this outcome. In assuming the (sometimes unwilling) role of 'authorised knowers' (Snider 2003), and consequently speaking on behalf of prisoners silenced by their lack of power, feminist reformers have themselves become party to increased levels of punishment, rather than the reformation of the institution of punishment, the prison. However, as will be discussed in the conclusion, such an outcome is not necessarily consequent upon women alone being the reformers.

This story begins in Kingston, Ontario, where the Prison for Women opened in 1934. Almost from its inception the prison was criticised as being unfit for its purpose: it was many hundreds of miles from most of the prisoners' homes, while its physical structure limited the development of a constructive regime and contributed to its becoming an unsafe prison. In the years following its opening many commissions and inquiries called for the prison's closure, but it was not until 1990, when *Creating Choices: The Report of the Task Force on Federally Sentenced Women* was accepted by the government of Canada, that this became a possibility.

The distinctiveness of the Task Force which produced *Creating Choices* partially lay in its resolute focus upon the needs of imprisoned women: those responsible for bringing together the Task Force well understood that the needs of men had for too long determined planning for women. Yet the Task Force was unique in another way, being comprised of almost equal numbers of civil servants and representatives from the voluntary sector. Among the latter, the Canadian Association of Elizabeth Fry Societies (CAEFS) and the Native Women's Association of Canada (NWAC) were particularly influential. Representatives of CAEFS and the Correctional Service of Canada (CSC) jointly chaired the two Task Force committees: the Working Group and the Steering Committee. Both voluntary organisations joined the venture reluctantly. For CAEFS the stumbling block was a reluctance to contribute to planning what it knew would be a continuation of imprisonment,[2] whereas for NWAC it was the fact that imprisonment was not an Aboriginal construct: Aboriginal peoples have never formally assented to Euro-Canadian law. These organisations were finally persuaded of the need to join the Task Force by the condition of the Prison for Women, where two Aboriginal women had committed suicide during the previous year.[3]

As is clarified elsewhere (Hayman 2006) the Task Force was heavily influenced by its Aboriginal members, who were late additions to the project, yet played crucial roles on both of its committees. They powerfully impressed upon fellow members the consequences of Canada's colonial policies, which had directly led to the disproportionate criminalising and imprisonment of Aboriginal peoples, and stressed that Aboriginal federally sentenced women were as much victims of this colonial history as they were victimisers of others. Having accepted this characterisation of Aboriginal women prisoners, the Task Force found it impossible to differentiate between groups of federally sentenced women, recognising that most shared similar socio-economic backgrounds and histories of abuse and addiction. This was a view supported by research into offending women outside Canada (see Carlen 1983; Heidensohn 1985; Morris 1987; Smart 1976), but only beginning to be more widely discussed within Canada (see Adelburgh and Currie 1987).

The Task Force was also reluctant to label federally sentenced women as potentially, or actually, violent, believing that the changed environment of the new prisons would reduce their challenging behaviour and make their management easier. Consequently, the Task Force reluctantly identified just 5 per cent of federally sentenced women as being in need of extra support and security. The need to work to consensus, and to provide a final report that could not be filleted by an unsympathetic implementation team, contributed to the Task Force's creating a uniform 'woman' as the focus of their planning. This left its report, *Creating Choices*, with a crucial omission at its heart, which was the failure to plan sufficiently, or prescriptively enough, for the women who did not fit their model.

In defining women as victims of their socio-economic circumstances and, in the case of Aboriginal federally sentenced women, as being dislocated from their culture, the Task Force challenged the traditional stereotyping of the criminal woman. They reflected points highlighted by Heidensohn (1985) and others, who focused on the way that offending women were seen as 'doubly deviant', in that they offended both against the law and notions of appropriate feminine behaviour. Locating federally sentenced women firmly within socio-economic boundaries demonstrated their lack of agency and showed that the choices they made were largely circumscribed by poverty and addiction. The Task Force showed that much of the 'deviance' flowed from the dominant Euro-Canadian culture, which had excluded and marginalised these women. In doing so, the Task Force provided supporting evidence for the work of those first feminist criminologists, as it also did by recognising the stigma attached to such marginalisation and then challenging the basis of its construction. 'Chivalry' was not so much of an issue for the Task Force because, in one sense, it had played to the advantage of federally sentenced women, with judges being reluctant to sentence women to federal terms of imprisonment, because of the inadequacy of the Prison for Women.

Following months of intense work, which had taken its members across Canada to consult with those working most closely with, or for, federally sentenced women, and the women themselves, the Task Force finally called for the closure of the Prison for Women and its replacement by five regional prisons, including an Aboriginal Healing Lodge.[4] The locations of the proposed prisons were carefully identified and took account of what local communities could offer, so that the new prisons might be seen as a shared responsibility, rather than simply an imposition by CSC. The new prisons were to be dramatically different from the old Prison for Women and would incorporate 'all environmental factors known to promote wellness ... natural light, fresh air, colour, space, privacy and access to land' (TFFSW 1990: 115). They would be cottage-style and without fences and would depend upon dynamic security, which presupposed a different style of staffing. Like the Prison for Women, the new prisons would be multi-level, in that women of all security categories would be held on the same site, but without the attendant high levels of visible security.

The Healing Lodge was a complete departure from previous correctional norms in that the Task Force envisaged a great deal of input from Aboriginal staff, communities and Elders, with Aboriginal principles of justice informing the lodge's day-to-day operation. All Aboriginal federally sentenced women would be able to choose to go there at any stage of their sentence, regardless of their security classification. The concept of the healing lodge was not greatly expanded upon in *Creating Choices*, as it was acknowledged that Aboriginal people themselves needed to be responsible for its planning. However, the Task Force did suggest that at its heart would be a 'large round room to be used for ceremonies, teaching [and] healing' (minutes of the Working Group, October, 1989). As with the language used to describe the other new prisons, the custodial element of the proposed prison was disguised by the euphemisms employed, perhaps most importantly in its name.

The Task Force's conclusions were supported by a mass of commissioned research, which finally identified the multifarious faces of federally sentenced women, information that CSC itself surprisingly lacked (see Shaw 1991; Shaw *et al.* 1991a; Shaw *et al.* 1991b). The Task Force finally provided a blueprint for women's imprisonment that seemed to transcend the philosophical and physical constraints of planning for women prisoners elsewhere. It used the language of second-wave feminism to explain the rationale for change, but avoided any claims to being a feminist document by referring to *Creating Choices'* content as being 'women centred'. At the heart of the report lay the principles that provided a context for the Task Force's decision-making: empowerment; meaningful and responsible choices; respect and dignity; supportive environment and shared responsibility. Central to these was the belief that women could be empowered to make responsible choices, and the Task Force assumed that such choices were dependent upon the prisons providing 'meaningful options' for the women (TFFSW 1990: 107). It was also presupposed that choices should be relevant to the women themselves, at the time they were making those choices, rather than simply relevant to what would enable women to pass correctionally imposed hurdles, leading to an ultimate release date.

In many sections of the report the language was explicitly feminist and this usage inadvertently allowed its eventual incorporation into the harsher language of penality, and its later reinterpretation, once the implementation of *Creating Choices* became almost solely the responsibility of CSC. This appropriation of the language of feminism disturbed Kendall, who wrote that she was 'concerned that the language of feminism [was] being appropriated and stripped of its subversive potential by corrections in order to facilitate the correctional agenda' (1994: 3). Yet, even as the Task Force was adopting the language of feminism, it resorted to euphemisms throughout the report, which discussed new 'facilities' rather than prisons; 'staff' rather than guards or correctional officers; 'bedrooms' rather than cells. The prisons contained 'cottages' and as implementation took place CSC developed an 'enhanced unit', which was actually a maximum security place of containment: the disciplinary aspect of the prisons, and the involuntary nature of the prisoners' incarceration, was effaced. Such circumlocution, or 'Controltalk' (see Cohen 1983), continued with subsequent CSC policy documents, but the Task Force first enabled CSC to adopt them by resorting to such language in *Creating Choices* (see also Faith 1993; Bruckert 1993).

Following the government's acceptance of the report, and with CSC officially in charge of implementation, co-operation with its pre-eminent partner, CAEFS, broke down. Some two years after the publication of *Creating Choices* CAEFS withdrew from the venture, amid allegations that CSC was withholding information about proposals for the new prisons. (The Task Force's carefully considered locations for the new prisons were ignored in three of the five cases, and later some communities actively campaigned against hosting the new prisons.) NWAC remained with the implementation process and its representatives were involved in the planning of the Healing Lodge, but this did not necessarily mean that they were always in a more advantageous position. Budgetary constraints limited the scale of their planning and the healing lodge ended up with fewer facilities than in those which may be termed the 'Euro-Canadian' prisons (even though some also held significant numbers of Aboriginal women).

In 1994, at a time when CSC was in the midst of building the new prisons, and publicly committed to the new philosophy underpinning their planning, an event at the Prison for Women led to a Royal Commission of Inquiry, headed by Madam Justice Arbour. 'Event' seems too light a description of the mistreatment of eight women at the prison, which only publicly came to light when a video of the occurrences was broadcast on the Canadian Broadcasting Corporation's *Fifth Estate* programme almost a year later (see Shaw 1999). Following a series of escalating protests, eight women were removed from their cells in the middle of the night by an all-male institutional emergency response team (IERT) and strip-searched. CSC subsequently conducted its own inquiry, but Arbour found this to have been compromised by the relationship of the investigators to CSC. Arbour's report found that CSC chose to disregard 'the Rule of Law' whenever it suited its purposes and had a 'disturbing lack of commitment to the ideals of justice' (Arbour 1996: 198). Presciently, she suggested that: 'despite its recent initiative [the Task Force on Federally Sentenced Women], the Correctional Service [of Canada] resorts invariably to the view that women's prisons are or should be, just like any other prison' (Arbour 1996: 178).

Arbour's report was published in March 1996 and reminded the public that CSC was about to open new prisons. Edmonton Institution for Women opened in November 1996, closely followed by Nova Institution for Women in Truro (Nova Scotia) and the Okimaw Ohci Healing Lodge (Saskatchewan).

Edmonton was almost completely closed within five and a half months of its opening, following a number of walk-aways by some women, 13 incidents of self-injury, two attempted suicides, two assaults on staff, and one murder, initially thought to be suicide. Stated baldly, these seem an extraordinary series of events within a prison anticipated to break the conventional mould of women's imprisonment. What is missing from this summary is the context to these events, in that the prison was incomplete when it opened; had many more maximum security women than it could safely accommodate (among whom were many Aboriginal women refused permission to transfer to the Healing Lodge); had few programmes in place; and deployed new staff who were, largely, unfamiliar with correctional work (see Hayman 2006; Hannah-Moffat 2001; Chrumka 2000; CSC 1996a, 1996b). Additionally, most of Edmonton's prisoners were also struggling with the new style of corrections and a radically different style of prison architecture. Conditions within each of the new living houses were strikingly different from anything the women had previously known in other prisons. The houses, as distinct from the enhanced unit, had no resident guards and fire regulations initially prevented their being locked. Each house held a maximum of eight women with widely varying needs and backgrounds, who had to assume individual responsibility for weekly budgeting and the smooth running of their living quarters. Disagreements were to be resolved communally and the women had to accustom themselves to prison staff who seemed more like social workers than guards. Many of the women had never experienced such a structured pattern to their lives, let alone within the confines of a prison.

The events at Edmonton delayed the opening of the prisons in Kitchener (Ontario) and Joliette (Québec). They also determined the removal of all maximum security women at Edmonton and Truro to small units within men's prisons, until more secure accommodation could be constructed. (The Healing Lodge was never permitted to accept maximum security women.) At a stroke this destroyed a central component of the Task Force's careful schema: that women of all security levels should be held together within prisons solely for women. (At that stage the Prison for Women was still open – and it did not finally close until 2000.)

While there are many aspects of the Task Force's work that deserve closer attention (see Hayman 2006; Hannah-Moffat 2001; Hannah-Moffat and Shaw 2000) this chapter will concentrate on two: the consequences of the Task Force's failure to plan prescriptively for women termed 'difficult to manage'; and the unintended consequences of a benevolent attempt at penal reform.

Providing for the 'difficult to manage' women

As has already been made clear, the Task Force was reluctant to label women as either violent or requiring extra levels of support (largely because of perceived mental health needs), as it believed that a changed environment would have a positive impact upon them. The Task Force, having conceded that 5 per cent of the women might require additional security measures, then focused upon the way in which staff could support those women within a partially modified house, rather than a conventional maximum security block. While some on the Task Force questioned the wisdom of this, and CSC's representatives were among those pressing for the issue to be clarified, the demands of consensus ensured that the views of the majority prevailed. As a consequence, no specific plans for these women were outlined in the report and the omission made it possible for CSC later to decide how best they should be managed. (*Creating Choices* gives no hint of the debate and the information is only clarified in the minutes of Task Force meetings.) Within two years of accepting the report, CSC had doubled to 10 per cent the Task Force's figures relating to the 'difficult to manage' women and was planning secure accommodation in what it termed 'enhanced units', which were traditional concrete and iron structures, far removed from the supportive house environment envisaged by the Task Force. The units conveyed the message that some women were intrinsically different from the others and made it harder for maximum security prisoners, who had prepared for a new style of imprisonment, to imagine making the step towards the houses occupied by other women.

One of the underlying premises of the Task Force's planning was that security should be 'dynamic' and this meant that relationships between staff and prisoners would be based on one of *Creating Choices'* core 'principles', which encompassed respect and dignity. This phrase implied a mutuality of respect between prisoners and staff and its importance lay in the expected outcome, which was that levels of security would be reduced because of improved relationships. To achieve this, the Task Force envisaged staff 'from a wide variety of backgrounds and educational traditions' who would receive compulsory training in areas such as 'counselling, communications and negotiation skills', as well as 'issues relating to power and class' (TFFSW 1990: 116). This was a departure from the traditional prison officer model and, once it had been made clear to staff at the Prison for Women that they (and their 'culture') would not be relocated to the new prisons, ensured that most of the new staff were entirely new to corrections. The training they underwent emphasised what the prisoners themselves recognised as social work skills, rather than solely the correctional aspect of their new roles. Once the first 'Euro-Canadian' prisons opened (Healing Lodge staff received different instruction) and the training was put to the test, there was confusion. The staff found the requirement that they should provide 'support' (TFFSW 1990: 117) did not sit easily with their custodial function and the women could not reconcile their image of a guard with those who were attempting to mentor them. The women were largely experts in the old style of corrections, by virtue of their experience of imprisonment at the Prison for Women and provincial prisons, and this left them in the curious position of having a better 'sense' of imminent events than did the staff. But this knowledge also left the women uncertain of their own safety, because they did not trust the staff's ability to anticipate problems and intervene when necessary.

Events at Edmonton had a profound effect on the other prisons and also changed the way in which federally sentenced women were publicly perceived. Rather than being seen as women with 'high needs' while representing 'low risk', as they had been characterised by the Task Force, they were newly labelled as being potentially violent and hard to manage. As others such as Hannah-Moffat (2001) and Snider (2003) have noted, 'high needs' appeared to be coterminous with 'high risk', with the situation being exacerbated within CSC by the classification tools used to assess women upon admission to prison (see Hannah-Moffat and Shaw 2001). At the fatality inquiry (Chrumka 2000) into the murder of the woman at Edmonton, CSC's Deputy Commissioner for Women went so far as to suggest that many more women than first imagined did not fit the Task Force's model of imprisonment; indeed, that some were 'without the capacity for change'.[5] This changing public image of the ostensibly risky female offender took little account of the fact that the Creating Choices' model was never fully tested, thanks to Edmonton's unfinished state when the first prisoners arrived, and the disproportionate number of maximum security women the prison was forced to accept, yet could not safely accommodate.[6]

The closure of Edmonton left CSC uncertain about how to provide for the high-risk women and a decision was not forthcoming until September 1999, when CSC announced an Intensive Intervention Strategy. (The Healing Lodge was again exempt from this planning, but disproportionate numbers of Aboriginal women within the 'Euro-Canadian' prisons were to be affected by it.) The enhanced units (housing mostly maximum security women) would be upgraded and set entirely apart from the rest of each prison, while remaining within the perimeter fences. Additionally, minimum or medium security women with mental health and/or special needs would move to new supported living units (SLEs), where there would be 24-hour

Table 10.1 Bed capacity at the five new prisons*

Bed capacity	Regular beds	Enhanced unit beds	SLEs	Total
1995	258 (91%)	25 (9%)	n/a	283
March 2005	332 (80%)	50 (12%)	32 (8%)	414

*The figures for 2005 do *not* include beds available at the new federal Fraser Valley Institution for Women, in British Columbia, or in regional treatment/psychiatric centres.

supervision and support by staff. Women had the right to refuse placement in the SLEs, but risked transfer to a secure unit should they fail to cope with life in an ordinary house. It was estimated that 'approximately thirty women' would be in the secure units and 'approximately thirty-five women' (within the then federally sentenced women population) would be in the SLEs (CSC 1999).

Secure units also contain segregation cells, which are not counted as part of official capacity (yet were used as such when Edmonton first opened). This potential capacity is assessed in Hayman (2006) and, for the purposes of this chapter, should simply be noted because of the way in which it might contribute to an increase in provision for maximum security and difficult to manage women. Using figures published by CSC in 1995, and building upon those available for the five new prisons in March 2005, Table 10.1 shows that by 1995 CSC had planned for just under 10 per cent of available accommodation being for maximum security women, whereas the Task Force had envisaged 5 per cent. (The secure units were also expected to contain women newly admitted to prison and awaiting assessment.) Within ten years the percentages had altered considerably. As well as extended secure units and new SLEs, three of the prisons also had additional regular houses, which meant that in the intervening years total bed capacity at the five new prisons had increased by 46 per cent. By 2005, 20 per cent of the beds were designated for women needing extra levels of intervention and security, compared with 9 per cent when they first opened. The difference in secure unit provision is particularly marked, having moved from a posited 'approximately thirty women' (CSC 1995) to 50 beds.

Table 10.2 shows the total bed capacity across the entire federally

Table 10.2 Total bed capacity for all federally sentenced women, March 2006

Regular beds	Enhanced unit beds	SLEs	Total
387 (77%)	60 (12%)	67 (13%)	514

sentenced women's estate. It includes capacity at the Fraser Valley Institution for Women, the two psychiatric hospitals/prisons, and the minimum security Isabel McNeill House in Kingston. Some 25 per cent of all federally sentenced women are now potentially subject to some form of extra intervention, if SLE provision is added to that of the EUs. While emphasising that it is not CSC's practice to count segregation cells as part of official capacity, it should not be forgotten that the cells have been used as such before, if in extreme circumstances. Were the present 19 segregation cells to be added to these figures the total number of beds available for intensive supervision would be increased to 29 per cent.

But these developments have not signalled the end of CSC's planning for this group of women. A Management Protocol is now in place and covers those maximum security women who 'commit an act causing serious harm or seriously jeopardise the safety of others' (CSC 2004). Crucially, women placed on the Protocol are removed from one regional prison to another, taking them far from their home communities, in a complete reversal of all that the Task Force had intended – and also reversing the position adopted by CSC when *Creating Choices* was accepted by the government of Canada.

The Protocol has three stages, with Step 1 permitting the almost complete isolation, in a segregation unit, of a woman, with a level of security never envisaged by the Task Force. Step 2 allows for limited association with other women in the segregation unit and Step 3 envisages the woman's gradual reintegration into the secure unit. 'Once the inmate has maintained positive participation for a period of three months in the *Transition* Step [3] ... she can then be discharged from the Protocol' (CSC 2004: 10), and may be considered for relocation to her original prison. However, if the woman's behaviour becomes unacceptable at any stage of this process, she may be returned to Step 1 and have to rework her way through each step of the Protocol.

Theoretically, this suggests that some women could be subjected to unlimited periods of segregation. Although such a scenario is unlikely, the fact that it might even be a possibility raises concern, not least because such extended periods of segregation contravene the clear intention of Section 31 of the Corrections and Conditional Release Act 1992. This states that prisoners should not normally be kept in segregation for more than 30 days at a time (although this may be increased to 45 days if multiple convictions are involved; see Arbour 1996: 185). As has earlier been indicated, Arbour was fiercely critical of CSC's disregard of the law and feared that the old style of imprisonment might re-emerge in the new prisons (1996: 91). Even she could not have anticipated such a realisation of all her misgivings. Arbour noted the impact of segregation upon prisoners and the point was later pursued by Martel (1999), who assessed the deleterious impact of isolation upon prisoners' mental health. There is also the question of the way in which dynamic security is affected by such confinement: guards intended to be role models and mentors have little chance of assuming those functions. Yet perhaps the biggest concern of all resides in the design of the segregation cells, which are uniform in all the new 'Euro-Canadian' prisons. They are unsafe. They provide ready ligature points for distressed women and the standard sanitary fittings offer further opportunities for self-harm. As research demonstrates, women's response to the distress of imprisonment is frequently manifested in self-harm (see Shaw *et al.* 1991a; HM Inspectorate of Prisons 1999; Liebling *et al.* 2005).

The difficulty is that all prison systems have to provide for a very small group of persistently disruptive and/or dangerous prisoners, who do not fit a predetermined pattern. But, in focusing on subgroups within this already small group, CSC would appear to be suggesting that there is no limit to the refined degrees of security and segregation it might provide.

These developments have further consequences, in that Aboriginal federally sentenced women are disproportionately affected by them. Aboriginal women now comprise 29 per cent of the total federally sentenced women's population (whereas they are less than 3 per cent of the general population), and the Healing Lodge has never been permitted to house maximum security women,[7] even though Arbour (1996) and the Canadian Human Rights' Commission (2003) recommended that it should be. Aboriginal women are disproportionately likely to be classified as maximum security, or to be seen as in need of extra levels of support, as provided in the SLEs. (In July 2003 they comprised 46 per cent of all women classified as maximum security.) The development of the new secure units contributes to Aboriginal women being further isolated from other federally sentenced women and, perhaps more importantly, from the Aboriginal environment of the Healing Lodge. Bearing in mind that the Aboriginal members of the Task Force joined the Task Force out of desperation at the plight of Aboriginal federally sentenced women within the unsafe Prison for Women, this outcome is particularly worrying.

Assessing the consequences of benevolence

As the beginning of this chapter made clear, the Task Force itself was a departure from correctional norms, in Canada and elsewhere. That particular combination of civil service and voluntary sector representatives reflected the increasing feminist discourse within most reaches of Canadian government during the 1980s, although 'femocrats'[8] were sometimes suspect within the wider bureaucracy and many civil servants would have been wary of being too closely identified with women's issues. Nevertheless, the Task Force's feminist credentials were apparent throughout *Creating Choices* and also in the way in which the Task Force commissioned research, so that federally sentenced women and their backgrounds would be properly known. (CSC did not have accurate information on this client group.) Although two on the Task Force had themselves been federally sentenced prisoners, most other members had theoretical, rather than practical, knowledge of the barriers and inequities confronting women within Canadian society. Indeed, the profile of the Task Force generally resembled that of the early 'maternal' prison reformers in the United States (see Rafter 1985), and the Task Force's members unsurprisingly provided solutions for the prisoners which reflected their own middle class ways of knowing. (See Rumgay, Chapter 14 in this volume, for discussion of related issues.) Having consulted federally sentenced women, the Task Force assumed their voices and collectively became the 'authorised knowers' (Snider 2003) of what was best for them, without explicitly acknowledging that the women could never adequately be heard, simply because they were not free. The Task Force subsequently planned for its idealised 'woman', and also attempted to provide pathways into the community for her during her period of imprisonment, but its primary solutions were grounded in the prison.

The Task Force's relationship with CSC, particularly that of its voluntary sector members, had important consequences. In many cases it was far more than benevolence that inspired the Task Force members' participation: it was despair. They knew that women were dying within the Prison for Women; that the prison removed autonomy from the women's lives; that the prison generally did not restore women intact to their homes and communities once their sentence was completed. Yet Task Force members also knew they were not being given a choice about whether or not imprisonment itself should be challenged: the only choice was between retaining the *status quo* (the Prison for Women) and another form of imprisonment. The plight of federally sentenced women ensured their participation, because they could not stand on principle and see more women harmed. Despite grave reservations they joined the venture and, as the April 1989 Working Group minutes revealed, remained concerned that their work might lead to further 'oppression' of federally sentenced women, a fear that was particularly prevalent among the voluntary sector members. So the question to be answered in relation to these reformers is one posed by Snider (2003: 356): why is it that 'arguments intended to alleviate oppression perpetuate oppressiveness'?

The answer lies partially in the fact that groups attaining the status of 'authorised knowers' derive their knowledge from three sources: their own experience of working alongside criminal and criminalised women; other observers' theoretical and/or practical knowledge of these women; and the women themselves. Of these three groups, the true experts are the women, but their knowledge is too often mediated through the voices of others and, in this instance, the women's voices were further modified and overlaid by the decision that the Task Force should work to a consensus model. The initial 'woman' had an Aboriginal identity, shaped by historic victimisation and low socio-economic status, and this identity was eventually believed to reflect that of other federally sentenced women. The Task Force finally provided for a group of women with high needs and low risk (of violence), suggesting that 'where women do present risks, these risks tend to be to themselves' (TFFSW 1990: 89). It also envisaged a 'holistic' treatment of women's needs, with a move away from fixed programming, wherein 'categorised needs [were] defined not by the women, but by the programme leader, or corrections officials'. The preference was for an approach that allowed for more individualised strategies and greater individual support for each woman (TFFSW 1990: 85). Many members of the Task Force assumed that, even though they could not fully challenge the need for imprisonment, they could at least ameliorate some of its harm.

However, the programmes produced by those finally responsible for the implementation of the Task Force's plan did not allow for such an individualised approach. Moreover, the programmes tended to focus upon a woman's perceived psychological needs and upon the behavioural patterns that had brought her into prison. The reasons for offending were located within each woman, rather than in the wider community from which she had emerged. As earlier suggested, the Task Force's adoption of the language of feminism facilitated and validated CSC's subsequent reinterpretation of that same language, as is now particularly evident in the way that the 'principles' underpinning *Creating Choices* have undergone a subtle transformation. The 'choices' the women were encouraged to make regarding programming eventually became choices that satisfied the needs of the correctional authorities, rather than the women themselves. Their 'responsible choices' did not always reflect the needs they had individually identified, but reflected the requirements of CSC and, by extension, the parole board. This 'responsibilising' strategy actually removed autonomy from the women, rather than empowered them.

As the discourse changed, so did the interpretation of 'need': in many cases it became synonymous with risk (of violence), despite the fact that risk in relation to federally sentenced women initially meant risk of recidivism (see Carlen and Worrall 2004; Hannah-Moffatt 2001). CSC, by its reaction to events at Edmonton, transformed federally sentenced women into offenders presenting high (mental health) needs and high risk (of violence). This directly led to 25 per cent of total bed space in the new prisons being made more secure and highlighted the shift from 'dynamic' security, with its emphasis on relationships between staff and prisoners, to a 'static' security of high fences and cameras.

How could the benevolent intentions of the Task Force have led to such an outcome and should any of this have been foreseen? An examination of the history of women's imprisonment provides easy parallels, as Rafter (1985) makes clear. The early reformatories for women in the United States began with the same intention of restoring women to their communities, albeit to the gendered roles then thought appropriate. The reformers projected middle-class values on to the relatively few women with whom they dealt and the consequence was actually a greater level of intervention in the women's lives. These Canadian reformers were focused upon providing a Canadian solution to the problems confronting federally sentenced women and were not necessarily interested in penal history, or always aware of the lessons that might have been learned. Their overriding priority was to provide a safer environment than that of the Prison for Women. They could not fully acknowledge that their work might lead to failure, or greater 'oppression', because that would have highlighted their compromised principles and made working with the civil servants impossible. Conscience, as much as benevolence, ensured their participation. Yet while this might suggest that only those from the voluntary sector had the best interests of federally sentenced women at heart, this was far from the case. The civil servants acknowledged the inadequacy of the Prison for Women and were also committed to change – but change within a penal environment.

The consequence has been that the voluntary sector is now inextricably linked in the public mind to the new regional prisons, despite having played no part in the planning that followed the government's acceptance of *Creating Choices* (see Hayman 2000, 2006). (The Healing Lodge is the exception to this.) Task Force members, having worked so hard to produce a plan benefiting all federally sentenced women, now see that their careful work has been distorted to fit the changing characterisation of federally sentenced women.

Much of the literature on contemporary imprisonment for women focuses on the ways in which women are uniquely affected by their confinement (see Carlen 1983; Dobash *et al*. 1986; Eaton 1993). However, generally it would be wrong to suggest that the efforts of women reformers led to harsher outcomes than reform attempted by men, even though it might appear to be the case in this instance. In terms of offending the gender gap has historically determined the needs of men taking priority over those of women. Feminist criminologists redressed that balance theoretically, while reformers have done so in a practical sense, at the same time generally underpinning their conclusions with empirical evidence. Reformers' reports have clarified in painstaking, informed detail the areas requiring the most attention from correctional authorities (see TTFSW 1990; Prison Reform Trust 2000). Such a wealth of detail encourages wide provision by those responsible for implementation of such plans, as happened in Canada. It is the very scale and thoroughness of feminist reformers' efforts, and their commitment to using the language of feminism as an explicator, that enables others to refashion their work. The more reformers delineate, the greater the possibility of later subversion. The Task Force replicated the historic pattern in the penal sphere of 'generalising', except that this time they were not reaching conclusions based on generalising from the needs of men: they were generalising from the needs of women and then assuming a commonality of women's experience. In doing so they helped create expectations of what would be appropriate responses from their idealised 'woman' and her failure to respond as expected allowed other interventions to be designed. The outcome would be the same if male reformers prepared equally ambitious plans and created the conditions for others to interpret their plans: the prison always triumphs.

While a reading of the literature on prison reform might have prepared these Canadian reformers for the reinterpretation of their plans, and their diminished influence, what should not be underestimated is the power of the prison itself. The institution of imprisonment stands resolute, resisting all moves towards its reformation, even as it appears to invite change. The paradoxical success of the prison (as a means of disciplining the deviant) is dependent upon its continuing failure as a place of rehabilitation – and upon others then agitating for its reform. The prison cannot afford to succeed, because success would limit its power. The prison must therefore be in a perpetual state of working towards reform while acknowledging its flaws, if it is to retain its authority to discipline – and it is this cycle that entraps the benevolent. This cycle is partially explained by Carlen's use of the term 'carceral clawback' (2002). Most reformers, as did these Canadians, understand the damage caused by imprisonment, yet simultaneously acquiesce in the supposition that the state will never agree to an alternative. This understandable wish to lessen harm determines the reformers' complicity, because they find it impossible simply to observe and comment while individuals are being hurt. Their good intentions thus legitimise the prison, as they imply that the prison might have a function beyond punishment. It does not.

Such a conclusion is not to adopt the view that change should never be attempted, but is to suggest that any partnership in prison reform should frankly acknowledge the inherent limitations. Perhaps the terminology is wrong and 'reform', in the sense of making situations better, is not the most accurate word to use. Reformers might most accurately be called 're-formers', in that they form again, or re-fashion, the prison. Their endeavours might alter aspects of the prison for the better, but its function – punishment – will not be hidden from view.

Mason (see Chapter 9 in this volume) counters the traditional story of the consequences of prison reform, yet the overwhelming lesson from the historical literature is one of failure. Individuals, given the choice, do not voluntarily turn to the prison for improving programmes and do not see deprivation of liberty and autonomy as a benevolent act. They know that they are imprisoned in order to be punished. This Canadian story therefore demonstrates the potency of Snider's earlier suggestion that attempts to 'alleviate oppression [actually] perpetuate oppressiveness' (2003: 356). It also highlights Shaw's position, that the Task Force's work and *Creating Choices* diverted attention from 'rethinking the use of imprisonment' (1996: 195). The Task Force on Federally Sentenced Women accepted, albeit reluctantly and understandably, the premise that imprisonment itself could not be challenged and, in doing so, helped legitimise imprisonment. The Task Force thus became a further footnote in the history of attempts to repair what is fundamentally irreparable.

Glossary

CAEFS	Canadian Association of Elizabeth Fry Societies
CCRA	Corrections and Conditional Release Act 1992
CSC	Correctional Service of Canada
EU	Enhanced unit
IERT	Institutional emergency response team
NWAC	Native Women's Association of Canada
SLE	Structured living environment
TFFSW	Task Force on Federally Sentenced Women

Notes

1 Federal prisoners are those who have been sentenced to terms of at least two years and are the responsibility of the federal government. Anyone sentenced to less than two years of imprisonment becomes a provincial prisoner and is subject to the law of the province where they are detained.
2 CAEFS adopted an abolitionist stance in June 1993.
3 Two women took their lives during the period of the Task Force and a further three committed suicide in the following year. All were Aboriginal women.
4 The report actually called for six new regional prisons, but recognised that the imminent opening of the Burnaby Correctional Centre for Women, in British Columbia, precluded a new prison in that province.
5 Tom Barrett, 'Warden Says Danger Was Unforeseen', *Edmonton Journal*, 9 September 1998.

6 The findings of the Arbour Report (1996) increased pressure on CSC to close the Prison for Women and transfer all federally sentenced women to regional prisons.
7 See Hayman (2006) for a discussion of the reasons.
8 A term coined by Australian feminists to cover feminists working in a government bureaucracy (see Stetson and Mazur 1995).

References

Adelburgh, E. and Currie, C. (eds) (1987) *Too Few to Count*, Vancouver: Press Gang Publishers.

Arbour, Hon. L. (1996) *Commission of Inquiry into Certain Events at the Prison for Women*, Ottawa: Public Works and Government Services.

Bruckert, C. (1993) *Creating Choices: The Report of the Task Force on Federally Sentenced Women, A Critical Analysis*, Ottawa: University of Ottawa.

Canadian Human Rights' Commission (2003) *Protecting Their Rights: A Systemic Review of Human Rights in Correctional Services for Federally Sentenced Women*, Ottawa: Public Works and Government Services.

Carlen, P. (1983) *Women's Imprisonment*, London: Routledge and Kegan Paul.

Carlen, P. (2002) 'New Discourses of Justification and Reform for Women's Imprisonment in England', in P. Carlen (ed.) *Women and Punishment: The Struggle for Justice*, Cullompton: Willan Publishing: 220–36.

Carlen, P. (ed) (2002) *Women and Punishment: The Struggle for Justice*, Cullompton: Willan Publishing.

Carlen, P. and Worrall, A. (2004) *Analysing Women's Imprisonment*, Cullompton: Willan Publishing.

Chrumka, A. G. (2000) *Report to the Attorney General: Public Inquiry into the Death of Denise Fayant*, Alberta: Department of Justice.

Cohen, S. (1983) 'Social-Control Talk: Correctional Change', in D. Garland and P. Young (eds) *The Power to Punish*, London: Heinemann Educational Books: 101–29.

Cohen, S. (1985) *Visions of Social Control*, Oxford: Blackwell.

Cook, S. and Davies, S. (1999) *Harsh Punishment: International Experiences of Women's Imprisonment*, Boston: Northeastern University Press.

CSC (Correctional Service of Canada) (1992) *Regional Facilities for Federally Sentenced Women Draft #4 Operational Plan*, Ottawa: Correctional Service of Canada.

CSC (1994) *Board of Investigation – Major Disturbance and other Related Incidents – Prison for Women, from Friday April 22 to Tuesday April 26, 1994*, Ottawa: Correctional Service of Canada.

CSC (1995) *Regional Facilities for Federally Sentenced Women*, Ottawa: Correctional Service of Canada.

CSC (1996a) *Lessons Learned for the Future*, Federally Sentenced Women's Program, Ottawa: Correctional Service of Canada.

CSC (1996b) *Board of Investigation Report into a Suicide in February 1996, and Other Major Incidents at Edmonton Institution for Women*, Ottawa: Correctional Service of Canada.

CSC (1999) *Backgrounder: Intensive Intervention Strategy*, Ottawa: Correctional Service of Canada.

CSC (2004) *Management Protocol*, Ottawa: Correctional Service of Canada.

Dobash, R., Dobash, R. and Gutteridge, S. (1986) *The Imprisonment of Women*, Oxford: Blackwell.

Eaton, M. (1993) *Women After Prison*, Buckingham: Open University Press.

Faith, K. (1993) *Unruly Women: The Politics of Confinement and Resistance*, Vancouver: Press Gang Publishers.

Freedman, E. (1981) *Their Sisters' Keepers: Women's Prison Reform in America, 1830–1930*, Ann Arbor: University of Michigan Press

Garland, D. and Young, P. (eds) (1983) *The Power to Punish*, London: Heinemann Educational Books.

Hannah-Moffat, K. (2001) *Punishment in Disguise: Penal Governance and Canadian Women's Imprisonment*, Toronto: University of Toronto Press.

Hannah-Moffat, K. and Shaw, M. (eds) (2000) *An Ideal Prison? Critical Essays on Women's Imprisonment in Canada*. Halifax: Fernwood Publishing.

Hannah-Moffat, K. and Shaw, M. (2001) *Taking Risks: Incorporating Gender and Culture into the Classification and Assessment of Federally Sentenced Women in Canada*, Ottawa: Status of Women Canada.

Hayman, S. (2000) 'Prison Reform and Incorporation', in K. Hannah-Moffat and M. Shaw (eds) *An Ideal Prison? Critical Essays on Women's Imprisonment in Canada*, Halifax: Fernwood Publishing: 41–51.

Hayman, S. (2006) *Imprisoning Our Sisters: The New Federal Women's Prisons in Canada*, Montreal: McGill-Queen's University Press.

Heidensohn, F. (1985) *Women and Crime*, Basingstoke: Macmillan.

HM Inspectorate of Prisons (1999) *Suicide is Everyone's Concern: A Thematic Review*, London: Home Office.

Kendall, K. (1994) 'Therapy Behind Walls: A Contradiction in Terms?', *Prison Service Journal*, 96: 2–11.

Liebling, A, Tait, S., Durie, L., Stiles, A. and Harvey, J. (2005), 'Safer Locals Evaluation', *Prison Service Journal*, 162: 8–12.

Martel, J. (1999) *Solitude and Cold Storage: Women's Journeys of Endurance in Segregation*, Edmonton: Elizabeth Fry Society of Edmonton.

Morris, A. (1987) *Women, Crime and Criminal Justice*, Oxford: Blackwell.

Prison Reform Trust (2000) *Justice for Women: The Need for Reform* (The Wedderburn Report), London: Prison Reform Trust.

Rafter, N. H. (1985) *Partial Justice: Women in State Prisons 1800–1935*, Boston: Northeastern University Press.

Shaw, M. (1991) *The Federal Female Offender: Report on a Preliminary Study*, Ottawa: Solicitor General of Canada.

Shaw, M. (1996) 'Knowledge Without Acknowledgement: Violent Women, the Prison and the Cottage', paper presented at the 48th annual meeting of the American Society of Criminology in Chicago, 1996.

Shaw, M. (1999) 'A Video Camera Can Change Your Life', in S. Cook and S. Davies (eds) *Harsh Punishment: International Experiences of Women's Imprisonment*, Boston: Northeastern University Press: 250–71.

Shaw, M. *et al.* (1991a) *Survey of Federally Sentenced Women: Report to the Task Force on Federally Sentenced Women on the Prison Survey*, Ottawa: Solicitor General of Canada.

Shaw, M. *et al.* (1991b) *Paying the Price: Federally Sentenced Women in Context*, Ottawa: Solicitor General of Canada.

Smart, C. (1976) *Women, Crime and Criminology*, London: Routledge and Kegan Paul.

Snider, L. (2003) 'Constituting the Punishable Woman: Atavistic Man Incarcerates Postmodern Woman', in *British Journal of Criminology*, 43(2): 354–78.

Stetson, D. M. and Mazur, A., (eds) (1995) *Comparative State Feminism*, London: Sage.

TFFSW (1990) *Creating Choices: Report of the Task Force on Federally Sentenced Women*, Ottawa: Correctional Service of Canada.

Zedner, L. (1991) *Women, Crime and Custody in Victorian England*, Oxford: Clarendon Press.

Introduction

Frances Heidensohn

Arguably, feminist perspectives have been the most important new approaches to be introduced to criminology in the late twentieth and early twenty-first centuries. As well as challenging and changing the core of the subject, they have stimulated new areas of growth. These are not only in the conventional fields such as victimisation, but also in the study of masculinity. However, it can also be claimed that there remain major gaps in, and limitations to, theoretical contributions (Gelsthorpe 2002). The selection presented in this part of the book is intended to show some exciting possibilities for renewal and development. This is not, any more than elsewhere in this volume, an exhaustive list. Historical studies might have been included (Walker 2003; Barton 2004; and see Heidensohn and Gelsthorpe 2007) for instance. Hegemonic masculinity has already been noted as a major product of gendered approaches directly applied to criminality (Connell and Messerschmidt 2005).

Nicole Rafter's chapter takes her work on Lombroso, the first notable criminologist, to write about women and crime and shows how feminist criminology has developed in relation to his work and to other biosocial studies. She insists that the new biosocial sciences pose significant challenges to feminist criminologists, which they will need to address and cannot ignore.

The next two chapters both incorporate the term 'human rights' in their titles, evidence of the extension of the gender agenda, but they have very distinctive takes on the theme, despite illustrating it empirically. Marisa Silvestri begins by addressing the limitations of criminology in general: its failure to address questions of power, for example. She then outlines the history of the human rights discourse before applying its framework to the specific issue of women's imprisonment. Using this example she is able to show this much discussed issue in a new light. It is illuminating to review the case studies in the second part of this volume from this perspective.

Oliver Phillips weaves together a series of approaches in his comparative study of gender, justice and rights in two post-colonial societies. He draws on an exceptionally wide range of concepts in his analysis – sexuality, customary law, differing notions of gender. He provides a powerful illustration of 'intersectionality' – of how gender may be one, albeit key, part of a theoretical construct which may need to incorporate notions of race, diverse forms of justice and the role of colonial and post-colonial history.

The final chapter is another case study, but of an altogether distinctive type. Judith Rumgay studied the rise, success and relative decline of a voluntary society dedicated to the welfare of the most difficult female offenders. In a very neat paradox, she deploys a gendered analysis to explore a declaredly non-feminist organisation. Her study is also distinctive in providing a natural history of a women's network and of female networking at the highest social and political levels.

In essence, these authors propose new sets of tools, of ideas and approaches for use in twenty-first century criminology. Human rights, biology, customary or colonial law, they insist, all can play a part, as can settings as varied as Southern Africa or élite salons of late twentieth century London.

References

Barton, A. (2004) *Fragile Moralities and Dangerous Sexualities*, Aldershot: Ashgate.

Connell, R. and Messerschmidt, J. (2005) 'Hegemonic Masculinity: Rethinking the Concept', *Gender and Society*, 19(6): 829–59.

Gelsthorpe, L. (2002) 'Feminism and Criminology' in M. Maguire *et al.* (eds) *The Oxford Handbook of Criminology*, 3rd edn, Oxford: Oxford University Press.

Heidensohn, F. and Gelsthorpe, L. (2007) 'Gender and Crime', in M. Maguire *et al.* (eds) *The Oxford Handbook of Criminology*, 4th edn, Oxford: Oxford University Press.

Walker, G. (2003) *Crime, Gender and Social Order in Early Modern England*, Cambridge: Cambridge University Press.

Chapter 11

Gender, genes and crime: an evolving feminist agenda

Nicole Rafter

Biological theories of crime pose difficult questions for feminists, who are often deeply invested in sociological explanations of behaviour. Not only do biological theories in general hold that crime is caused (at least in some ultimate sense) by biology, but the subdivision of evolutionary psychology argues that the same evolved mental modules or genetic factors that cause crime are also deeply implicated in the sex/gender organisation of society. In their general outlines, then, and in many of their details, biological theories seem to challenge feminist hopes for equality and self-determination. They do so, moreover, by claiming the imprimatur of hard science and at times by dismissing socio-feminist explanations as misguided, unsophisticated, or both (Campbell 2006; Walsh 2002; Wright 1994). Feminists, in turn, are often dismissive about biological theories of crime, consigning them *en masse* to the trash heap of sexist conservatism. And yet, few if any feminists would want to dismiss Darwinism or new genetic discoveries out of hand, and many of us would like to find ways to reconcile our feminist convictions with the biological sciences.

This chapter explores the implications for feminist criminology of biological theories in general and the explanations of evolutionary psychology in particular. It does so by retracing my own path over the past three decades through the thickets of thinking about gender and crime. Building on my efforts over the last several years to come to terms with biocriminology, I hope to at least stimulate discussion among other sociologically trained feminists who find themselves confronting the sciences in this, the much-heralded 'century of biology'.

The blank-slate position of the 1970s and 1980s

In the nature–nurture debate over the source of gender differences, participants in second-wave feminism, myself included, placed our bets on nurture. Of our many reasons for seeking the sources of inequality in social factors, most important was the recent memory of what the Nazis had done in the name of biology. We were also deeply influenced by the civil rights movement, grounded as it was on the belief that racial disparities originate in prejudice and inequity, not innate differences. Moreover, in the 1970s it was natural to turn to social explanations, for sociology provided the framework for criminological research. Another factor pushing us towards nurture-type explanations was annoyance at the way criminology ignored crime by women. 'The deviance of women is one of the areas of human behaviour most notably ignored in sociological literature,' Frances Heidensohn wrote (1968: 160) on page one of the founding document of what became feminist criminology. Similarly, Dorie Klein (1973: 3) sounded the first note in US feminist criminology with the observation that 'Female criminality has often ended up as a footnote to works on men that purport to be works on criminality in general'. Men simply wrote women out of the picture – a result, we believed, of social power, not biology.

In line with our preference for nurture over nature explanations, we distinguished between gender and sex, defining sex in terms of the body, as a biological given, and gender in terms of social roles, as the superstructure built on the foundation of sexual characteristics. 'Gender is not a natural fact but a complex social, historical, and cultural product,' wrote Kathleen Daly and Meda Chesney-Lind in their definitive 'Feminism and Criminology' article (1988: 504); 'it is related to, but not simply derived from, biological sex differences and reproductive capacities'. Gender was to sex what nurture was to nature, mind was to body, and the social was to the biological.

Although we thought in terms of these and other dualisms, few of us tried to tackle the tough political and philosophical issues that the dualisms implied. Indeed, I doubt that in the 1970s I understood that a 100 per cent nurture claim *did* imply a dualism. Nor did I understand that my stance was in some ways the mirror-opposite of what the newly hatched 'sociobiologists' were saying. While E. O. Wilson (1975) and other sociobiologists claimed that human nature lay in the genes – in the ways in which humans had evolved – I claimed that it lay in social circumstances – in the ways in which societies had evolved. I was no more prepared than E. O. Wilson to admit to one-sided thinking.

Life with Lombroso

The sociobiology of the 1970s was in fact not an entirely new field but rather an updated version of nineteenth-century evolutionism, particularly the work of Herbert Spencer and Charles Darwin, which explained human behaviour in terms of natural selection and a struggle for survival. Such work had depicted human females as inferior to males – more passive, less variable, less capable, and less civilised. In criminology, far and away the most famous proponent of evolutionism had been the Italian psychiatrist Cesare Lombroso (1835–1909), the founder of criminal anthropology and self-proclaimed first scientific criminologist. Far from arguing against the blank-slate position or nurture position, Lombroso began by assuming that there is no slate at all: we are what our biology dictates, be it males, females, prostitutes, political assassins, or born criminals.

My own thinking about biology, gender and crime has been shaped by involvement, with my colleague Mary Gibson, in the production of new translations of Lombroso's criminological work. Initially I knew very little about how Lombroso's atavism theory of crime, according to which criminals are throwbacks to a more primitive evolutionary stage, related to the scientific thought of his day. I was drawn to retranslate Lombroso because, like Mary Gibson, I found it impossible to study the history of criminology with the fragmentary and inaccurate English translations of Lombroso's work then available. In addition, I was fascinated by what Lombroso said (or seemed to have said, to judge from those suspect translations) about criminal biology. The great criminologist of the body, Lombroso had been at ease with criminalistic freaks, obscene tattoos, and violent death. Even more than 1970s deviance theorists, he had been drawn to the marginal and bizarre, the edgy and transgressive – attractions I shared.

However, Lombroso's name was infamous among feminist criminologists. Mainstream criminologists, although they had long since rejected Lombroso's biologistic explanations of male crime, continued to draw on the Italian's work to explain female crime (see, for example, Mannheim 1965). Thus Lombroso's name became synonymous with a regressive, sexist positivism and Lombroso himself became a kind of avian centaur: sitting duck in front, whipping boy behind. He was a sitting duck because, to judge from *The Female Offender* (Lombroso and Ferrero 1895/1915) – at the time, the only English translation of his work on female crime – he had made a great many offensive remarks about women. He could serve as our whipping boy not only because he was dead, and thus unable to protest, but also because he evidently had been a hardcore biological positivist – the opposite of what we wanted to be as criminologists. And so we lashed away, ridiculing what we thought Lombroso had said and failing to understand his work because few of us (but see Smart 1976) knew how to situate it historically.

As Mary Gibson and I worked from the original text of 1893, we discovered that the translator of *The Female Offender* had covered only a quarter of Lombroso's original. Whereas Lombroso and his assistant Guglielmo Ferrero had titled their work *La donna delinquente, la prostituta e la donna normale*, *The Female Offender* omitted much of the material on prostitutes and all of the commentary on 'normal' women – material crucial to Lombroso's argument. It also omitted nearly all the passages on the sexual characteristics of female criminals, such as lesbianism, virility, and anomalies of the breasts and genitals. In good Victorian fashion, moreover, it sanitised Lombroso's language and thought. Reading *The Female Offender*, one would never guess that Lombroso had a keen interest in sexual pathology or that he had contributed to the development of sexology as a field of study. (Our new edition [Lombroso and Ferrero 2004] includes all four parts of the original text and restores the sexual material excised and bowdlerised by *The Female Offender*. Following Lombroso's original, we titled the new edition *Criminal Woman, the Prostitute, and the Normal Woman*.)

It would be difficult to overstate Lombroso's carelessness as a scientist. Moreover, he was deeply steeped in the 'scientific' racism and sexism of his day, and he did indeed uncritically accept the then current precepts of biological determinism. But, as our new translation of his *Criminal Man* (Lombroso 2006) shows even more clearly, he was not a strict biological determinist, for his criminological theory took social factors into account as well. And whether or not one likes what he said, his historical significance is undeniable: it was Lombroso who first conceived of criminology as a science; it was he who first formulated an evolutionary theory of crime; and it was he who anticipated current genetic theories of crime (Rafter 2006). He was, moreover, crucial to the development of the positivist tradition that, for better or worse, remains dominant in criminology and without which the field would not exist at all.

Furthermore, Lombroso produced the first book-length study of female crime – a work that for a long time remained the only such study of its kind. Arguably, Lombroso was the first person to take female criminality seriously. And while he did indeed sexualise female criminality, as the early critics complained, and portray 'good' women as submissive housewives, it is important to recognise that he was not inventing his evil women out of whole cloth but rather drawing on ancient and pervasive myths about women's nature. Indeed, the madonna–whore dichotomy predated him by at least 2,000 years.

The emergence of evolutionary criminology

By the late 1980s, sociobiology had begun to segue into evolutionary psychology (or EP, as it is commonly called). Within a few years, EP became one of the most fertile, if contentious, fields in contemporary science and a seemingly bottomless source of best-sellers in pop psych. According to EP, we are psychologically what we have evolved to be – what our genetic make-up has become through natural selection and other evolutionary processes.

Central to EP is the contention that men and women differ in basic predispositions with regard to reproduction and the sexual division of labour. Women, we are told, are more passive than men and less interested in sex; what we want most is a good man to provide for our children. Gender traits, EP further holds, are genetically determined. From this basic picture it is not difficult to get back to the madonna–whore dichotomy that had pervaded Lombroso's work on female crime, a move many evolutionary psychologists have been quick to make. These EP enthusiasts include *New Republic* editor Robert Wright, who explains that 'From a Darwinian standpoint, loose women are in some ways great *sex* partners, because they're so easy to get'. Men 'won't always insist on marrying a Madonna, of course, virgins being scarce ... Still men do often draw a morally colored distinction ... viewing some kinds of women as full-fledged human beings ... and other kinds as something more like pieces of meat' (Wright 1994: 40, emphasis in original).

Evolutionary psychologists have been much criticised for the shoddiness of some of their science, the rapidity with which they reach sweeping conclusions on the basis of guesses about what must have happened Back Then, and the conservative political slant of much of their work (Rose and Rose 2000). And yet criminologists, including some with little or no background in evolutionary biology, have been quick to apply EP principles to offending. Most notoriously, they have used EP to explain rape:

According to the evolutionary theory of rape, the male reproductive advantage derived from having multiple sex partners has resulted in natural selection favoring genes promoting brain patterns for 'pushiness' in pursuit of sexual intercourse. In some males, genes may carry pushiness to the point of actual force . . . [O]ver generations, pushy males will probably be more successful at passing on their genes, including any genes coding for readily learning pushy sexual behavior, than will less pushy males. (Ellis and Walsh 1997: 234–35)

Criminologists have also applied EP to homicide and other offences (e.g. Daly and Wilson 1998; Ellis and Walsh 1997; Walsh 2002). And sexual harassment, in the EP view, is simply a misunderstanding between naturally chilly women and naturally hot-blooded men (Wright 1994).

EP has created a kind of sluiceway, refilling the criminological pool with sexist notions that feminists have spent decades bailing out. Yet evolutionism and feminism are not necessarily at odds. Using a Darwinist-feminist framework, Brown University biologist Anne Fausto-Sterling and her colleagues have recently explained teen pregnancy among poor girls – and proposed a feminist solution to the problem (Fausto-Sterling *et al.* 1997). In *Not by Genes Alone: How Culture Transformed Human Evolution*, Peter Richerson and Robert Boyd (2004) have advanced a fascinating Darwinist argument according to which culture sometimes 'walks evolution on a leash'; although not itself feminist, their theory appears to be compatible with a feminist perspective. What is problematic is the way Darwinism has at times been introduced into criminology by evolutionary psychologists with very little evidence but in ways that reinforce gender hierarchies and family configurations that went out with the 1950s. EP has been used, as evolutionism was used in the nineteenth century and sociobiology was used in 1970s, to further conservative political agendas.

Feminist criminologists have been slow to enter the 'Darwin wars'. This hesitation is probably sensible, given that like most other criminologists, few of us have a background in evolutionary psychology or genetics. However, we can and should argue back, on empirical as well as theoretical grounds, against the claim that there is something natural and therefore excusable about rape and sexual harassment. In addition, we should counter EP claims about women's weaker sex drive, relative to men's, and their relative sexual passivity; so far as I know, there has never been an adequate study of human female sexual interests and capacities. More positively, feminist might want to look further into EP, if they can push aside the sexist underbrush, for EP offers intriguing possibilities for theorising about the origins of violent behaviours and sex differences in overall crime rates.

These possibilities have been explored by psychologist Anne Campbell, who brings not only EP expertise but also a feminist perspective to explaining variations in crime by women and men. Campbell (1999) and Campbell *et al.* (2001) view female evolutionary adaptations as positive developments, not simply the obverse or slow versions of male adaptations. Instead of looking at women's experiences only when the topic is sex crime, Campbell includes women's adaptations across the criminological spectrum. She treats patriarchy as an aspect of culture that pathologises female aggression, reinforcing the gender hierarchy; and she recommends rewarding women economically and socially for child-rearing. Campbell's feminised criminological EP will find its critics, just as EP more generally does. But her work is more scientifically plausible and far more carefully argued than most other EP theories of crime, and it offers a good example of ways in which evolutionary criminology and feminist criminology can converge.

Rediscovering the body

The sex/gender debate that we thought had been settled in the 1970s re-erupted in the 1990s. Thomas Laqueur's *Making Sex* (1990) dissolved formerly clear boundaries between sex and gender, male and female, showing that our understanding of sexual difference is historically contingent. Judith Butler's *Bodies That Matter* (1993) turned our epistemologies upside down, making us question our formerly confident distinctions between sex and gender. About the same time, Marjorie Garber's witty study of cross-dressing, *Vested Interests* (1992), sensitised us to the fluidity of sexual orientations and sex/gender identities. Meanwhile, through transplants, implants and excisions, women and men ventured ever further into the uncharted seas of sexual ambiguity, defying both bodily givens and social taboos. Women grew beards, men sprouted breasts, lesbians got pregnant, and young western women covered themselves with tattoos like Japanese yakuza. Such adventuresomeness proved again and again that sex and gender, far from being fixed, are rather in constant flux. Today in feminist theory one seldom finds the simple nature/nurture, body/mind and social/biological divides of earlier discussions; instead, one finds a search for ways to surmount dichotomies (see also Lorber 1993).

As I started to teach and write about biological theories of crime, the terms of the debate shifted for me. I became less interested in the theoretical significance of the sex/gender distinction and more in the relationship of the individual body to culture and the social circumstances into which it is born. Geneticists, I found, had long ago rejected biological determinism; some had even ceased giving biology causal primacy over environment. The more I read, the more I wanted to get beyond the denial of nature with which I had begun. Moreover, like other feminists I was becoming dissatisfied with constructivist positions and hoped to replace them with a more 'embodied' epistemological understanding.

Although I am still searching for a fully satisfactory way of understanding relationships between bodies and their social contexts, I have found two helpful models. First, in an article on 'Genes, Environment and the Development of Behaviour', animal behaviourist Patrick Bateson of the University of Cambridge rejects the old dichotomies of nature versus nurture and innate versus learned behaviour to propose a 'jukebox' model of development. Bateson begins with an example involving grasshoppers:

> Some normally green grasshoppers growing up on African savannah blackened by fire are also black and prefer black backgrounds. As a result they are less easily detected by predators. However, their offspring, developing among new grass, suppress the mechanisms making black cuticle and are once again green. ... [C]ases are known where particular genes are only expressed in special environmental conditions ...

> The study of individual differences in behaviour has been revolutionised in recent years by the discovery of similar cases throughout the animal kingdom. More and more examples of striking differences in reproductive behaviour are being found between members of the same species which are of the same sex and age. Each individual is capable of developing in more than one way – a jukebox with the potential for playing many tunes but, in the course of its life, playing only one. The particular tune it does play is triggered by the conditions in which it grows up. (Bateson 1998: 161, textual references omitted)

Bateson's vision of a complex, dynamic interplay of organism and environment – of a genetic jukebox – offers a model in which genes and their environments interplay with a multitude of possibilities, working in unison and reciprocally rather than hierarchically or in temporal sequence. Moreover, his observation about the 'striking differences in reproductive behaviour ... being found between members of the same species which are of the same sex and age' fits with my own evolving sense of sex and gender as continua of possibilities.

A second, more explicitly feminist model turns up in Anne Fausto-Sterling's new work (2005), 'The Bare Bones of Sex'. Examining how 'culture shapes bones', Fausto-Sterling rejects 'the nature/nurture dualism', even though it has been 'a mainstay of feminist theory', in favour of 'dynamic systems theories [that] can provide a better understanding of how social categories act on bone production' (Fausto-Sterling 2005: 1 of 23). Fausto-Sterling urges us to 'work with the idea that we are always 100 per cent nature and 100 per cent nurture' (2005: 9 of 23). 'The sex-gender or nature-nurture accounts of difference', she concludes (2005: 10 of 23), 'fail to appreciate the degree to which culture is a partner in producing body systems commonly referred to as biology – something apart from the social'.

The dynamic systems theory that Fausto-Sterling sets forth in this article (and in a followup Part 2 on race) allows for multi-causality and body–society interrelatedness, not only in bones but also in sex, gender and – although she doesn't discuss it – criminality. The model ties culture and body together inextricably. Genes and environment, body and society, interact, with the causal arrows going in both directions. A criminological example can be found in the phenomenon of maternal malnutrition, which can damage a fetus, causing mental retardation that can then feed into criminal behaviour, if only by producing a person susceptible to manipulation by more criminally inclined others. In this example, the causal sequence begins with social factors – the poverty and lack of dietary information that lead to malnutrition. The policy implications seem obvious and fully in line with feminist goals: anti-poverty and maternal education programmes.

Neither feminist theory nor the field of biology is likely to stop evolving, and the two models that I find helpful today will doubtless prove less satisfying in the future. But these models have the great virtue of fitting comfortably with both science and feminism. They offer ways to think about feminist theory and biological theories of crime simultaneously. They require neither the easy determinisms of some EP explanations nor some of EP's essentialist statements about men's and women's nature. We can entertain the models while pursuing the feminist dream of equality *and* absorbing contemporary genetics.

We will have even greater need of such flexibility in decades ahead as the 'century of biology' moves into its future and the consequences of the genome project become increasingly apparent. We are going to have to come to terms with the new genetics. We will also need to find new ways to combine feminism and criminology if we want feminist criminology to remain a vital alternative to mainstream criminology.

Feminists need to engage more confidently and forcefully in their encounters with the biological sciences. We need to push ourselves and our students to integrate biological findings that seem sound and relevant, and to critique biocriminological theories of the past and present. We need to trace the genealogies of ideas such as the low-intelligence explanation of criminal behaviour to show how it changed over time, responding to new scientific and social circumstances. Central to my course on biological theories of crime are these questions; what is science, and how do we recognise it when we see it? I ask students to spot the holes in EP arguments and in other biological work on crime, current and historical. We discuss how the biological and social sciences can supplement one other in the study of criminal behaviour. I ask them to steer clear of simple dichotomies and to recognise change (in individuals, in societies, in sciences) over time. Just as feminists have a lot to learn from the biological sciences, so too does biocriminology have a lot to learn from feminist social scientists, and we should not hesitate to add our voices to emerging discourse on biology etc.

References

Bateson, P. (1998) 'Genes, Environment and the Development of Behaviour', in *The Limits of Reductionism in Biology*, Novartis Foundation Symposium 213, New York: John Wiley and Sons: 160–70.

Butler, J. (1993) *Bodies That Matter: On the Discursive Limits of Sex*, New York: Routledge.

Campbell, A. (1999) 'Staying Alive: Evolution, Culture, and Women's Introsexual Aggression', *Behavioural and Brain Sciences*, 22: 203–52.

Campbell, A. (2006) 'Feminism and Evolutionary Psychology', in J. H. Barkow (ed). *Missing the Revolution: Darwinism for Social Scientists*, Oxford: Oxford University Press: 63–99.

Campbell, A., Muncer, S. and Bibel, D. (2001) 'Women and Crime: An Evolutionary Approach', *Aggression and Violent Behavior*, 6: 481–97.

Daly, K. and Chesney-Lind, M. (1988) 'Feminism and Criminology' *Justice Quarterly*, 5(4): 497–535.

Daly, M. and Wilson, M. (1988) *Homicide*, New York: Aldine de Gruyter.

Ellis, L. and Walsh, A. (1997) 'Gene-based Evolutionary Theories in Criminology', *Criminology*, 35(2): 229–76.

Fausto-Sterling, A. (2005) 'The Bare Bones of Sex: Part 1 – Sex and Gender', *Signs* 30(2): 1491–1528. Downloaded from http://0-galegroup.com.ilsprod. ib.neu.edu on 4 December 2005.

Fausto-Sterling, A., Gowaty, P. A. and Zuk, M. (1997) 'Evolutionary Psychology and Darwinian Feminism', *Feminist Studies*, 23(2) (Summer): 403–18. Downloaded from http://0-find.galegroup.com on 4 December 2005.

Garber, M. (1992) *Vested Interests: Cross-Dressing and Cultural Anxiety*, New York: Routledge, Chapman and Hall.

Heidensohn, F. (1968) 'The Deviance of Women: A Critique and an Enquiry', *British Journal of Sociology*, 19(2): 160–75.

Klein, D. (1973) 'The Etiology of Female Crime: A Review of the Literature', *Issues in Criminology*, 8(2): 3–30.

Laqueur, T. (1990) *Making Sex: Body and Gender from the Greeks to Freud*, Cambridge, MA: Harvard University Press.

Lombroso, C. (2006) *Criminal Man*, ed. and tr. M. Gibson and N. Rafter, Durham, NC: Duke University Press.

Lombroso, C. and Ferrero, W. (1895/1915) *The Female Offender*, New York: D. Appleton and Company.

Lombroso, C. and Ferrero, G. (2004) *Criminal Woman, the Prostitute, and the Normal Woman*, ed. and tr. N. Rafter and M. Gibson, Durham, NC: Duke University Press.

Lorber, J. (1993) 'Believing is Seeing: Biology as Ideology', *Gender and Society*, 7(4): 568–81.

Mannheim, H. (1965) *Comparative Criminology: A Textbook*, Vol. 2. London: Routledge & Kegan Paul.

Rafter, N. (2006) 'Cesare Lombroso and the Origins of Criminology: Rethinking Criminological Tradition', in S. Henry and M. M. Lanier (eds) *The Essential Criminology Reader*, Boulder, CO: Westview Press: 33–42.

Richerson, P. J. and Boyd, R. (2004) *Not by Genes Alone: How Culture Transformed Human Evolution*, Chicago: University of Chicago Press.

Rose, H. and Rose, S. (eds) (2000) *Alas, Poor Darwin: Arguments Against Evolutionary Psychology*, New York: Harmony Books.

Smart, C. (1976) *Women, Crime and Criminology: A Feminist Critique*, London: Routledge & Kegan Paul.

Walsh, A. (2002) *Biosocial Criminology*, Cincinnati: Anderson Publishing.

Wilson, E. O. (1975) *Sociobiology*, Cambridge, MA: Belknap Press.

Wright, R. (1994) 'Feminists, Meet Mr. Darwin', *The New Republic*, 28 November: 35–46.

Chapter 12

Gender and crime: a human rights perspective

Marisa Silvestri

As criminology progresses into the twenty-first century, discussions about its state of health continue to abound. The diagnosis is mixed, and readings of the past, present and future states of criminology vary enormously. One thing we can be sure about is that the impact of feminist perspectives is clearly observable on criminological research, policy, and practice agendas. Writers interested in gender have taken on the challenge of making women, and more recently men, visible within the criminological enterprise. With the impact of feminist perspectives so clearly visible, there is much to be proud of. Indeed, one might question the need to pursue new directions and approaches to the study of gender and crime. Despite the significance of feminist perspectives, the extent to which mainstream criminology has acknowledged such contributions remains a contested point. Comack (1999) argues that feminism and those with a gender agenda remain very much on the margins of the discipline. Criminology's response to feminist work is described by Heidensohn (2000: 4) as a 'token genuflexion, rather than true respect and consideration of gender issues'. This chapter responds to calls for new approaches by considering the usefulness of a human rights framework for the study of gender and criminal justice. Exploring new directions offers us the opportunity to restate the continuing significance of gender within criminology. In doing so, we can try to avoid the empirical and conceptual complacency that often descends on disciplines and remain vigilant of the evolving and ever-changing nature of the field. Above all, this chapter provides an opportunity to combat the growing mantra in criminal justice and broader circles that 'all things are equal now' and ensures that we keep gender on the agenda. The chapter is divided into three main parts. The first part will consider the state of criminology and maps out the logic behind searching for new directions within the study of gender and crime. The second part introduces readers to the development and growing importance of a human rights discourse. The third and final part outlines the significance of a human rights framework for the study of gender and crime by considering the female prisoner in greater depth.

The state of criminology

In summing up the debates about the state of criminology, South (1998: 122) argues that criminology 'is either in deep crisis, close to being dead and buried, or else has come through a period of conflict, resolution and consolidation, to reach a point of renewed vitality'. He concludes that criminology seems to be in a rather vigorous state of good health, producing new directions and some reflexive debate. Before giving criminology a clean bill of health, however, it might be prudent not to overstate its vigour. If we look at the indices being used to map its condition, for example, Walters (2003) reminds us that the traditional markers, normally associated with health, in this case, the growth of criminological centres, journals, programmes and student numbers, are not necessarily evidence of a discipline in a healthy or productive state; in many cases, he argues, it may indicate the converse. Some commentators have bemoaned the lack of theoretical innovation within criminology (Rock 1994) and others have pointed to the 'perverse' and 'deeply disturbing trends in the *content* of criminology' (Hillyard *et al.* 2004, original emphasis). Hillyard *et al.* offer an insightful discussion on the current state of the criminological research agenda. They argue that 'alongside the noise of criminology – the ceaseless chatter advocating the extension of criminal justice practices and "solutions" – there stands a series of telling, sustained silences' (2004: 371). In particular, they note the absence of questions about power within criminological research agendas and detail the lack of attention dedicated to investigating state criminality and liability. Such characterisations of criminology are easy to make given the ongoing influence of Home Office funded research in criminology. Described as an almost entirely atheoretical fact-gathering, narrow and policy-friendly body, it should also come as no surprise that in orientation its agenda is couched in 'practical, policy relevant concerns rather than in terms of the theoretical development of an academic discipline' (Morgan 2000: 71).

On a more optimistic note, it may be that, as predicted by Heidensohn (2000), change is afoot, with some innovative work being conducted today by newer generations in criminology. Indeed, the 'Reawakening of the Criminological Imagination' was the key theme of the British Criminology Conference in 2005. When thinking more specifically about the issues of gender and criminology, we can see that the relationship between women, femininity and crime, and increasingly men, masculinity and crime, continues to assume an increased visibility and political significance within both criminology and the public arena. Not only have such works assumed a greater visibility, they have also matured within criminology. As the disciplinary boundaries become increasingly blurred in most fields, criminological works have become much more interdisciplinary in nature. If we scan the criminological literature that has emerged over recent years, it becomes fairly evident that some of the more interesting work has taken on the task of engaging with new vocabularies, new terms, and concepts outside of the discipline. In support of this position, Heidensohn (2000: 3) notes that 'criminology has to be renewed every so often from external sources or outside visitors'. In the quest for new directions, new vocabularies and new concepts, this chapter is underpinned by an interest in human rights. One of its key aims is to provoke greater discussion about the location and operation of power through highlighting the role of the state with regard to those it imprisons.

The development of a human rights discourse

Though the language of rights has enjoyed a long history, the 'human rights project', to which this chapter refers to, should not be confused with the historical concept of 'natural rights'.[1] Contemporary references to human rights are those that refer to the rights that belong to every human being solely by virtue of his or her membership of humankind. In this sense human rights are frequently held to be 'universal'. The various international principles of human rights were developed in response to the world's outrage when the full account of Nazi atrocities became public knowledge. On 9 December 1948, the UN General Assembly approved the Convention on the Prevention and Punishment of the Crime of Genocide. On the very next day, 10 December 1948, the UN General Assembly adopted and proclaimed the Universal Declaration of Human Rights (UDHR). The declaration itself goes far beyond any mere attempt to reassert all individuals' possession of the right to life as a fundamental and inalienable human right. It is a declaration that represents a statement of principles or moral guidelines for the recognition and protection of fundamental human rights throughout the world (Kallen 2004; Nickel 1992). Articles 1 and 2 of the UDHR set out the three cardinal principles of human rights – freedom, equality and dignity – as rights and freedoms to which everyone is entitled without distinction of any kind. The 28 articles that follow identify particular rights and freedoms exemplifying the three central principles. A more in-depth and critical discussion of the origins of the 'human rights project' can be found in Woodiwiss (2005).

With human rights firmly established on the statute books since 1948, some important changes have taken place in the past decade that have forced the issue of human rights firmly back on to both national and international agendas. During this time, there has been a clear shift in the way in which we think about human rights and our ability to access them; this is particularly true when thinking about human rights at a national level. In December 1996 Jack Straw, the then Shadow Home Secretary, and Paul Boateng MP produced a consultation paper, *Bringing Rights Home*, which set out the Labour Party's proposals to incorporate the convention rights into United Kingdom law. Infused with optimism, the paper claimed that the Human Rights Act would 'nurture a culture of understanding of rights and responsibilities at all levels in our society ... result[ing] in a human rights culture'. The Human Rights Act (1998) came fully into force on 2 October 2000, enabling the European Convention on Human Rights (ECHR) to be relied on directly in our domestic courts.[2] So what was once a discourse reserved for dealing with international abuses of communities and individuals whose access to power was severely limited, the ability to claim one's human rights at the beginning of the twenty-first century is now taking place at a national and domestic level.

The sales pitch accompanying the Human Rights Act (1998) has been impressive so far. Described as having the potential for being one of the most fundamental constitutional enactments since the Bill of Rights over 300 years ago, the Joint Committee on Human Rights (2002: para 9) states that the Act would 'help to inaugurate a gradual transformation of civil society', creating a 'more humane society', working to 'deepen and widen democracy by increasing the sense amongst individual men and women that they have a stake in the way in which they are governed'. Others have been even more ardent in their support. Baroness Helena Kennedy declares: 'something is happening: a different *Zeitgeist*, a shift in the legal tectonic plates'. Professor Wade observes a 'quantum leap into a new legal culture' (cited in Costigan and Thomas 2005: 51).

Given the ongoing rampant and atrocious nature of some international human rights abuses, there may be some commentators who question the need to draw on human rights at a domestic level; British citizens do, after all, enjoy the benefits that come with living in a democratic state. Kallen (2004: xiv) makes a strong case for focusing on democratic states when she argues: 'If all human rights scholars shifted their attention away from democratic societies, what could well happen is that we neglect to "clean up our own back yards".' The very fact that our democratic societies' laws and social policies are predicated upon human rights principles of justice and equity for all citizens may blind us to the very real violations that might occur. If having access to one's human rights is about confirming our civilised condition (Woodiwiss 2005), then focusing on the human rights of *all* citizens is an important project, domestic offenders included. Drawing on a human rights framework then, becomes much more about understanding how justice and equality are defined and delivered in society. Woodiwiss (2005: xiii) neatly sums this up when he states that the 'coverage, content, inclusions, and exclusion of rights tells us not only who is protected against what, but also the sort of people and the aspects of social relations that are especially valued (or not) by the governmental body responsible for constructing, approving and enforcing the regime'.

In October 2002, the government noted the complementary nature of equality and human rights in its consultation paper *Equality and Diversity: Making it Happen*. The paper reflected the government's vision of a society based on 'fair and equal treatment for all and respect for the dignity and value of each person' (Women and Equality Unit 2002: para 9.3). Following a series of consultation papers, the government accepted the strong case for developing a single commission, and so on 30 October 2003 the Secretary of State for Trade and Industry and Minister for Women, Patricia Hewitt, announced the decision to proceed with a single Commission for Equality and Human Rights. The Commission is expected to come into existence from 2007. While it may be somewhat premature to begin to speculate about its impact, achieving equality is no longer simply a question of discrimination but is now firmly associated with achieving human rights. The power of a human rights approach within this context rests on its capacity to provide redress for those experiencing social exclusion and who lack the power or necessary agency to change their disadvantaged status. And this is where criminology enters the debate. For achieving one's human rights is inextricably bound up with achieving justice, an obvious and central concern for criminologists. So what can a human rights discourse offer the study of gender and crime? How can we begin to draw on these developments to improve women and men's experiences of criminal justice? This chapter forms part of a broader study on gender, crime and human rights. In Crowther-Dowey and Silvestri (2007) we go beyond the focus of this chapter, the female prisoner, and maintain that human rights is uniquely placed to take on board the concerns of both women and men as offenders, victims and criminal justice professionals.

What can human rights offer women in prison?

The closed nature of the penal system in itself makes all those held in detention, be they women or men, particularly vulnerable to breaches of their human rights. Furthermore, prisoners often share backgrounds and characteristics, which heighten their vulnerability. The Chief Inspector of Prisons, Anne Owers (2004: 110) describes this dialectic:

> It is particularly the marginalised who need the protection of human rights: by definition, they may not be able to look for that protection to the democratic process, or the common consensus. And most of those in our prisons were on the margins long before they reached prison (look at the high levels of school exclusion, illiteracy, mental disorder, substance and other abuse); and may be even more so afterwards (with difficulty in securing jobs, homes, continued treatment, and even more fractured family and community ties). Prisons exclude literally: but they hold those who are already were and will be excluded in practice.

With the female offender absent from governmental, policy and criminological thinking for much of the time, the dramatic and alarming increase in the number of women in prison in the last decade[3] has seen her return on to government and criminological agendas. More specifically, a concern over the quality of care that women in custody receive has been the focus of various criminological, official and campaigning studies.[4] The overwhelming consensus of these studies is that women in custody are particularly vulnerable on entering the criminal justice system and that the experience of prison impacts on them in a particularly damning way. Research has shown that women suffering from poor physical and mental health, the social effects of poverty, addictions and physical and sexual abuse are over-represented in the prison population (Carlen 2002). A recent Home Office study found that 66 per cent of female prisoners were either drug dependent or reported harmful hazardous levels of drinking in the year prior to custody. Half the women in one Home Office survey said they had experienced domestic violence and the true figure is likely to be higher (cited in Fawcett Commission 2004). The same report shows that the majority of women in prison have experienced some form of abuse, and that a history of abuse is one factor among others contributing to the risk of offending and of a range of associated problems, including drug and alcohol problems, mental health problems and self-harm (Fawcett Commission 2004). With a higher proportion of women than men entering prison with a mental health problem, Carlen and Worrall (2004) argue that women's physical and mental healthcare needs in prison are more varied and complex than men's.

It would be inaccurate to portray the female prisoner as devoid of any formal rights. In claiming the authority to imprison one of its citizens, Mathiesen (2000) reminds us that the state is undertaking a responsibility for the prisoner's health, safety and physical well-being that is qualitatively greater than that owed to free citizens. And, while prisoners may lose much when they enter prison, they also maintain and acquire some rights. The Prisons Inspectorate does already rely heavily on international human rights standards in setting its 'expectations' against which it measures conditions for prisoners (HMIP 2004). The standards are broad based and incorporate every aspect of prison life, including transportation and reception, healthcare, education, legal rights and protection from harm. They also extend to the need to seek alternatives to custody, through preventative measures, and the reintegration of prisoners into society. While most principles apply to all prisoners, some are gender or age specific, and others relate to the issue of racism or other forms of discrimination in prison (Scraton and Moore 2004).

There are some positive procedures that are designed to encourage the special status of women's rights. So far as possible, men and women should be detained in separate institutions. In those institutions holding men and women, 'the whole of the premises allocated to women shall be entirely separate' (United Nations 1955: 8,a). In women's prisons there must be a special provision for prenatal and postnatal care. Where possible, babies should be born outside prison. When babies are permitted to stay with their mothers in prison, there should be nursery provision staffed by qualified personnel (United Nations 1955: 23,2). Women's prisons should be staffed predominantly by female officers. Although it is permissible for male members of staff, such as doctors and teachers, to carry out professional duties, male members of staff should not enter the part of the prison set aside for women unless accompanied by a woman officer (United Nations 1955: 53,1).

Carlen and Worrall (2004) remind us that not all of the rights are 'absolute' and the 'rule of law' in a civilised society limits and qualifies some of them. They also argue that the prison service has shown a high degree of complacency about the impact of the Human Rights Act. Despite this, there are now some cases being brought which challenge prison treatment generally (under Article 3), the prison disciplinary system (under Articles 6 and 7) and restrictions on contact with families (under Article 8). The state is also obliged to ensure effective independent monitoring and inspection processes. Where there are grounds to believe that a violation of human rights has taken place, the state is under an obligation to conduct a 'prompt and impartial investigation' or ensure than an inquiry takes place (United Nations 1999: Article 9: para 5). The United Kingdom has also recently signed up to the *Optional Protocol to the Convention against Torture and other Cruel, Inhuman or Degrading Treatment or Punishment*, adopted by the United Nations in December 2002. The object of the Protocol is 'to establish a system of regular visits undertaken by independent international and national bodies to places where people are deprived of their liberty, in order to prevent torture and other cruel, inhuman or degrading treatment or punishment' (United Nations 2002).

The following section focuses on three main issues that face the female prisoner: their over-representation in suicide and self-harm statistics, contact with their children and families, and the experience of girls in prison. In doing so, I consider the relevance of Article 2: the right to life, Article 8: the right to private and family life, and the United Nations' Convention on the Rights of the Child.

Suicide and self-harm: the right to life

When a person is in the custody of the state, the state has a particular duty to safeguard their right to life. More specifically, the prison service claims to operate the concept of the 'healthy prison'. Drawn from international human rights principles, the prisons inspectorate uses the World Health Organisation's four tests of what constitutes a healthy custodial environment to measure and assess the prison regime. In determining whether or not an establishment is 'healthy', it tests whether: prisoners are held in safety; if they are treated with respect and dignity as human beings; if they are able to engage in purposeful activity; and if they prepared for resettlement (Scraton and Moore 2004). Upholding the right to life is especially significant regarding women prisoners who are clearly over-represented in the suicide and self-harm statistics (Liebling 1994). While women constitute 6 per cent of the prison population in England and Wales, 20 per cent of prison suicides from January to August 2004 were women (Asthana and Bright 2004). From one female suicide in custody in 1993, the next decade saw a dramatic rise in which 14 women and girls killed themselves while in prison (Home Office 2003).

As part of the overall development of the 'healthy prison' and following a growing concern over the level of suicide and self-harm in women's prisons, there have been a number of important changes to the delivery of healthcare within prisons in recent years. Since the publication of two critical reports from Her Majesty's Chief Inspectorate of Prisons (HMCIP) in 1990 and 1999, on the way in which the prison service perceives and deals with suicide, there has been a recognition of the need within the prison service to develop strategies directed towards identifying and meeting the needs of women and young prisoners. The reform in healthcare in prisons has at its centre the principle of equivalence in standards of healthcare with that of healthcare in the community. In 1997, Her Majesty's Inspectorate of Prisons went on to favour an integration of the healthcare for prisoners with that of the National Health Service. CARAT teams (counselling, assessment, referral, advice and throughcare) now operate in all prisons, offering assessment and referral services for the high numbers of women in prison with substance abuse problems.

Such developments suggest that the prison service has recognised its official obligations towards its inmates. Recent investigations into the healthcare of women in prison, however, portray a prison service working at odds with the concept of a 'healthy' environment. While prisoners retain the right to have healthcare equivalent to that available to those outside the prison, research points to an inconsistent picture within the prison estate. The quality between prisons varies considerably: some prisons providing healthcare broadly equivalent to NHS care, but many are characterised by low-quality care, with inadequately trained and professionally unsupported doctors, which fails to meet proper ethical standards (Reed and Lyne 1997). More specifically, the worrying lack of proper detoxification programmes for women has the effect of creating unsafe environments in which women are neither held decently nor able to be effectively assessed and prepared for resettlement (HMCIP 2005). Lowthian (2002) also stresses the poor regimes that characterise women's prisons in England and Wales. In particular, she notes poor healthcare and hygiene standards; a lack of holistic needs-based programmes for women; an overemphasis on security and discipline over 'non-mandatory' tasks due to staff shortages; an inappropriate allocation of prisoners; and an overall inadequate standard of care due to staff shortages.

It is these very conditions that have come to define the experience of imprisonment for many women. This chapter has already stressed that on entering prison women bring with them a distinctive type of vulnerability. With this in mind, Liebling (1992, 1995) emphasises the significance of the prison environment in contributing to the risk of suicide. She notes that for certain groups of prisoners, 'the situational aspects of their prison lives may be decisive' and that those most vulnerable are 'expected to undergo an experience whereby the demands made may exceed the resources available' (Liebling 1995: 183). There is little doubt that the cumulative effects of the conditions outlined above pose serious problems for women and may well serve to increase the risk of self-harm and suicide. Recent work undertaken by the Commission on Women and the Criminal Justice System (Fawcett Commission 2004) confirms these findings and further points to a lack of throughcare upon release back into the community.

It was specifically because of the special vulnerability of people in detention that the Northern Ireland Human Rights Commission decided to make the human rights of prisoners one of its strategic priorities. Following the controversial death of 19-year-old female prisoner Annie Kelly in Northern Ireland in 2002, the highly critical HMCIP (2003) report on Mourne House revealed that the Northern Ireland Prison Service had no dedicated policy or strategic plan for the treatment of women and girls in custody. It pointed to a number of alarming conditions, including an inappropriate level of security; a regime based on lengthy periods of lock-up offering an insufficiently busy and active day; an unhealthy balance of male staff to female prisoners; the strip-searching of women without reasons being given; insufficient information and support for women on their first night in prison; and no structured induction programme. The inspectors were especially critical of the treatment of suicidal and self-harming women, noting the inappropriate use of the main male prison hospital and punishment blocks for distressed women prisoners.

Following publication of this report, Scraton and Moore (2004: 142) confirmed the concern about the punitive context within which physically and mentally disturbed women and girls are treated. Critical of the lack of available counselling and therapeutic provision for those with mental health needs, they noted: 'Holding women prisoners, particularly girl children for 28 days in bare cells with nothing to read, listen to or look at amounted to a real and serious deprivation.' Furthermore, 'the use of the strip cell with no mattress, no pillow, a heavy duty blanket, a potty for a toilet to be slopped out and no in-cell access to a sink was degrading and inhumane and, possibly in breach of Article 3 of the European Convention on Human Rights and of Article 3 of the Human Rights Act' (2004: 144). In sum, their findings raise serious concerns about the extent to which the treatment of women and girls in custody is compliant with international human rights law and standards. Their findings point to a prison service operating a disregard for the concept of the 'healthy prison', which 'at best neglected the needs of prisoners and at worst added to the hopelessness, helplessness, and desperation experienced by many prisoners made vulnerable through their incarceration' (2004: 83).

While the capacity of the prison service to uphold its duty of care to those it imprisons remains questionable, several recent landmark cases of deaths in custody have forced the issue firmly within a human rights framework. When taken together, the Amin[5] case, related to the death of teenager Zahid Mubarek at Feltham Young Offenders Institution in 2000, the Middleton case[6] concerning the suicide in prison of Colin Middleton in 1999, and the Sacker case,[7] in which Sheena Creamer was found dead while on remand at New Hall prison in 2000, establish the important principle that deaths of people in custody should be effectively and thoroughly investigated and that the investigation should cover the measures taken to safeguard an individual's life (Scraton and Moore 2004). In March 2004, following the inquests into the death of Colin Middleton and Sheena Creamer, the House of Lords ruled that juries in inquests into jail deaths are to be allowed to blame failings in the prison system for contributing to an inmate's suicide. Five law lords unanimously ruled that an earlier ruling virtually barring jurors from blaming shortcomings in the prison system for contributing to a prisoner's death no longer applied. The Human Rights Act, with its guarantee of the right to life, now meant that jurors were entitled to say not only 'by what means' a prisoner had died, but also 'in what circumstances', the judges ruled (Dyer 2004). These landmark cases are pivotal in confirming the state's obligation to protect life.

Imprisoning mothers: the right to private and family life

Despite their incarceration, prisoners have the right to a private and family life (Article 8). In order to facilitate this, where possible prisoners should be held in institutions reasonably near their home. The state also has a duty to provide assistance to a prisoner's children. Further rights for the children of prisoners can be found in the broader United Nations Convention on the Rights of the Child (UNCRC). The UNCRC is important in that it emphasises that all the rights it identifies apply to *all* children and that there should be no discrimination on the grounds of the activities or status of the child's parents.

Article 9 of the Convention states that the child has a right to maintain regular contact with both parents unless it is contrary to their interests. In real terms, however, the structural configuration of women's prisons has very real and detrimental consequences for women's ability to maintain contact with their families. The small number of establishments that accommodate women means that they are, on average, more likely to be located further from their families than men are. The Chief Inspector of Prisons reported that 60 per cent of women surveyed were more than 50 miles from home (HMCIP 2005). One of the ways in which the prison service has responded to the concept of maintaining family life has been to allow women to keep children with them in prison. For women with a child under 18 months, mother and baby units are available. The units are staffed by trained prison officers and employ professional nursery nurses and the prison accepts a duty of care towards the baby in relation to health issues.

In their work on prisons in Northern Ireland, Scraton and Moore (2004: 143) report that the right of women in prison and their children to a meaningful family life was not respected. They found that women were restricted to brief periods of unlock during which they could make telephone calls to their children, and there were no special arrangements made for family visits. Women complained that they were often only able to see their children for 45 minutes each week. It is worth reiterating here that the deleterious effects on family life of imprisoning mothers continues well after they have served their sentences and are released back into the community. Women's vulnerability also extends beyond their time in custody. While women have many of the same resettlement needs as men, there are additional factors relating to their caring responsibilities, histories of abuse and discrimination in the labour market that further compound their vulnerability. Director of the Prison Reform Trust Juliet Lyon (2004) describes the consequences of imprisonment for women:

> There is a high price to pay for overuse of custody. Imprisonment will cause a third of women to lose their homes, reduce their future chances of employment, shatter family ties and separate more than 17,000 children from their mothers.

With the female prisoner more likely to be the primary carer of dependent children than her male counterpart, the National Association for the Care and Resettlement of Offenders (NACRO) found that a significantly higher proportion of the children of female prisoners than male end up in care; and for those children that are taken into care, there is an increased likelihood of them becoming offenders themselves (Fawcett Commission 2004). Furthermore, Caddle and Crisp (1997) found that the children of imprisoned mothers displayed a variety of behavioural problems, including sleeping and eating problems, bed-wetting, becoming withdrawn and problems in developing overall social skills.

While the establishment of mother and baby units may appear at first glance to be an attempt to address the specific vulnerability of women offenders with children, Carlen and Worrall's (2004) argument that their very existence is also said to encourage courts to send mothers with babies to prison instead of seeking out the alternatives is perhaps a more convincing one. The very idea of imprisoning women with children, together with the current organisation of the women's prison estate, hinders and indeed militates against the possibility of achieving the right for private and family life. An interesting point is raised by Carlen and Worrall (2004) when they ask what rights prisoners' children have among all this. Their answer is simple: 'not many'. There is clearly much to be gained from thinking outside of the 'penal box' (Hannah-Moffat 2002). We have much to learn from penal systems further afield. The Ter Peel experiment in the Netherlands is often cited as a model of provision. Here, children remain with their mothers up to the age of four years but attend nurseries outside the prison on a daily basis (cited in Carlen and Worrall 2004). In Russia, mothers of children under the age of 14 who are convicted of all but the most serious offences are routinely given suspended sentences until the child reaches 14. In Germany, women are housed under curfew with their children in units attached to prisons but outside the gates (Fawcett Commission 2004: 49).

Children – the incarceration of girls

With the United Kingdom currently locking up more young people than any other country in Europe (Howard League 2002), the issue of children and young adults in the prison system continues to take centre stage for penal reformers. This chapter has so far emphasised prisoners' vulnerability in making its case for a human rights approach. The issue of vulnerability is ever more pressing for children who come into contact with the criminal justice system. Goldson (2002: 7) observed that children in prison can be 'innately' and/or 'structurally' vulnerable. They have more often than not suffered family breakdown, poverty, educational failure and various forms of abuse. As a result, he argues that the social circumstances of the children who inhabit our prisons are invariably 'scarred by multiple and inter-locking forms of disadvantage and misery' (2002: 27).

A core principle of the UNCRC and other international human rights standards is that the 'best interests' of the child should be the primary consideration in all actions and interventions concerning the child (Article 3). Given their special vulnerability, children have the right to protection from harm and to have their physical integrity protected (Article 19). The detention of children should be used only as a measure of last resort and for the shortest appropriate period of time. Further, every child deprived of liberty shall be treated with humanity and respect for the inherent dignity of the human persons and in a manner that takes into account the needs of person of his or her age (Article 37).

The vulnerability of girls who encounter the criminal justice system has long been a concern for academics. Research has pointed to the overly harsh treatment that girls receive throughout their interactions with the criminal justice system. Conceptualised as 'wayward' and in need of 'protection', girls are invariably harshly sanctioned for non-criminal offences and trivial misdemeanours. It is here that the criminal justice system operates a double standard. Often, girls have broken moral and not legal rules and find themselves being punished for behaviour that flaunts normative expectations (Chesney-Lind and Shelden 1998; Phoenix 2002).

The vulnerability of girls is intensified and exacerbated on reaching prison. Unlike boys, girls are held in inappropriate establishments, where it is difficult to meet their specific needs. A report conducted by the Howard League for Penal Reform in 1997, *Lost Inside*, found that a number of girls under the age of 18 were being held alongside adult women in adult jails. The report also found that staff had little or no training in dealing with vulnerable girls. Yet the vulnerability of girls was marked: 2.2 per cent had self-harmed; 6.5 per cent had experienced family breakdown; 40 per cent had been in care; and 41 per cent reported drug or alcohol abuse. Despite the human rights principle that children have a right to family life, and that contact with family is crucial in terms of children's rehabilitation, Scraton and Moore (2004) found that there was no evidence of any appropriate and essential provision by the prison service to ensure that children and young prisoners were given as much access as possible to family and friends. It is within this context of vulnerability that 19 children killed themselves in prison in England and Wales between 1993 and 2003 (Joint Committee on Human Rights 2003).

Following the publication of *Lost Inside*, the Howard League has challenged a number of breaches of human rights through the courts. It supported and gave evidence at a judicial review of Home Office policy concerning the holding of girls under 18 alongside adult prisoners.[8] The court ruled that it was unlawful for the Secretary of State automatically to place children in an adult prison. In 2002 the Howard League successfully challenged the prison service insistence that the protection of the Children's Act 1989 did not apply to children in prison.[9] Since then there have been some important developments regarding the holding of girls in the penal system. In April 2004 the government announced its intention to remove girls from adult prisons and embarked on a building programme of four specialist units for detaining teenage girls.

While the intention to separate girls from adult prisoners is a welcome one, to suggest that such a move will act as a remedy for dealing with the multiple problems that girls in custody face is rather short-sighted. Frances Crook, director of the Howard League, reminds us that

Specialist units for girls in adult prison have been tried and failed not least because it is impossible to detach them totally from the rest of the prison. Even if physically separated from the adults, girls held in prison are still living in a punitive adult culture with high levels of self-harm, suicide, poor staff training and low staff ratios. (Howard League 2004)

Such a position is echoed in Lord Carlile's (2006) *Inquiry into the Treatment of Children in Penal Custody*, which found that some of the treatment children in custody experience would in another setting be considered abusive and could trigger a child protection investigation. More significantly, the Inquiry underlines the importance of human rights by asserting that the rule of law and protection of human rights should apply to all children equally, regardless of whether they are detained in custody or in the community.

Conclusion

This chapter has provided a brief insight into some of the ways in which a human rights framework might be applied to understanding women's experience of custody. Despite its potential, there is much uncertainty about the future of the human rights agenda. The extent to which a rights-based culture will develop in Britain remains to be seen but early indications are not encouraging. Work by Costigan and Thomas (2005: 44) indicates that despite the initial anticipation among legal commentators of the deluge of work that would be generated with the advent of such law, this new avenue to recourse has resulted in a 'trickle of cases' and that 'going down the human rights way is often a last refuge for a lawyer who hasn't got a case, rather than the first port of call'. Sedley (2005) adds to the critique of the legal profession by pointing out that very few of those in the profession know about the actual operationalisation of human rights law. More specifically, he bemoans the pedagogic shortfall within university curriculums in training our future legal professionals. The implications of this are considerable. If the legal profession are not fully immersed in the potential of a human rights discourse, the public are almost certainly not. It is unlikely then, that we will be in a position to promote, let alone protect, the human rights of offenders, who after all remain a politically unpopular and undeserving group.

While a rapidly rising prison population and a reducing budget are often used to explain the shortcomings of the penal system, the lack of appropriate care given to prisoners goes beyond financial and administrative concerns. The integration of the 'healthy prison' concept will not, of itself, overcome the uneasy relationship that exists between the delivery of care within punitive containment (Sim 1990). Hannah-Moffat's (2002) account of failed penal reform in women's prisons in Canada illustrates this well. Despite a well-intentioned, women-centred strategy of reform, she argues that a major barrier to the realisation of any meaningful structural reform is its 'denial of the material and legal reality of carceral relations embodied in the prison' (Hannah-Moffat 2002: 203). Her work serves as a powerful reminder of the very real limits of reform within existing penal systems where prisoners are not perceived as deserving of their basic human rights.

The current contradictory nature of government policy on women's imprisonment provides further grounds for concern. There is nothing concrete to suggest that the government is committed to reducing the number of women in prison. The promise by government to pilot radical new approaches to meet the specific needs of women offenders, to tackle the causes of crime and reoffending among this group and to reduce the need for custody, outlined in the Comprehensive Spending Review in 2004, has been accompanied by an expansive building programme. Two new private prisons are being built to hold a further 800 women and £16 million is being spent on juvenile jail units (Lyon 2004). These developments have taken place against a backdrop of recommendations aimed at developing a national network of local women's supervision and rehabilitation support centres linked to local custodial units (Wedderburn 2000; Fawcett Commission 2004). This failure to invest in innovative penal practice is best summed up by Lowthian (2002: 164) when she states that such policies indicate 'a disregard for meaningful change and unwillingness to genuinely foster new approaches'.

It is precisely during such times of disregard and contradiction that we should strive to keep the human rights of the offender on the agenda. To reiterate, the language of human rights offers a vocabulary for those interested in understanding the location and operation of power within a gendered criminal justice system. If approached in this way, the vulnerability of women who inhabit our prisons will become glaringly obvious. More broadly, adopting a human rights perspective offers us an opportunity to rethink and fracture our conception of the offender, and while offenders may continue to be unpopular, we might begin to conceive of them as deserving of their human rights. It is through the re-framing of prisoners as people with rights rather than privileges conditional upon good behaviour that the potential of a human rights agenda may be realised. As the delivery of punishment increasingly moves to private hands, the need to be ever vigilant about what goes on behind closed doors becomes ever more pressing.

Notes

1 'Natural rights' were not rights held solely by virtue of one's humanity. Rather, natural rights, in reality, were rights of dominant westerners: white European men. Some 80 per cent of all human beings were excluded. (Kallen 2004)

2 The Scotland Act 1998 and the Northern Ireland Act 1998 had already brought the European Convention on Human Rights into United Kingdom law in 1998.

3 The figure for women in prison at 10 March 2006 stands at 4,450 (www. womeninprison.org.uk). This is in sharp contrast to the number in 1993, where the average number of women prison stood at 1,500 (Howard League for Penal Reform).

4 The publication of the wide-ranging *Thematic Review of Women in Prison* in 1997 marks a turning point for official discourses on women in prison. The Scottish Office published *Women Offenders – A Safer Way: A Review of Community Disposals and the Use of Custody for Women Offenders in Scotland* in 1998 (Social Work and Prisons Inspectorates for Scotland 1998). For England and Wales, the government's *Strategy for Women Offenders* was published for consultation in 2000. The key findings of the consultation that followed have fed directly into the development of the Women's Offending Reduction Programme (WORP), a three-year programme to address the factors that affect women's offending.

5 R (*Amin*) v Secretary of State for the Home Department [2003] UKHL 51. The *Amin* case related to the death of teenager Zahid Mubarek, who in March 2000 was beaten to death by a racist prisoner sharing his cell in Feltham Young Offenders Institution. Zahid Mubarek's family lawyers argued that Article 2 of the ECHR entitled the family to a public hearing and the House of Lords ruled in October 2003 that there should be a public inquiry into the death. The subsequent inquiry into his death and the surrounding issues is ongoing.

6 R (*Middleton*) v West Somerset Coroner and another [2004] UKHL 10. The Middleton case concerns the suicide of Colin Middleton in January 1999. The case concerned the state's procedural obligation to investigate a death possibly involving a violation of Article 2. The House of Lords ruled in March 2004 that, while not attributing criminal or civil liability, an inquest should find out 'how' the person died, not simply 'what means' but also 'in what circumstances'. Middleton's mother, who had brought the initial

case, did not seek a fresh inquest, just an order that the jury's findings be publicly recorded.

7 R (*Sacker*) v West Yorkshire Coroner [2004] UKHL 11. The Sacker case relates to the death of 22-year-old Sheena Creamer, who was found dead in August 2000 while on remand at New Hall Prison. The coroner had ruled that the inquest jury could not attach a rider of 'neglect' to its verdict. The House of Lords judged in March 2004 that the inquest has been deprived of its ability to address the positive obligation of Article 2 to safeguard life and ruled that a new inquest should be held.

8 R v Accrington Youth Court, ex parte Flood [1998] 1 WLR 156.

9 R (*on the Application of the Howard League for Penal Reform*) v Secretary of State for the Home Department [2002] EWHC 2497 (Admin).

References

Asthana, A. and Bright, M. (2004) 'Suicides rise as weekend jail fails women', *Observer*, 11 August.

Caddle, D. and Crisp, D. (1997) *Imprisoned Women and Mothers*, Home Office Research Study 162. London: Home Office.

Carlen, P. (ed.) (2002) *Women and Punishment: The Struggle for Justice*, Cullompton: Willan Publishing.

Carlen P. and Worrall, A. (2004) *Analysing Women's Imprisonment*, Cullompton: Willan Publishing.

Lord Carlile (2006) *Inquiry into the Treatment of Children in Penal Custody*, London: Howard League for Penal Reform.

Chesney-Lind, M. and Shelden, R. G. (1998) *Girls, Delinquency and Juvenile Justice*, Belmont, CA: Wadsworth.

Comack, E. (1999) 'New Possibilities for a Feminism "in" Criminology? From Dualism to Diversity', *Canadian Journal of Criminology*, 41(2) April: 161.

Costigan, R. and Thomas, P. (2005) 'The Human Rights Act: A View from Below', in L. Clements and P.A. Thomas (eds) *Human Rights Act: A Success Story?* Oxford: Blackwell Publishing.

Crowther-Dowey, C. and Silvestri, M. (2007) *Gender and Criminal Justice: A Human Rights Perspective*, London: Sage.

Dyer, C. (2004) 'Inquest juries blame suicides on jails, law lords rule', *Guardian*, 12 March.

Fawcett Commission (2004) *Commission on Women and the Criminal Justice System*, London: Fawcett Society.

Goldson, B. (2002) *Vulnerable Inside: Children in Secure and Penal Settings*, London: The Children's Society.

Hannah-Moffat, K. (2002) 'Creating Choices? Reflecting on the Choices', in P. Carlen (ed.) *Women and Punishment: The Struggle for Justice*, Cullompton: Willan Publishing.

Heidensohn, F. (2000) *Sexual Politics and Social Control*, Buckingham: Open University Press.

HMCIP (1990) *Suicide and Self-harm in Prison Service Establishments in England and Wales*, London: HMSO.

HMCIP (1999) *Suicide is Everyone's Concern: A Thematic Review*, London: Home Office.

HMCIP (2003) *Report of a Full Announced Inspection of HM Prison Maghaberry*, Northern Ireland Prison Service, 13-17 May 2002.MH.01.

HMCIP (2004) *Expectations: Criteria for Assessing the Conditions in Prisons and the Treatment of Prisoners*, London: HMSO.

HMCIP (2005) *Annual Report of Prisons for England and Wales, 2003–2004*, 26 January.

Hillyard, P., Sim, J., Tombs, S., Whyte, D. (2004) 'Leaving a Stain Upon the Silence: Contemporary Criminology and the Politics of Dissent', *British Journal of Criminology*, 44(3): 369-90.

Home Office (2003) www.homeoffice.gov.uk/rds/pdfs/2/s95women03

Howard League (1997) *Lost Inside: The Imprisonment of Teenage Girls*, Report of the Howard League Inquiry into the Use of Prison Custody for Girls Aged Under 18, Howard League for Penal Reform.

Howard League (2002) Submission to the UN Committee on the Rights of the Child, *Children in Prison – Barred Rights*, Howard League for Penal Reform.

Howard League (2004) www.howardleague.org/press/2004 04.htm.

Joint Committee on Human Rights (2002) *The Case for a Human Rights Commission*, Sixth Report HL, (2002–03 67), HC (2002–03) 489, para 9.

Joint Committee on Human Rights (2003) *Inquiry into Human Rights and Deaths in Custody*, written evidence from Inquest, 15 December.

Kallen, E. (2004) *Social Inequality and Social Injustice: A Human Rights Perspective*, Hampshire: Palgrave Macmillan.

Liebling, A. (1992) *Suicides in Prison*, London: Routledge.

Liebling, A. (1994) 'Suicide Amongst Women Prisoners', *Howard Journal of Criminal Justice*, 33(1): 1-9.

Liebling, A. (1995) 'Vulnerability and Prison Suicide', *British Journal of Criminology*, 35(2): 173–87.

Lowthian, J. (2002) 'Women's Prison in England: Barriers to Reform' in P. Carlen (ed.) *Women and Punishment: The Struggle for Justice*, Cullompton: Willan Publishing.

Lyon, J. (2004) 'High price to pay for jailing women', *Observer*, 18 July.

Mathieson, T. (2000) *Prison on Trial*, 2nd edn, Winchester: Waterside Press.

Morgan, R. (2000) 'The Politics of Criminological Research', in R.D. King and E. Wincup (eds) *Doing Research on Crime and Justice*, Oxford: Oxford University Press.

Nickel, J. (1992) *Making Sense of Human Rights: Philosophical Reflections on the Universal Declaration of Human Rights*, Berkeley, CA: University of California Press.

Owers, A. (2004) 'Prison Inspection and the Protection of Human Rights', *European Human Rights Law Review*, 2: 108–17.

Phoenix, J. (2002) 'Youth Prostitution Policy Reform: New Discourse, Same Old Story', in P. Carlen (ed.) *Women and Punishment: The Struggle for Justice*, Cullompton: Willan Publishing.

Reed, J. and Lyne, M. (1997) 'The Quality of Healthcare in Prison: Results of a Year's Programme of Semi Structured Inspections', *British Medical Journal*, 315:,1420–24.

Rock, P. (1994) 'The Social Organisation of British Criminology', in M. Maguire, R. Morgan and R. Reiner (eds) *The Oxford Handbook of Criminology*, Oxford: Oxford University Press.

Scraton, P. and Moore, L. (2004) *The Hurt Inside: The Imprisonment of Women and Girls in Northern Ireland*, Northern Ireland Human Rights Commission, Northern Ireland.

Sedley, S. (2005) 'The Rocks or the Open Sea? Where is the Human Rights Act Heading?' in L. Clements and P.A. Thomas (eds) *Human Rights Act: A Success Story?*, Oxford: Blackwell Publishing.

Sim, J. (1990) *Medical Power in Prisons*, Milton Keynes: Open University Press.

South, N. (1998) 'Late-Modern Criminology: "Late" as in "Dead" or "Modern" as in "New"?', in D. Owen (ed.) *After Sociology*, London: Sage.

Straw, J and Boateng, P. (1996) *Bringing Rights Home: Labour's Plans to Incorporate the European Convention on Human Rights into UK Law* (text published 1997) E.H.R.L.R. 71–80.

United Nations (1955) *Standard Minimum Rules for the Treatment of Prisoners*, Office of the High Commissioner for Human Rights.

United Nations (1999) *United Nations Declaration on the Right and Responsibility of Individuals, Groups and Organs of Society to Promote and Protect Universally Recognised Human Rights and Fundamental Freedoms*, Article 9: para 5.

United Nations (2002) *Optional Protocol to the Convention against Torture and Other Inhuman or Degrading Treatment or Punishment*, Office of the High Commissioner for Human Rights.

Walters, R. (2003) 'New Modes of Governance and the Commodification of Criminological Knowledge', *Social and Legal Studies* 12(1): 5-26.

Wedderburn, D. (2000) *Justice for Women: The Need for Reform*, London: Prison Reform Trust.

Women and Equality Unit (2002) *Equality and Diversity: Making it Happen*, London: Women and Equality Unit.

Woodiwiss, A. (2005) *Human Rights*, Abingdon: Routledge.

Chapter 13

Gender, justice and human rights in post-colonial Zimbabwe and South Africa

Oliver Phillips

Introduction

In the struggle against colonial power, twentieth-century African nationalism subordinated women's rights to the demands of political and economic independence;[1] gender equality was either expected to develop automatically with liberation, or dismissed as 'a new form of cultural imperialism' (Seidman 1984: 432). But in twenty-first century post-colonial Africa an unprecedented array of international and regional legal instruments now promise to advance women's rights. As the site of considerable interaction between transnational and local governmental and non-governmental organisations this objective remains vulnerable to accusations of 'western' interference, a refrain all too familiar to the many post-colonial feminists obliged to negotiate the dialectic of local resistance to women's empowerment and universalist presumptions in western feminism (Narayan 1997: 1–40; Gilligan 1993; Menon 2000). The least contested campaigns for women's rights have frequently been those perceived to be 'above' culture and in the wider national interest; for instance, health-related and reproductive rights (e.g. reducing maternal mortality, teenage pregnancy and sexually transmitted infections), overlapping with violence against women (VAW) through a narrative of sexual harm.[2] Indeed, these areas delivered substantial alliances between feminists from across the world, ensuring greater integration of sexual and reproductive freedoms into women's rights through the Declarations at Vienna (1993), Cairo (1994) and Beijing (1995).[3] As women have developed increasingly global alliances, so they have needed to account more carefully for the differentials of culture and history.

> As feminism has sought to become integrally related to struggles against racialist and colonialist oppression, it has become increasingly important to resist the colonising epistemological strategy that would subordinate different configurations of domination under the rubric of a transcultural notion of patriarchy. (Butler 1993: 46)

Early feminist interventions in criminology (Heidensohn 1968, 1985; Smart 1977) focused primarily on the key questions of equality, informal social control, victimisation and deviance, and initiated the growth of an array of feminist critiques across the field. These impacted significantly on criminological studies of masculinity, sexuality and race, but the intersection of these (and other markers of identity) was brought into sharpest relief in the cross-cultural debates within feminist politics, bringing about a newly invested reflexivity.

> Universal images of 'the Third World woman' (the veiled woman, chaste virgin etc.) – images constructed from adding 'the Third World difference' to 'sexual difference' – are predicated upon (and hence obviously bringing into sharper focus) assumptions about Western women as secular, liberated, and having control over their own lives. (Mohanty 1991: 74)

As a result, definitions of 'feminism', 'gender' and 'sexuality' have been repeatedly interrogated by African women, with some writers explicitly criticising western gender dichotomies and theories as inappropriate for analysis in Africa (Amadiume 1997; Oyewumi 1997). Yet, it is these same conceptual categories that are used to deliver formal rights through legal instruments (whether national or international), that are imported through discourses of development, and that are often cited in their claims to justice by those unversed in these cosmopolitan, intellectual debates of semantics. The inherent dynamism of cultures, compounded by the post-colonial imperative of reinvention (Hobsbawm and Ranger 1991), leaves key definitions susceptible to both assertion from above and reinterpretation from below. Consequently, Uma Narayan suggests that critiques of their local culture by Third World feminists should be seen as 'just one prevailing form of intracultural critique', whose similarity to western feminism springs from the universal ubiquity of gender inequality, and whose mobilisation will be informed by their own experience of local culture (1997: 9–10).

Zimbabwe and South Africa are both societies where these issues are manifest in national politics today, as the treatment of gender, sexuality and cultural authenticity has become central to their concepts of justice and nationhood. A sudden increase in the discussion and visibility of sexuality is rooted in long-contested gender struggles and is heavily implicated in attempts to define each nation at its moment of post-colonial delivery. This post-colonial context invests discussion of gender and sexuality with a significant political dimension that is absent in the western world. Feminist and criminological analyses have to take into account that gender equity frameworks, mechanisms of social regulation, notions of deviance, victimisation, rights and duties are all hostage to the many legacies of colonisation. Furthermore, where criminal justice systems have lacked popular legitimacy, human rights have provided a framework for alternative visions of justice and been more explicitly included in the development of criminal justice and criminology. Not only does this provide a more 'insightful and critical' framework for thinking about crime (Silvestri, Chapter 12 in this volume) but it also certifies that the interpretation of 'rights' is subject to local negotiation rather than wholesale importation.

This chapter aims to illustrate these post-colonial complexities through reference to gender and justice in South Africa and Zimbabwe today, and to consider how sexual hierarchies and gender relations become either entrenched or transformed in specifically post-colonial moments of fissure and reinvention.[4] It will focus primarily on the three legal constructions that regulate relationships of sexuality and gender, and that frame their contested definitions in these countries. These are: first, the creation and present treatment of African customary law; second, the discourse of rights within colonial and post-colonial contexts; and third, the efficacy and credibility of the judiciary and constitution. The political debates that surround these three elements will be shown to reflect competing visions of justice in a post-colonial world that remains demonstrably unjust (and unequal). Focusing on this interaction of historical legacy and contemporary politics will highlight the fact that gender and sexuality, as sites of intersection for claims to cultural authenticity and equal rights, are key signifiers in contested definitions of post-colonial justice in Zimbabwe and South Africa.

This was most pointedly signified in the mid 1990s through contradictory approaches to homosexuality. Within months of

Zimbabwean President Mugabe's proclamation that 'I don't believe they [homosexuals] should have any rights at all,'[5] and the labelling of Zimbabwean homosexuals as the 'festering finger endangering the body' that government must 'chop off',[6] South Africa became the first country in the world to ratify a Constitution that included a prohibition of discrimination on the grounds of sexual orientation. The Constitutional Court has since ruled that sexual orientation should be no bar to absolute equality[7] in relation to employment benefits, adoption of children, immigration through partnership,[8] and most recently, marriage.[9] As these measures deliver specific rights of formal equality and unsettle the gendered hierarchy so fundamental to exclusive heteronormativity, they are more than a symbolic inclusion of homosexuals into the social body. They contrast markedly with neighbouring Zimbabwe's rejection of homosexuality as a 'white man's disease' integral to the colonialist corruption of 'traditional' African society. Elsewhere, I have analysed the role this 'whitewashing' of homosexuality played in discrediting the increased sexual autonomy of Zimbabwean women, positioning such autonomy as another alleged form of western imperialism (see Phillips 1997a, 1999, 2000). Both the sexual inclusivity of citizenship in the new South Africa and the sexual exclusivity of citizenship in Zimbabwe are intrinsic to the gendered construction of notions of entitlement and belonging in the post-colonial vision of these states. In each case, sexuality has been inherently integral to, and explicitly recruited to serve as, an index of citizenship and national identity at key moments of state transformation.

The subject of colonial and customary law

The contrasting treatment of gendered and sexual rights in present-day Zimbabwe and South Africa is partly driven by their different negotiation of a shared post-colonial dynamic. This is the difficult but practical reconciliation of a 'traditional' lineage-based culture with the development of universal rights and equality in a 'modern' nation state.[10] A situated analysis of the discourse of rights and the development of law will show that it is simplistic to view this as a crude conflict between 'tradition' and 'modernity'. Instead, Comaroff suggests that the legacy of the colonial state in Africa is one of 'alternative modernities', 'one based on the liberal ethos of universal human rights, of free, autonomous citizenship, of individual entitlement; the other assertive of group rights, of ethnic sovereignty, of primordial cultural connection' (2001: 64, cited in Van Zyl 2004: 158).

Comaroff ascribes these dynamics to the contradictory registers of 'radical individualism' and 'primal sovereignty' that simultaneously framed the colonial discourse of rights, not only providing the colonisers with their motivating rationalisations, but also distributing 'new forms of subjectivity, sovereignty and identity among Africans' (Comaroff 1997: 198). The register of primal sovereignty was predicated on the collective sense of identity that was reframed and emphasised with the colonial interventions in definitions of ethnicity,[11] for the colonial discourse of rights involved 'a discourse in which local peoples were made into ethnic subjects, racinated, and recast in an often antagonistic dialectic of construction and negation' (Comaroff 1997: 234). Counter-colonial forces frequently developed these 'contradictory registers' in constructing a nationalist politics that would unify the various ethnic and linguistic groups contained within the newly defined borders of the colonial state, thereby continuing this 'antagonistic dialectic'. This is also evident in the *African Charter on Human and Peoples' Rights* where individual rights and freedoms are qualified by group rights over the individual, as well as individual duties to the collective, to an extent not reflected in other international human rights instruments.[12] For the purposes of this chapter, however, the most pertinent manifestation of this 'antagonistic dialectic' is the historical treatment of women living under African customary law in both colonial and post-colonial periods.

In codifying customary law, colonial authorities distinguished those customs they thought merited validation into law, from those that had no need of legal status or were discerned to be 'repugnant to natural law, justice or morality'.[13] But before sifting through specific customs, it was necessary to validate their collective origins, and identify distinct groups of people who could be distinguished by their customs.

> 'Custom' came to be a crucial index of group identity … And as different groups became increasingly linked together in the colonial society and economy under a single administration which forced them to settle many of their disputes in its courts and according to its forms, claims about custom became more rigid. As people took a stand on their own customs in

'inter-tribal' cases, so the claims they made about them became more competitive and more explicit. And these explicit claims about custom were being made in a period of great upheaval and disruption ... Literacy changes the mutability of custom, but not automatically. Not all customs become fixed: there is competition about what will become part of the immutable tradition. (Chanock 1985: 9)

Law came to be seen as constitutive not only of the 'authenticity' of cultural norms, but also of those group identities to which individual complainants and offenders were assumed to be attached. For particular customs became associated with particular tribal groupings, and once inscribed in law, what had previously been customary possibilities became specific expectations of an affiliated identity. This problematic failure to easily distinguish ideal exhortations from normative behaviour was compounded by the fact that 'authoritative' interpreters of custom were most likely to present the position which most suited their own established interests and needs.

It is in this 'needs rather than knowledge' that the essential clue to the nature of African evidence about customary law is to be found. For the statements which were (and are still) made about it are not so much statements about what the law was in the past, as claims about what it ought to have been in the past and what it ought to be in the present. The question which faces us is not 'Are these statements true about the period of which they were being made?' but 'Why is there a need to present the past in this way?' (Chanock 1985: 8)

Diana Jeater's (1993) review of the development of the laws around marriage and adultery in colonial Rhodesia makes clear that the people testifying about the content of customary laws can be described as predominantly elder men of standing within their communities. This is unsurprising given the gerontocratic and patriarchal social structures out of which they would have come, to be heard by colonial authorities whose own notion of society was so hierarchically structured, and whose initial desire to emancipate African women from what were perceived to be 'primitive' structures of kinship was rapidly replaced by a recognition that colonial authority could not function without relying on African chiefs and headmen (Jeater 1993). For this reason, some of the early colonial laws impacting directly on women and their sexual independence were redolent with Comaroff's 'antagonistic dialectic of construction and negation' (1997: 234) as they demonstrated precisely the tension between definitions of personhood that were located in lineage and collective identity, and definitions of 'emancipated' individual subjectivity that adhere to the modern state.

The 1901 Native Marriage Ordinance (NMO), evincing this initial emancipatory concern, had the contradictory aims of constructing a legal framework to support African marriages while attempting to prevent African women from being forced into marriage. Consequently, it immediately bestowed on women a measure of potential autonomy from the men who, under customary law, were perpetually their legal guardians:

> The African idea that sexual identity was an aspect of lineage membership, and that individual members were answerable to the family group for the uses they made of their sexuality, was undermined at a stroke by the Ordinance's provision that no woman should be made to marry against her will. The women's rights were given priority over the rights of the lineage ...

> In effect, the State was usurping the rights of family heads to control the sexual choices of members of their households and lineages. The shift from answerability to the ancestors and the lineage to answerability to the State had major political implications in terms of the authority of 'big men' over the people, presenting client men and women as individuals not necessarily bound by or wholly defined in terms of lineage membership. (Jeater 1993: 81)

Ironically, this shift from lineage to state regulation was subsequently compounded by the attempts of family heads to use the colonial law to bring women back into their control. In persuading the colonial authorities to pass the 1916 Native Adultery Punishment Ordinance (NAPO), they specifically prohibited married African women from an act that was permitted for anyone else.[14] While this was aimed at restricting their agency, it also brought African women's particular social status increasingly within the realm of legal regulation. Women were legal subjects in so far as they could be held responsible for committing the offence of adultery, but they did not have the subjective legal status to be offended by a man's adulterous behaviour, nor did they have any further capacity to act in law other than through their male guardian. Nevertheless, in constituting the criminality of women's sexual autonomy, the NAPO implicitly relied on a notion of women's independent action and their specific responsibility for this agency.

Both the NMO and the NAPO initiated a transfer of control from lineage to state and suggest a shift from the power of the patriarch to the rights and obligations of an individual, but in reality they transferred on to women a partial subjectivity that was expedient for maintaining traditional relations of power. This subjectivity was partial in two senses: first, it was a negative subjectivity, as it was restricted to giving women the status to be arrested as offenders; and second, it was an incomplete subjectivity, as women had no legal standing of their own but could only operate in law through a male guardian, so it did not deliver direct or proper recourse to the protection offered by the law.[15] But it was also expedient as it was invested in women 'solely as adjuncts to the group, means to the anachronistic end of clan survival, rather than as valuable in themselves'.[16]

The lingering historical effects of this partial subjectivity remain a key issue in relations of gender and sexuality in contemporary Southern Africa. It is the reason that claims to sexual autonomy (for women and/or homosexuals), which invoke a sexuality owned by the self rather than rooted in lineage and family, foment such great anxieties. It is precisely this tension between 'traditional' lineage-based guardianship ('primal sovereignty') and the contrary notion of an individual autonomous legal subjectivity ('radical individualism' – arguably fundamental to claiming human rights[17]) that fuels the vacillating attempts of the Zimbabwean government to initially empower and then restrain women. In Zimbabwe an ambivalent approach to this tension undermines commitment to gender equality, whereas in South Africa a clear commitment to gender equality is enshrined in legal formalism, but remains to be realised where the legacy of women's partial subjectivity is deeply embedded.

Reconciling the authority of lineage-bound relationships with the authority of the state has significant implications for the procedure and practice of criminal justice as a whole. As an institution of the nation-state the criminal justice system engages with defendants in their individual capacity. Individual defendants bear specific responsibility for particular alleged offences. Theories of retribution, (specific) deterrence and rehabilitation are all primarily oriented towards the individual offender. On conviction, it is the individual offender who will serve the sentence handed down. In contrast, traditional practices rely on a model of restorative justice whereby responsibility for restitution is collective (e.g. family), rather than individual. This is because the negotiation of penalties (usually the payment of damages) is preoccupied with the re-establishment of equilibrium and the restoration of consensus, rather than with establishing individual responsibility for specific offences. Thus, when a man rapes a woman, under common law the state assumes the burden of prosecuting the individual offender and on conviction it is he personally who is punished. But under customary law, the representatives of the families will negotiate compensation for damages relating to the woman's value (as determined by bridewealth). Her lack of legal subjectivity in this regime means that any damages paid are given to the family as a whole in the person of her male guardian. Similarly, the underlying principle of restitution may even require the rapist to marry his unmarried victim. While in practice many women will have some active participation in this process, there is no guarantee of this. However, even if restitution has been agreed and paid between the families, the state still has a duty to prosecute cases that come to its attention, and in practice it does. Such duplication leads convicted offenders inevitably to complain that they are being punished twice for the same offence, and that this inflicts unjust economic hardship on their families as the cost of damages is dramatically compounded by the imprisonment of a key breadwinner (Phillips 1999: 133–78).

Post-colonial constitutional frameworks

The key distinction between South African and Zimbabwean negotiation of the relationship between 'radical individualism' and 'primal sovereignty' is clearly reflected in their constitutions. South Africa's new Constitution makes customary law explicitly subject to its equality clause prohibiting multiple forms of discrimination (Cap.2, s.9(3)), while Zimbabwe's Constitution contains a clause explicitly exempting customary, family and personal law from the fundamental rights and freedoms granted in its bill of rights (S.23(3)(a)and(b)). The significant impact this has on the development of rights, gender relations, and concepts of justice is clarified through analysis of the drafting and subsequent interpretation of each country's constitution.

South Africa's transition to democracy was phased across more than four years leading up to the first fully democratic elections in 1994.[18] The drafting and adoption of a new constitution was the 'primary objective' of the multi-party talks (Spitz and Chaskalson 2000: 34), in a two-stage process that would rely on an interim constitution to frame the first democratic elections, after which the final constitution could be legislated. An extraordinarily wide consultative process framed the negotiation of each constitutional provision in detail by participants with widely divergent initial positions. The process tempered these positions, and the final document was 'a moderate, liberal outcome' that emerged 'at the expense of both institutional protections for minority privilege and the more radical socio-economic reforms which many still regard as essential to long-term stability and justice' (Black 1999: 97).

Apartheid systematised inequalities through separation, differentiation, and the explicit provision of partial subjectivities according to race. The interim constitution made explicit that its premise was the transcendence of the 'divisions and strife of the past, which generated gross violations of human rights' (Spitz and Chaskalson 2000: 412). Similarly, the new (final) constitution speaks explicitly of 'diversity' and affirms the principle that differences between people should be reconciled to become a positive asset in building a strong democracy. This was put into practice through the unprecedented initiation of a Truth and Reconciliation Commission (TRC), but it is primarily enshrined in the constitution's 'Equality Clause'. This implicitly rejects partial subjectivities as it prohibits discrimination 'on any one or more grounds including race, gender, sex, pregnancy, marital status, ethnic or social origin, colour, sexual orientation, age, disability, religion, conscience, belief, culture, language and birth' (Chapter 2, S.9(3) of the South African Constitution 1996). 'Many of the categories listed above can be problematised,' writes Mikki Van Zyl,

> but as a broad collection they represent many of the concepts that have formed the basis of critiques about exclusions in existing interpretations of citizenship in modern democracies: five out of the sixteen are related to gender and sexuality, and six link to racialisation. Hence, it could be argued that the Equality Clause in the South African Constitution represents a quantum leap in formal rights for previously excluded groups. (Van Zyl 2004: 159)

The constitution explicitly guarantees social and economic as well as civil and political rights, and expressly authorises affirmative action (Cap 2, s.7(2)). To oversee this, Chapter 9 establishes the Commission on Gender Equality 'to promote respect for gender equality and the protection, development and attainment of gender equality'. But of most pertinence here is the clear decision not to dilute the Equality Clause with any exemptions for customary law, despite the entreaties of traditional leaders who perceived a direct threat to the patriarchal structures of customary relations.[19] Comaroff's conflict between 'radical individualism' and 'primal sovereignty' is thus resolved firmly in support of the former, as is made clear by Penuell Maduna, Minister of Justice and Constitutional Affairs (1999–2004):

> The new constitutional order cannot avoid placing the individual at the center of things … The individual is … linked to all sorts of groups – for example to a trade union, a parent-teacher association, or a church. But these entities cannot be allowed to dictate the individual's rights … For the majority of South Africans, customary law rights are not primary rights … One of the customary rights is the right of the traditional leader to lord it over you. I have never for one second in my life lived under a traditional leader, and I'm very much a black South African. Traditional law plays no role at all in my life … To follow the traditional law of succession, my son is my heir and my daughters wouldn't get anything. Is that what I want to happen to my children? They would live perpetually under male domination, and I honestly, seriously and utterly believe in the equality of the sexes … There is a tension between a Western-oriented society, as some people want to impose on us, and a pure African, 'Africanist' society. I think we are a mixture of all sorts of things but essentially, we place the individual at the center of human activity. (quoted in Spitz and Chaskalson 2000: 391)

The democratic process of the constitution's drafting delivered crucial legitimacy and authority to a court bound to uphold the constitution's sovereignty over Parliament and the Executive. Subsequent decisions by the Constitutional Court have asserted clear jurisdiction over both Parliament and the executive office of government without invoking significant challenge.[20] However, more recently, government drafted a constitutional amendment that would give the Minister of Justice responsibility for, among other things, courts' administrative and budgetary arrangements, the appointment of acting Constitutional Court judges, and the power to make rules for all superior courts.[21] Both the General Council of the Bar of South Africa and the International Bar Association have strongly criticised the proposed amendment, stressing that financial and administrative autonomy is fundamental to the independence of the judiciary.[22] At the time of writing President Mbeki had instructed his Justice Minister to review the Bill in light of this concern.[23]

There has also been considerable debate about the transformation of a judiciary that in 1994 consisted of 160 white males, three black males, two white females and no black females. Of the 53 judges appointed between then and April 2006, 90 per cent are black, and more than 20 are women.[24] While there is clear consensus about the need to transform the composition of the judiciary, there is disagreement over how to balance the speed of change with the need for juridical experience, particularly if the efficacy and independence of the judiciary is to be maintained. In 2004, heated arguments involving both race and judicial independence flared up in the Cape High Court, attracting considerable attention in the national press. The furore was fuelled by a comment from the ruling ANC that there was a need to transform the 'collective mindset' of the judiciary to bring it into line with the aspirations of the 'masses'; however, they denied that this was an attack on white judges, asserting that it was simply a reference to the transformation envisioned by the constitution.[25] The Chief Justice and heads of superior courts subsequently established an 'ongoing process' in each court and in judicial education and training programmes of measures that would ensure a 'conscious effort to break down racial and gender stereotypes, and to promote a culture of open discussion around such issues'.[26]

Both these recent debates around the independence and transformation of the judiciary have taken place openly, with some degree of passion and a modicum of invective, but no interference or vitriol has emanated from the executive arm of government thus far. The tone and content reflects the historical frustration and intense engagement that legitimately characterises discussion about the key issues of political transformation and accountability in South Africa today. These debates suggest that the constitution serves as a clear framework through which a just solution to these issues can be developed, so that institutions such as the courts can be transformed with their independence and authority intact. In practice, the consensus that has thus far sustained the jurisdictional authority of the courts arises from the constitution's exceptional legitimacy. This is derived from both the unusually inclusive process of its drafting and the power of the discourse of rights (whether civil, political, social, or economic) in a state whose prior absence of rights dramatically and until recently highlighted their necessity for all citizens.

In Zimbabwe there was never any similarly far-reaching and deep-seated attempt to develop consensus on the fundamental shape of the future state, nor was there any concerted attempt to reconcile through an open process of accountability such as the TRC. The political settlement that finally delivered independence was negotiated not in Zimbabwe but in London where the British government brokered negotiations between the different parties. The constitution currently in place in Zimbabwe was not produced through detailed discussion, but emerged from a very brief three months of talks whose preoccupation was the mechanics of a transition to democracy (ceasefire, re-entry of refugees, integration of armed forces, first election, etc.) (Chan 2003: 11–14). It contains a weak bill of rights and standard clauses that appear in the post-independence constitutions of other former British colonies in Africa, suggesting a default model. However, two key provisions (both now expired) reserving some white parliamentary seats and inhibiting the redistribution of land, led the ruling party ZANU-PF to view the constitution as an unwelcome obstacle in the country's transformation into an independent post-colonial state.[27] Consequently, where the constitution has prevented government from implementing its political will, President Mugabe has frequently lambasted it as a 'British' document and sought to sidestep it. At the same time, the weakness of the bill of rights and the authoritarian facility of the document, has suited government on those numerous occasions where they have implemented 'emergency' measures or been challenged on issues of human rights or civil liberties.[28] More recently, government has passed legislation that restricts political activities,[29] the freedom of the press,[30] freedom of movement, and most pertinently, judicial review of state appropriation.[31]

In 2000, government attempted to enact a new constitution but, partly as a result of its determination to increase executive powers in the face of popular opposition, it lost the referendum necessary to do so. This draft Constitution of 2000 did, however, confirm the government's dedication to promoting the register of 'primal sovereignty' and the accompanying partial subjectivity of women, as it included provisions affirming that the majority of women should not have the right to own property and offered a generally reduced commitment to women's rights.[32] President Mugabe is said to have been personally responsible for a clause that allowed for the overriding of any individual right in the name of 'public morality and public security', specifically including a prohibition of gay marriage (Chan 2003: 167). The 2000 referendum was the first electoral defeat for ZANU-PF in 20 years of rule, and their subsequent dismay was reflected in increasingly draconian legislation and unprecedented political violence. What followed was the invasion of commercial farms by 'war veterans'[33] and concerted attacks by government-sponsored youth militia on farmworkers and urbanites suspected of being sympathetic to the opposition.[34]

By 2001, the Supreme Court was regularly finding that government suppression of political opposition, its censorship of media and its implementation of land reform, were exceeding the bounds of the constitution. Furthermore, the courts entertained opposition complaints of localised rigging in the 2000 parliamentary elections. Such independence brought the Supreme Court into direct conflict with the Executive arm of government who repeatedly defied rulings of the High and Supreme Courts, and publicly attacked the integrity of those judges who showed some degree of judicial independence.

> The Minister of Justice questioned the desirability of white judges, 'war veterans' stormed the Supreme Court on 20 November 2000, and on 14 December Mugabe himself told a ZANU-PF congress that 'the courts can do what they want. They are not courts for our people and we should not even be defending ourselves in these courts'. (Chan 2003: 167)

Claiming the need to 'indigenise' the courts, government forced the retirement of senior judges. But the fallacy of this 'indigenisation' subsequently became apparent with the promotion of those judges who had ruled consistently in favour of government (ignoring constitutional restraints), over the heads of those black judges who were more senior, but had a record of judicial independence and political impartiality.[36] Ten out of the twenty judges on the Supreme and High Court benches resigned between 2001 and 2005, a number of whom alleged serious threats of violence from government agents,[37] and all of whom cited as reasons for leaving 'the erosion of the rule of law, outright harassment, demeaning acts and remarks targeted at the judiciary, and the government's contemptuous disregard of court orders'.[38] At least four of these ten judges were black, and many of them felt obliged to flee the country.[39]

In these first years of the twenty-first century, the relationship between executive and judicial arms of government is therefore demonstrably different in Zimbabwe and South Africa, and a key reason for this is arguably the relationship between the substantive content and the political credibility of their constitutional frameworks.

This relationship also facilitates or limits each constitution's role as a platform for gender equality. In South Africa lengthy consideration led to the explicit inclusion of many gender-related issues in its list of prohibited grounds of discrimination, whereas in Zimbabwe in 1996 the 14th amendment to the Constitution removed 'sex' from this list and replaced it with 'gender.' Previously, while discrimination on the grounds of biological sex was prohibited, discrimination on the grounds of gender was not, so that even those women who were living under civil law were vulnerable to the many gender stereotypes of socio-cultural origin that underpin discrimination. Subsequent to the 1996 amendment, discrimination on anatomical or biological grounds (e.g. pregnancy, menstruation, childbirth, lactation, or physical attributes) was no longer prohibited by the constitution. This fudging contrasts markedly with the careful articulation of so many different forms of discrimination in South Africa's Equality Clause.

> The current Constitution of Zimbabwe seems unclear about the distinction between sex and gender. Its drafters appear to have thought sex and gender were interchangeable synonyms. For if they were clear about this distinction and why both (sex and gender) should be prohibited as grounds for discrimination, then one can only conclude that our Constitution has been crafted deliberately to discriminate against women. (Zimbabwe Human Rights NGO Forum 2001: 2)[40]

Deliberate or not, the end result is that the rights offered to women through the constitution are limited on a number of counts. Their partial subjectivity is reinscribed through section 23 of the constitution where the priority of customary law over the bill of rights means that women's recourse to law is contingent on either their detachment from the traditional security of lineage or on their attachment to a man – and even after these conditions are realised, their right to equality is further limited to gender (excluding biological sex). The provisions of the constitution will inevitably obstruct advances in sexual rights, as the framework of the law does not anticipate even formal equality. This is despite the fact that Zimbabwe is a signatory to both the United Nations Convention for the Elimination of All Forms of Discrimination Against Women (CEDAW) and also The Declaration on Gender and Development passed by the Southern African Development Community (SADC) Council of Ministers in February 1997. This latter declaration contained a strong commitment to mainstreaming gender equality in national policy and 'ensuring the eradication of all gender inequalities in the region.'[41] Yet government policy on this matter is ambivalent at best, and counter-productive at worst; for instance, in 1999 the Women's Coalition began a campaign to remedy the lack of specific provision in law and police practice for dealing with domestic violence. After much campaigning the Domestic Violence Bill was drafted in 2003, but it still awaits enactment.

Legislating gender and producing politics

During Zimbabwe's Independence, ZANU-PF had been openly supportive of the principle of gender equality,[42] and soon after assuming power it passed the Legal Age of Majority Act (LAMA)(1982). This conferred legal subjectivity on all Zimbabweans over the age of 18 – immediately granting women the unprecedented possibilities of legal independence. Thus, women no longer need the consent of their guardian to enter into a civil marriage. But the majority of Zimbabwean women still marry under customary law rather than civil law. Section 23 of the constitution means that this majority of women still find themselves under the authority of a male guardian, have no legal subjectivity of their own, and their recourse to the fundamental rights and freedoms listed in the constitution is strictly limited by custom. The most explicit example of this in practice is the Supreme Court ruling in *Magaya* v *Magaya*, where the property accumulated by a woman was given to a younger brother who had had no role in its accumulation.[43] The decision provoked outrage as women's groups and human rights NGOs accused the Supreme Court of a regressive judgement that reversed any progress in women's rights made since 1980. But their anger should rightfully have been directed at a constitution that was, in fact, correctly interpreted (Bigge and von Briesen 2000: 289–313).

For Zimbabwean women the LAMA came to represent government's ambivalent flirtation with gender equality, as it was followed by increased censure of independent women. During the 1980s, the state carried out random street clear-ups in major urban areas of any women not possessing a marriage certificate or proof of employment (Jacobs and Howard 1987: 39–42), and during the 1990s facilitated a social atmosphere that led mobs of men to strip women naked in the street if their skirts were 'too short' (Phillips 1999: 238–44; and Jackson 1993: 25–6). In all of these cases, the harassment of women was justified with their denunciation as *mahure* (prostitutes), a word frequently used to describe women who display economic independence, or most particularly a sexual autonomy. The widespread application of this label to independent women is epitomised by a statement made in the early 1980s by the then Minister of Home Affairs that the abolition of *lobola* (bridewealth) would 'legalise prostitution' as 'a woman for whom *lobola* was not paid could easily move to another man' (Seidman 1984: 432).[44] While he was referring to those women who did not undertake a 'customary' marriage, this absolute resistance to sexual autonomy also reflects the perceived 'dangers' of lesbianism. Lesbians present an even greater challenge in that they choose to survive without men, and not just without men as their guardian. This has significant implications as a woman who does not marry (e.g. a lesbian) will bring no *lobola* into the family, thereby affecting the ability of her brothers to pay *lobola* for their own wives, and undermining the economic base of reproductive culture and kinship structures. This is a direct illustration of the conflict between the register of 'primal sovereignty' whereby sexual relations are defined in relation to lineage, and 'individual rights' whereby sexual relations are the distinct manifestation of individual autonomous choice.

Accepting that a woman can choose her partner is a fundamental precondition for her recognition as a fully entitled legal subject, for sexual independence is implicitly connected to broader structures of social and economic power. The refusal of this independent choice has been at the root of women's sustained partial subjectivity, for it was the key concern of both those Zimbabwean men who persuaded colonial authorities to pass the NAPO in 1916, and those who railed against homosexuals in 1995/6. The denigration of homosexuals invariably invoked cultural signifiers to depict them as foreign to Zimbabwean culture,[45] thereby relating the issue specifically to the register of 'primal sovereignty' and suggesting that homosexuality was being imposed at western insistence:[46]

> Homosexuality is unnatural and there is no question ever of allowing these people to behave worse than dogs and pigs, ... What we are being persuaded to accept is sub-animal behaviour and we will never allow it here. If you see people in your areas parading themselves as Lesbians and Gays, arrest them and hand them over to the police. (President Mugabe to ZANU-PF Women's League, 11 August 1995, quoted in *The Herald*, 12 August 1995).

This statement was made in Shona, which gives 'dogs' (*imbwa*) particular idiomatic significance consistent with Mugabe's calls for a return to 'our traditional values that make us human beings'.[47] He thereby invokes notions of *ubuntu* [48] (or *munhu* in Shona) that refer to the African conception that the humanity of individuals is derived from the society around them.[49] He also makes explicit his reliance on the register of primal sovereignty and applies it to the exclusion of individual rights. While this interpretative strategy might be consistent with the Zimbabwean Constitution, it is quite different from that which has emerged from the South African Constitution.[50]

In South Africa, distinguishing 'living' customary law from the 'formal' customary law that was constructed in the colonial encounter (as outlined earlier) allows the Constitution Court to critically appraise and reproduce it in a more organic rights-receptive form. Thus, while the Equality Clause will always trump customary law, considerable value is still given to 'living' customary law so that it is 'receptive to changing conditions and ... could be applied and developed in light of the rights and values of the Constitution' (Jagwanth and Murray 2002: 294). The decisions in *Moseneke*[51] and *Amod*[52] each deal with a widow married under different customary or religious arrangements and provide that 'proper consideration has to be given to ... the dignity of widows and their ability to enjoy a rightful share of the family's worldly goods'.[53] This renders impossible the ruling that was so unavoidable for the Zimbabwe Supreme Court in *Magaya*, even though customary arrangements of inheritance are historically similar in the two countries. Furthermore, the South African Recognition of Customary Marriages Act (120 of 1998) gives women full majority status and the right to acquire property in their own names, thereby recognising the value of customary law in many people's lives, while formally removing the constraints of women's partial subjectivity. Predictably, the new constitution has also fostered a considerable amount of equality legislation of direct application to all women,[54] most of which would be impossible under the Zimbabwean Constitution.

However, one particular Constitutional Court ruling provides an indication of the limits of sexual autonomy and individual rights in the new South Africa. In the case of *Jordan*,[55] the majority judgement found that where the Sexual Offences Act criminalised sex workers but not their clients (sex purchasers), there was no gender discrimination as the prohibition on prostitution applied to both men and women sex workers. While Justices O'Regan and Sachs dissented from that particular finding,[56] there was unanimous agreement that the prohibition of sex work was consistent with the constitutional rights to privacy, dignity, freedom, security of the person, and economic activity, and that its decriminalisation was a matter for the legislature rather than the Constitutional Court. This seems an unusually cautious approach for the Constitutional Court to take with regard to its jurisdiction. The failure of the court to recognise sex workers (acknowledged to be predominantly women) as frequently representative of the most marginalised groups in society is surprising, as it is they who are most desperately in need and most explicitly deprived of rights (social, economic, civil and political). There are persuasive public health arguments for decriminalisation, and it is arguable that these are also the logical extension of many of the constitution's founding principles. But these arguments depend on the effective removal of sexuality and law from a discourse of morality and reproduction, adopting instead a framework of health, harm reduction, and labour. The *Jordan* ruling ignores the need to promote a context in which sex workers might develop greater agency and better working conditions. On the contrary, their criminality and vulnerability are certified and the moral borders that signify the acceptable limits of sexual agency are established. The unanimity in the *Jordan* decision suggests that sex workers are seen as having so remote a claim on 'innocence'[57] that even a body so accepting of rights as the South African Constitutional Court could not grant their entitlement to legitimate status. In this way, some aspects of the historical sexual hierarchies so clearly articulated by Gayle Rubin (1984) remain unchanged, and the limits of South Africa's transformative trajectory are clearly delineated.

The decision in *Jordan* is consistent with the claim by Jagwanth and Murray that much of the gender litigation in the Constitutional Court has involved relatively privileged groups, whereas those marginalised in multiple ways – those whose interests the constitution was most intended to protect – are in fact the people who have received the least benefit (2002: 291). It is, moreover, important to recognise that these are formal rights that still need to be properly embedded in order for them to be accessed and realised by all but the most litigious. In this regard, Mikki Van Zyl suggests that the constitution should be seen as an 'enabling tool':

Though the first steps have been won through the enshrining of sexual rights in the Constitution, the struggle is far from over. The actual articulation of those rights still depends on positionality, agency, and the manner in which those rights are interpreted, negotiated and implemented or practised within the institutions of governance. (Van Zyl 2004: 161)

The explicit inclusion of sexuality in the Equality Clause, along with the political strength of the various organisations supporting it, forecloses a hyper-masculine, 'homophobic' stance of the type proclaimed in Zimbabwe. Even if he were inclined to do so, President Mbeki could not engage the same rhetorical devices as Mugabe without contradicting fundamental constitutional values. The promise of sexual rights in the constitution therefore shelters Mbeki from delivering unsolicited comment while it obliges him to honour them in principle. It cannot oblige him to have the political will to advance them through an energetic implementation of policy or to prioritise them in competing demands for limited resources. The fundamental issues of gendered agency that are packed into sexual relations determine one's ability to negotiate safe sex and so are presently a matter of life or death in a country with a high level of HIV infection and limited access to treatment.[58] Yet the controversy around Mbeki's refusal to acknowledge the link between HIV and AIDS (attributing AIDS primarily to poverty rather than sexual transmission) and his scepticism about the benefits of anti-retroviral treatment, have caused him to avoid interviews on the subject. His comments on sexuality in this context have been preoccupied with 'sexually charged representations of African bodies as central epistemological features of nineteenth- and twentieth-century European racism' (Hoad 2005: 101). Meanwhile his government's refusal of treatment led activists to successfully petition the Constitutional Court to oblige them to develop a national treatment programme; while government eventually developed such a plan, a distinct lack of political will is evident in its very slow implementation.[59] This demonstrates both the power and the limits of the constitution as a medium for active intervention in governance. Similarly, the constitution's clear provision of sexual rights provides Mbeki with a shelter beneath which he is absolved of the need to speak to them, discreetly allowing him to neglect the serious engagement with gender power, sexual relations and sexual violence that sexually transmitted HIV necessitates. However, there are two recent developments that threaten to bring the issue of sexual rights further into a domain where comment and commitment will be required and their constitutional inviolability will be tested.

The first of these is the constitutional court declaration that the Marriage Act (25 of 1961) contravenes the Equality Clause, and that the legislature must, within 12 months, amend it so that same-sex and heterosexual partners have equal access to its provisions.[60] Rather than granting the litigants (a lesbian couple wanting to marry) an instant remedy (as was in his power), Justice Sachs chose to require parliament to amend the legislation, stipulating that amendments had to accord with the full equality granted by the court. He also stipulated the precise words that were to be automatically inserted to render the Act non-sex specific if parliament failed to act within 12 months. In explaining this ruling, Sachs affirmed that the democratic and legitimating power of legislative passage would assure more steadfast progress towards equality for lesbians and gays:[61]

> Parliament should be given the opportunity in the first place to decide how best the equality rights at issue could be achieved. Provided that the basic principles of equality as enshrined in the Constitution are not trimmed in the process, the greater the degree of public acceptance for same-sex unions, the more will the achievement of equality be promoted. (para 139)

The ruling of the Constitutional Court is unanimous,[62] incontrovertibly rooted in the constitution, and has since been explicitly supported by the ruling ANC.[63] However, radio talk shows and other public discussions of the decision clearly reflected the results of a 2003 survey, indicating that 78 per cent of adult South Africans think that sexual relations between two adults of the same gender are 'always wrong'.[64] Traditionalist and religious groupings have indicated a clear intention to lobby parliament on this issue over the next 12 months, so it seems inevitable that tensions between the registers of 'primal sovereignty' and 'radical individualism' will be central to the debate. This is likely to be the most testing trial to date of the ANC's commitment primarily to sexual equality, but also to the values of the constitution and the authority of the constitutional court.

The second possible challenge to the security of sexual rights arises from a similar disjunction between populism and formal constitutionalism. The defence presented by ex-Deputy President Jacob Zuma in his rape trial signalled a significant shift in the official consensus that exists around issues of sexual agency and gender equality. At issue in the trial was whether the penetration that took place was consensual, and while Zuma's defence had other more conventional dimensions, his reliance on traditional Zulu conceptions of appropriate gendered behaviour is of most interest here. Every detail of the trial has been widely reported and intensely discussed across South Africa. Despite his fluency in English, Zuma chose to testify entirely in isiZulu, requiring court interpreters to translate even the most mundane phrases.

> He invoked the culture and spoke in an idiom that would make language activists proud. He told (the) Judge ... that the very charge of rape was a result of having acted in accordance with what he had been taught as a youngster growing up ... in northern KwaZulu-Natal. Zuma ... told the court that he had been taught that 'leaving a woman in that state [of sexual arousal]' was the worst thing a man could do.[65]

In explaining his belief in the woman's consent, Zuma invested significance in the fact that she was wearing a knee-length skirt ('It told me something') and that she did not sit properly in her skirt: 'she would cross her legs and wouldn't even mind if the skirt was raised very much ... I realised, well, there is something she is after, because of these things. Maybe she is trying to send a certain message to me by these actions'.[66] Zuma was explicit in court that he felt it was his duty as a Zulu man to respond to the woman's evident 'needs', and that 'I would have had my cows ready' had the woman's family requested *lobola* with a view to marriage.[67] He emphasises that he genuinely believed the woman to be consenting (under South African criminal law his belief merely has to be genuine to gain an acquittal, it does not have to be reasonable). But his defence is also a strategic engagement with the national audience that the trial of a man who may become president attracts; for it is firmly situated within the register of 'primal sovereignty' and directly challenges the values of sexual and gendered equality that may have formal recognition, but still lack popular support. Zuma's appeal to traditionalist values struck a populist chord; throughout the trial crowds of supporters danced and protested outside the court, engaged in the symbolic burning of 'g-strings' and specifically invoked Zulu signifiers that resonated with his return to a register of 'primal sovereignty'. His supporters also claimed that the trial was politically motivated and it seems pertinent that Zuma's defence built on his reputation as an uneducated man of the people, rooted in the soil of his fathers, in direct contrast to the educated, cosmopolitan President Mbeki.

The political narrative for the Zuma-ites is one of political betrayal. It is of a cynical Thabo Mbeki trampling African National Congress traditions to thwart Zuma's natural ascent to the top office. The backdrop ethos is of a noble struggle tarnished through the centralisation of authority and abuse of state institutions for partisan ends. The 'legitimate' response: Street power, replete with intimidation, stonings and the burning of images.

This depressing deeper political resonance of the trial ... is that Marx, finally, needs to be superceded by Machiavelli. In this vein, ideological politics have been reduced to tribal posturing and factional manoeuvring ... Whether the rape charges were politically motivated may or may not be true. What is beyond doubt, is that major political capital will be made by whichever camp stands to benefit from the judge's ruling.[68]

Zuma's defence is strategically directed at both criminal charge and political marginalisation, bringing the tension between Comaroff's registers of 'primal sovereignty' and 'radical individualism' more openly into the fields of criminal justice and mainstream politics. He has exposed the volatile political capital of a tension that was contained by the consensus underlying the constitution, and to the extent that Zuma has invested his considerable political authority in the populist appeal of 'primal sovereignty', so too have the sexual rights more readily associated with 'radical individualism' been challenged. Negotiating the balance between these registers is a constant practice in the daily lives of many South Africans, but it also goes to the heart of both principle and practice in justice and in politics. So while sexuality might well be the terrain that produces a heavily rhetorical and contested engagement with these registers in the next few years, the vast array of socio-economic and political factors that are the fodder of national and global politics will determine the measure of their reconciliation.

South Africa has such a high rate of sexual violence that researchers label it 'systemic' (Van Zyl 2004: 164). The limits of formal constitutional rights might be measured through their inability to ensure the success of policies designed to redress women's disproportionate vulnerability to sexual violence (and hence HIV).[69] But there is at least a constitutional platform to define the end-goal of strategic objectives, and this, combined with official recognition of the problem, has resulted in some (if inadequate) attempts on the part of the state to engage with it.[70] In Zimbabwe the political context since 2000 has produced a dramatic rise in reports of sexual violence: there are reports of coercive sex being used explicitly as an instrument of torture by state-sponsored militia in attacks upon the opposition and suspected sympathisers.[71] Far from attempting to prevent sexual violence, however, a pervasive impunity suggests that this violence has licence. Such an instrumental usage of sex would be less likely if there was a more developed context of women's subjectivity, making them fully entitled citizens with recourse to legal equality. For if women's identity were not thought to derive so directly from their attachment to men, their physical integrity might not represent a terrain of such appropriation. In both South Africa and Zimbabwe, the broader context of gender inequalities *has* to be addressed in order to properly develop the concept of sexual agency and the reality of sexual equality. The constitutional framework in South Africa appears to provide a starting point that is not present in Zimbabwe.

Conclusion

While it is important to acknowledge the limits inherent in the formalism of constitutional rights, a strong and effective constitution can provide a platform for popular interventions in democratic governance and the development of political agency. The constitution can serve as an 'enabling tool', through which attempts to challenge sexual inequality, violence and HIV/AIDS can be initiated, but their ultimate success will still depend on an effective reconciliation of the registers of 'primal sovereignty' and 'radical individualism' in the political arena. The tension between these two registers is likely to increase in pressure as the number of years between the constitution and the source of its legitimacy (the process of drafting) grows. This qualification does not diminish the significance of the constitution as a platform for advances in sexual rights and equality, but it does caution that the authority of the constitution and its court is not eternally immune to political machination. But for the moment, the Equality Clause is binding and the Constitutional Court retains the authority to exercise jurisdiction over the government. This is clearly an assumption that one cannot make in the context of Zimbabwe, where the government has perceived itself to be in conflict with its courts and constitution. Consequently, the repeated failure of challenges to the Zimbabwe government's obvious constitutional contraventions cast the possibilities of the South African Constitution in an ever more resplendent light.

But the formal recognition of equal rights is not so immediate and omnipotent a recipe as to provide all South African women with an indisputable agency that all Zimbabwean women are perpetually denied. That is too simplistic. There are many women in South Africa whose lives remain relatively unchanged by the primarily bourgeois petitions that have been made to the Constitutional Court, and there are similarly women in Zimbabwe who manage to engage a sexual agency unanticipated by the register of 'primal sovereignty'. But in both states, those women who do manage to exercise some real control over sexual choices (as they will in practice) may well do so through resorting to methods that will generally entail disproportionate responsibility taken without recourse to structural support.[72]

Current attempts to promote gender equality through legal interventions will stumble without parallel attempts to undo the constraints on women's agency in a broader social context. Sexual agency depends on the ability to exercise agency in the ordinary contexts that surround the sexual. Such agency cannot, alas, be conjured by an expression of will or by a proclamation of rights. We cannot simply wish it into being, even if by consensus, as we first need to undo the obstacles that inhibit its development, and restructure the habits, patterns and cultural institutions that are built on its absence. But the constitutional recognition of the prioritisation of equality clearly presents a platform from which an interpretation of custom that challenges women's historical partial subjectivity can emerge. This is only sustainable if the vision of justice that frames it can accommodate the politics of 'primal sovereignty' that prevail in the local context. For the more the Constitutional Court invests in the constitution's explicit prioritisation of the register of 'radical individualism' over that of 'primal sovereignty', the more it appears vulnerable to a popular backlash. Yet in both countries, it has required a strategic manipulation of primal sovereignty by Mugabe and Zuma to initiate a reaction. This suggests that allegiance to 'primal sovereignty' must be taken seriously in any attempts to advance towards gender equality; it cannot be ignored or rejected but must be incorporated into the process to pre-empt excessive polarisation of the registers. The Constitutions of the two countries engage very differently with the contrary registers of 'radical individualism' and 'primal sovereignty' and so establish very different platforms from which to develop and support women's agency. The South African

Constitution clearly resolves the tension between rights and cultural authenticity through the notion of 'living' custom. It ushers in a legal framework that attempts to engage positively with the 'traditional' institutions that appear at first glance to be antipathetic to gender equality. Innovative jurisprudence and clear principles have produced exceptionally rapid change in the legal arena, and provided a platform conducive to initiating the development of women's sexual agency. For this to deliver on its promise, the appropriate political will now has to remain in the ascendant. In contrast, the Zimbabwean situation illustrates the extent to which a constitution that has neither symbolic strength nor the practical advantage of an unambiguous dedication to human rights (whether civil, political, economic or social) cannot resist the political machinations of a determined opportunist, and can serve to exacerbate inequities of sex and gender. The political context can never be entirely anticipated, but where the legitimacy and popular credibility of a constitution are intimately connected to its vision of justice, the possibility of containing the opportunism of vested interests and promoting greater equality is far greater.

Notes

1 The lateness of the South African post-colonial moment gave the ANC Women's League a determination to be a notable exception to this historical subordination, resulting in (among other things) the ANC's commitment to reserving 30 per cent of all its parliamentary seats for women (Hoad *et al.* 2005: 20).

2 Alice Miller (2004: 16–47), while recognising reproductive rights and sexual harm as key engines in the advance of women's rights in the international sphere, critically appraises the limits of these strategic platforms and cautions that the resulting protection ultimately privileges 'respectability' undermining the fundamental goal of equality.

3 World Conference on Human Rights (Vienna 1993), International Conference on Population and Development (Cairo 1994) and the Fourth World Conference on Women (Beijing 1995). For critical appraisal of the specific advances and alliances of these conferences, see Petchesky 2003.

4 A model of 'sexual hierarchies' was first articulated by Gayle Rubin who also emphasises that conflicts over sexual values 'acquire immense symbolic weight' at times of nation-building or dissolution (Rubin 1984). These are conditions that might be used to characterise present-day South Africa and Zimbabwe.

5 Zimbabwe International Book Fair (ZIBF) Opening Speech and Press Conference, 1 August 1995. The theme of the ZIBF that year was 'Human Rights'.

6 Anias Chigwedere, MP, *Zimbabwe Parliamentary Debate*, 28 September 1995 Hansard pp. 2779–81.

7 *National Coalition for Gay and Lesbian Equality* v *Minister of Justice* 1998 (12)BCLR 1517; *Satchwell* v *President of Republic of SA* CCT45/2001; *Du Toit & Anor* v *Min of Welfare and Population Development*, CCT40/2001; *J & B* v *Director General, Dept of Home Affairs* CCT46/2002. For further discussion see Van Zyl (2004: 166–8).

8 This stands in marked contrast to Zimbabwe where the 1957 Immigration Act provides that the entry into the country of 'known prostitutes or homosexuals' is prohibited (Chapter 4:02 S.14(1)(f)). For a full discussion of the extent of the South African rights and a citation of relevant cases, see Van Zyl (2004: 166–8).

9 *Minister of Home Affairs and Another* v *Fourie and Another* (*Doctors for Life International and Others, Amicus Curiae*); *Lesbian and Gay Equality Project and Others* v *Minister of Home Affairs and Others* CCT60/04; CCT10/05.

10 For a discussion of the 'potential incompatibility' of collective and human rights, see Howard (1992: 97–9).

11 For more on the colonial creation of ethnic and linguistic identity in Southern Africa, see Vail (1989) and Beach (1980).

12 See the Preamble, and Articles 27 and 29. For a comment on the historical and cultural origins of this inclusion of social duties and collective interests, see Mutua (1995).

13 Section 14 of the Charter of the white settlers in colonial Rhodesia provided that in civil cases between 'natives' the courts were to be guided by 'native law' only in so far as that law was 'not repugnant to natural law, justice, or morality'.

14 The Native Adultery Punishment Ordinance (NAPO) of 1916 was intended to strengthen African marriages by making adultery a criminal offence for Africans, punishable by up to a year's imprisonment. While this referred to both men and women, the fact that African marriages were polygynous meant that its application was persistently gender bound. For a married woman to sleep with any man other than her husband would be committing adultery, while a married man could be convicted of adultery only if he slept with another man's wife. Thus, he could sleep with any woman who was not married to another man. So while the NAPO was superficially symmetrical in its design, in effect it penalised only married African women and the African men they slept with. Colonial authorities were reluctant to criminalise adultery, preferring to see it as grounds for divorce. But the key concern of African husbands was that women should honour their marital and lineage obligations; the idea that women might be granted the freedom

of divorce was thus anathema to them. The insistence of elder African men triumphed, as colonial authority relied on the support of traditional patriarchal structures for effective government. For more on this see Jeater (1993).

15 The NMO gave women the capacity to refuse a marriage, but they still could not contract a marriage without the authority of their guardian.

16 Thandabantu R. Nhlapo (1991) 'The African Family and Women's Rights: Friends or Foes?', *Acta Juridica* 135: 138–9 (quoted in Jagwanth and Murray (2002: 294)).

17 While human rights are expressed through social relationships, if they are to be equally attributed to all people regardless of status, they must, ultimately, rely on a notion of individual agency. 'Human rights are *claims by the individual against society and the state* that, furthermore, "trump" other considerations such as the legal (but not human) right of a corporation to property. Human rights are private, individual, and autonomous' (Howard 1992: 82).

18 Tentative contact about the possibility of establishing a framework for negotiating a peaceful settlement developed sporadically throughout the 1980s until 1989 when the election of President F. W. De Klerk brought a committed energy to the process. Liberation movements were unbanned in February 1990, the multilateral National Peace Accord was signed in September 1991, and the first non-racial democratic elections took place in April 1994. For an extensive account of the entire process, including the drafting of the Constitution, see Spitz and Chaskalson (2000).

19 Spitz and Chaskalson suggest that subjugating customary relations to the Bill of Rights resulted in part from the traditional leaders' 'refusal to accept a compromise which might have found sufficient consensus in the Negotiating council' (2000: 393). An initial openness to their submissions rapidly shrank as the intransigence of traditional leaders became apparent. Gender equality, by the 1990s, was so fundamental to the liberal democratic tenets that emerged as the broad consensus of all the different political parties negotiating the constitutional draft, that Contralesa (Congress of Traditional Leaders of South Africa), an already small force, found itself further isolated. The racial diversity of the African National Congress (ANC) and the South African Communist Party, as well as the role of women in both organisations, meant that division on this issue was limited and not persistent (2000: 379–99). Furthermore, the 'traditionalist' position of gender disparity that one might otherwise expect from an African nationalist movement was countered by the premise of equality reflected in the Freedom Charter (Van Zyl 2004: 157). This was a document drawn up in 1955 through an extraordinary process of mass participation that came to have enormous symbolic power as 'the will of the people', and unified as 'charterist' much of the South African liberation movement including the ANC (see Suttner and Cronin 1986).

20 Examples include *Soobramoney* v *Min of Health* (*Kwazulu-Natal*) Constitutional Court of South Africa, Case CCT 32/97, 27 November 1997; *Government of RSA and others* v *Grootboom and others* Case CCT 11/00, 4 October 2000: and also *Minister of Health and others* v *Treatment Action Campaign and others* 2002 (5) SA 721 (CC).

21 Constitional 14th Amendment Bill and Superior Courts Bill.

22 Quintal, A. (2006) 'World body worry at draft judicial reforms', *The Cape Times*, 25 April, p. 6. and also 'Bar Council concerned', 30 January 2006 http://www.news24.com/News24/South_Africa/News/0,,2-7-1442_1872258,00.html accessed 2 May 2006.

23 Quintal, A. (2006) 'World body worry at draft judicial reforms', *The Cape Times*, 25 April, p. 6.

24 Sharise Weiner, S. C. (2005) 'Is the face of the South African judiciary changing fast enough?' *The Times*, 18 October.

25 'ANC "not slating" white judges' 10 January 2005, http://www.news24.com/News24/South_Africa/Politics/0,,2-7-12_1645293,00.html, accessed 2 May 2006.

26 'Judiciary slates racism, sexism' 4 April 2005, http://www.news24.com/News24/South_Africa/News/0,6119,2-7-1442_1685065,00.html, accessed 2 May 2006.

27 These constitutional provisions were drafted in conjunction with political agreements obliging both Zimbabwean and British governments to contribute to the process of land appropriation and compensation respectively. Once agreement between the two governments about their fulfilment of these obligations collapsed their political relationship became markedly antagonistic. British Foreign Office Minister Peter Hain referred to Zimbabwean 'thuggery, licensed from on high' (*Observer*, 2 April 2000) while President Mugabe labelled Tony Blair's cabinet 'gay gangsters' and suggested that Peter Hain was the 'wife' of Peter Tatchell (a gay human rights activist who had twice attempted to arrest Mugabe for crimes against humanity) (Interview with David Dimbleby in *Rebellion*, BBC (Menthorn, Barraclough and Carey) 1998).

28 The draconian Law and Order Maintenance Act, inherited at Independence from Ian Smith's Rhodesian Front government, was kept in place and put to effective use.

29 The Law and Order Maintenance Act was replaced with the Public Order and Security Act (POSA 1/2002) which increases restrictions on political organising and includes the following clause at S.16(2)(b): 'Any person who publicly and intentionally makes any abusive, indecent, obscene or false statements about the president or an acting president whether in respect of his person or office shall be guilty of an offence'. The sentence for this can be up to one year's imprisonment.

30 Broadcasting Services Act 2001; Access to Information and Protection of Privacy Act 5/2002; Broadcasting Services (Access to Radio and Media during an Election) Regulations 2005.

31 Constitutional Amendment no. 17 (2005).

32 Other notable provisions of this draft constitution included poorer individual rights and greater press censorship. For more on this see Chan (2003: 143).

33 Chenjerai 'Hitler' Hunzvi, leader of the Zimbabwe Liberation War Veterans Association (despite the fact that he had never fought in the liberation war), gloried in his chosen *nom de guerre* as he directed the land invasions and attacks on government opposition with corresponding violence. While many of his members were genuine war veterans, other war veterans who despised the violence of Hunzvi's *modus operandi* and accused him of betraying the ideals of the liberation war, established the Zimbabwe Liberator's Platform (Campbell 2003: 137).

34 The draft constitution (2000) had included a clause giving government the right to appropriate commercial farmland without compensation, so ZANU-PF publicly attributed the loss of the referendum to the opposition of white commercial farmers. But it is arguable that the farmworkers' unions were more instrumental in the government's loss of popularity in rural constituencies, and that the unresolved issues of white land ownership were ideal pretexts for deliberate attacks on the approximately 400,000 farmworkers who were deprived of work, displaced and later disenfranchised.

35 Judges received serious threats, but ZANU-PF made it clear that if they remained on the bench, government would be unable to guarantee their safety. This obliged a number of judges to retire, the first of which was the Chief Justice Anthony Gubbay. See Pedzisai Ruhanya, 'Why I quit: Judge' *Daily News* :10 June 2001.

36 See 'Outcry Over Chidysausiku's Appointment', *Zimbabwe Independent*, 26 August 2001; 'Chidyausiku Sidelines Judges', *Daily News*, 18 September 2001; 'Chidyausiku Accused of Bias', *Daily News*, 20 September 2001; 'Why I quit: Judge', *Daily News* 10 July 2001; '2001: Judiciary's Major Turning Point', *The Herald*, 8 January 2002; 'The Law Society of Zimbabwe Attacks Supreme Court Judgements', *Daily News* 17 April 2002; 'ZANU-PF's Final Blow on Judiciary?', *Financial Gazette*, 20 November 2002.

37 Raath, Jan (2004) 'Zimbabwe Ruins' *The Times*, 17 August, available online at http://www.timesonline.co.uk/article/0,,200-1218911,00.html, accessed 2 May 2006.

38 Mangwende, B. (2004) 'Retired High Court Judges Recalled', *Financial Gazette*, 29 April.

39 'Judge Majuru Quits', (2004) *The Herald*; 29 January 2004 'Another Judge Flees', *Zimbabwe Standard*, 1 February 2004.

40 http://www.hrforumzim.com/frames/inside_frame_monitor.htm accessed 6 May 2006.

41 For discussion of this, see Klugman (2000).

42 'In 1980 ZANU's election manifesto listed 13 Fundamental Rights and Freedoms. Ranked at number eight was the right of women to equality

with men "in all spheres of political, economic, cultural, and family life". This gender equality was to be based on the principles of equal pay for equal work and free choice of partner for both parties to a marriage' (ZANU 1980: 16) (in Zimbabwe Human Rights NGO Forum 2001: 2).

43 *Magaya* v *Magaya* SC 1999(1) ZLR 100 (S). As a woman living under customary law, Venia Magaya's father nominally owned the property that she had accumulated. On his death, she claimed that property as the eldest child (of the first wife). But her claim was overruled in favour of a younger brother (from a second wife) who had had no role at all in its accumulation WSLA 2001.

44 ZANU-PF had previously claimed that its commodification and inflation had changed *lobola* from a traditional bond between lineage groups, to a capitalist transaction between men (Seidman 1984: 432). But when discussion arose around its abolition, the reaction of traditional patriarchs was such that ZANU-PF defended *lobola* as 'part of the national heritage, an essential element of stable social relations', which should resist 'western feminism ... a new form of cultural imperialism' (1984: 432).

45 This becomes most evident in the parliamentary debates, where the clearest example was given by Anias Chigwedere, MP, who stated, 'The homosexuals are the festering finger endangering the body and we chop them off' (*Zimbabwe Parliamentary Debate*, 28 September 1995, Hansard pp. 2779–81).

46 For a full discussion of the context surrounding the emergence of the 'gay issue' at the time of the resulting parliamentary debates on 'The Evil and Iniquitous Practice of Homosexualism and Lesbianism', and the contention that Mugabe was actively importing the not just homophobia, but also the hetero/homosexual binary into Zimbabwean culture, see Phillips 1997a, 1997b and 2000; also Dunton and Palmberg 1996.

47 'We have our own culture and we must rededicate ourselves to our traditional values that make us human beings', *The Citizen* 12 August 1995.

48 For more on *ubuntu* see Louw 1998.

49 However, this assertion of culture as exclusively heterosexual is predicated on the *a priori* concept of a binary division of hetero/homosexuality. This notion of a 'binary sexuality' fixed within individuals, is far from the integrated human potential of the *ubuntu* concept, but is a distinctly western European polarisation of individual erotic desire as homo/heterosexual, initially popularised by European sexologists in the late nineteenth century (Weeks 1989). What's more, Mugabe claims only one part of this binary (homosexual) to be a definitive signifier of cultural imperialism, when it is actually impossible to define the exclusive heterosexual without reference to the homosexual.

50 South African Constitutional Court Justice Yvonne Mokgoro has derided notions of a categorical definition of *ubuntu*: 'any attempt to define

ubuntu is merely a simplification of a more expansive, flexible and philosophically accommodative idea' (Mokgoro 1998: 16).

51 *Moseneke and Others* v *Master of the High Court* 2001 (2) BCLR 103 (CC) declared s.23(7)(a) of the Black Administration Act 38 of 1927 to be invalid. In doing so, it brought inheritance under customary law out of segregated administration and into the purview of all courts up to and including the Constitutional Court, thereby making it similarly bound by constitutional decisions.

52 *Amod* v *Multilateral Motor Vehicle Accidents Fund* 1999 (4) SA 1319 (SCA).

53 *Moseneke 2001* supra para 30.

54 Including the Prevention of Family Violence Act (Act 133 of 1993), the Choice on Termination of Pregnancy Act (Act 92 of 1996), the Employment Equity Act (Act 55 of 1998), the Maintenance Act (Act 99 of 1998), and the Promotion of Equality and Prevention of Unfair Discrimination Act (Act 4 of 2000). For discussion of these see Jagwanth and Murray (2002: 268–73), and Van Zyl (2004: 164–6).

55 *S* v *Jordan and Others* (*Sex Workers Education and Advocacy Task Force and Others as Amicus Curiae*) CCT31/01.

56 The minority opinion suggested that the majority decision undervalued the material context and ignored the integral parts played by gender and economics in the relations of exchange that constitute sex work. The minority decision also pointed out that this approach in effect made the prostitute into the primary offender, thereby reinforcing sexual stereotyping and applying double standards whereby men are expected to be active sexual agents, and women are not.

57 Carole Vance and Alice Miller have put forward the suggestion that claims to human rights tend to rely on narratives that invoke representations of innocence and victimisation, making claims to sexual rights particularly difficult (Vance and Miller 2004: 11). Narratives of commercial sex are inherently lacking in innocence, and it is arguably only through alleging coercion and abuse that a sex worker may be recast as 'innocent' (I am grateful to Carole Vance and Alice Miller for their engagement in lengthy discussion on this topic).

58 The Actuarial Society of South Africa estimates that over 300,000 people died of AIDS in South Africa in 2004 (TAC Electronic Newsletter, 31 January 2005). At December 2004, 27,000 people were receiving anti-retroviral treatment in the public sector (TAC Electronic Newsletter, 21 February 2005). Both sourced from www.tac.org.za, accessed 5 May 2006.

59 On 14 December 2001, the Pretoria High Court found in favour of the Treatment Action Campaign, the Children's Rights Centre and paediatricians and against the Minister of Health and government on the provision of anti-retrovirals (ARVs) to prevent mother-to-child HIV transmission, describing a countrywide MTCT prevention programme as 'an ineluctable obligation of the State.' Government appealed against the

decision to the Constitutional Court, but lost the appeal and was obliged to implement a national programme (*Minister of Health v Treatment Action Campaign* (2) 2002 (5) SA 721 (CC)). Similarly, in August 2003, government eventually made a commitment to a national programme deploying ARVs in the treatment of all who need them, explicitly declaring an aim to treat 53,000 people by March 2004. This had been achieved through vigorous political campaigning, backed up by litigation, the threat of litigation, and a reliance on the socio-economic rights enshrined in the constitution and supported in the Constitutional Court. By December 2004, only 27,000 people were receiving ARV treatment in the public sector. For more on this see www.tac.org.za.

60 *Minister of Home Affairs and Another v Fourie and Another (Doctors for Life International and Others, Amicus Curiae); Lesbian and Gay Equality Project and Others v Minister of Home Affairs and Others* CCT60/04 ; CCT10/05.

61 Sachs also explained that parliament might wish to amend the act so that it covers the many diverse forms of marriage (customary, religious, etc common in South Africa but currently excluded from the Act (*Minister of Home Affairs and Another v Fourie* para 140).

62 It was unanimous with one exception; O'Regan, J agreed with the main judgement but dissented on the 12-month suspension of the declaration of invalidity, arguing that the court should not wait for parliament but had a duty to grant immediate relief to the litigants.

63 Evans, J. (2005) 'Govt to respect gay marriage ruling' *Mail and Guardian*, December, available online at http://www.mg.co.za/articlePage.aspx ?articleid=258227&area=/breaking_news/breaking_news__national/, accessed 3 May 2006.

64 Human Science's Research Council (2003) *South African Social Attitudes Survey* (SASAS), available online at http://www.hsrc.ac.za/ media/2003/11/20031119_2.html, accessed 23 May 2006.

65 Fikile-Ntsikelelo M. (2006) '100 per cent Zuluboy', *Mail and Guardian*, 6 April, available online at http://www.mg.co.za/articlePage.aspx?articlei d=268739&area=/insight/insight__national/ accessed 3 May 2006.

66 Musgrave, A. and Evans, J. (2006) 'Zuma: She Gave Sexual Signs', *Mail and Guardian*, 4 April, available online at http://www.mg.co.za/articlePage.a spx?articleid=268573&area=/breaking_news/breaking_news__national/, accessed 3 May 2006.

67 Evans, J. (2006) 'Zuma: I would have had my cows ready', *Mail and Guardian*, 5 April, available online at http://www.mg.co.za/articlePage.a spx?articleid=268633&area=/breaking_news/breaking_news__national/, accessed 3 May 2006.

68 Burger, G. (2006) 'Political Style and Gender Power', *Mail and Guardian*, 12 April, available online at http://www.mg.co.za/articlePage.aspx?artic leid=269152&area=/insight/insight__columnists/, accessed 3 May 2006.

69 For a discussion of women's vulnerability to HIV in Southern Africa and the constraints on agency, see Akeroyd (2004), and Susser and Stein (2004).

70 South Africa has initiated law and criminal justice reforms and addressed police training with the intention of increasing women's access to effective remedies in cases of rape, sexual abuse and domestic violence. It has also begun to implement policies to improve standards of medical and psychological care and treatment, as well as the forensic medical examination of survivors of sexual violence. However, it is worth noting that prior to April 2002, government forbade doctors and nurses in state hospitals from providing rape survivors with anti-retroviral treatment as post-exposure prophylaxis against infection with HIV. The enforcement of this policy led to the ejection of the Greater Nelspruit Rape Intervention Project (GRIP) from the Rob Ferreira and Temba hospitals because they were supplying the drugs AZT and 3TC to rape survivors. This policy was consistent with the government's 'dissident' position on HIV/AIDS and their discrediting of ARVs as toxic. Enormous pressure eventually forced government to allow testing, counselling and provision of post-exposure prophylaxis for rape survivors at risk of HIV infection.

71 In January 2002, a respected Zimbabwean human rights organisation reported a new pattern of sexual violence after interviewing victims who were forced to rape other victims at the instigation of the militia in Mashonaland Central Province (Amani Trust 2001). 'By the end of March 2002, the Amani Trust documented further sexual assaults by militia, including incidents in which men were forced by militia to commit sexual assault on one another … Another human rights organisation, the Zimbabwe Women Lawyers' Association, estimates that some 1,000 women are being held in militia camps. In Masvingo, newspaper accounts describe farmworkers being beaten and forced to watch their wives raped by militia because they may have voted for the opposition' (Amnesty International 2002).

72 For a discussion of a similar dynamic in Latin America see Shepard (2000: 111–43).

References

Akeroyd, A. V. (2004) 'Coercion, Constraints, and "Cultural Entrapments": A Further Look at Gendered and Occupational Factors Pertinent to the Transmission of HIV in Africa' in E. Kalipeni, S. Craddock, J. Oppong and J. Ghosh (eds) *HIV/AIDS in Africa: Beyond Epidemiology*, Blackwell Publishing: Oxford: 89–103.

Amadiume, I. (1997) *Reinventing Africa: Matriarchy, Religion, and Culture*, London: Zed Books.

Amani Trust (2001) *Statement on Sexual Torture*. Available online at http://www.kubatana.net/html/archive/hr/020107amani.asp?orgcode=ama001a ndrange_start=1 accessed 23 May 2006.

Amnesty International (2002) 'Assault and Sexual Violence by Militia', Amnesty International Press Release, 5 April, AI Index AFR 46/032/2002 – News Service Nr. 59.

Beach, D. N. (1980) *The Shona and Zimbabwe, 900–1850: An Outline of Shona History*, Teaneck, NJ: Holmes and Meier.

Bigge, D. and von Briesen, A. (2000) 'Conflict in the Zimbabwean Courts: Women's Rights and Indigenous Self-Determination in *Magaya* v *Magaya*', *Harvard Human Rights Journal*, 13: 289–313.

Black, D. (1999) 'The Long and Winding Road: International Norms and Domestic Political Change in South Africa', in T. Risse, S. C. Ropp and K. Sikkink (eds) *The Power of Human Rights*, Cambridge: Cambridge University Press.

Butler, J. (1993) *Bodies That Matter*, London and New York: Routledge.

Campbell, H. (2003) *Reclaiming Zimbabwe: The Exhaustion of the Patriarchal Model of Liberation*, Cape Town: David Philip.

Chan, S. (2003) *Robert Mugabe: A Life of Power and Violence*, New York: I.B.Tauris.

Chanock, M. (1985) *Law, Custom and Social Order: The Colonial Experience in Malawi and Zambia*, Cambridge: Polity Press.

Comaroff, J. (1997) 'The Discourse of Rights in Colonial South Africa: Subjectivity, Sovereignty, Modernity' in A. Sarat and T. R. Kearns (eds) *Identities, Politics and Rights*, Ann Arbor: University of Michigan Press: 193–236).

Comaroff, J. L. (2001) 'Reflections on the Colonial State, in South Africa and Elsewhere: Factions, Fragments, Facts and Fictions', in A. Zegeye (ed.) *Social Identities in the New South Africa: After Apartheid – Volume 1*, Cape Town: Kwela Books and SA History Online, Maroelana.

Dunton, C. and Palmberg, M. (1996) 'Human Rights and Homosexuality in Southern Africa', *Current African Issues* 19, 2nd edn, Uppsala: Nordiska Afrikainstitute.

Gilligan, C. (1993) *In a Different Voice*, Cambridge, MA: Harvard University Press.

Heidensohn, F. (1968) 'The Deviance of Women: A Critique and an Enquiry' *British Journal of Sociology*, 19(2): 160–75.

Heidensohn, F. (1985) *Women and Crime*, London: Macmillan.

Hoad, N. (2005) 'Thabo Mbeki's AIDS Blues: The Intellectual, the Archive, and the Pandemic', *Public Culture*, 17(1): 101–27.

Hoad, N., Martin, K. and Reid, G. (eds) (2005) *Sex and Politics in South Africa*, Cape Town: Double Storey, Juta.

Hobsbawm, E. and Ranger, T. (eds) (1991) *The Invention of Tradition*, Cambridge: Canto (CUP).

Howard, R. E. (1992) 'Dignity, Community, and Human Rights', in A. An Na'im (ed.) *Human Rights in Cross-Cultural Perspective*, Philadelphia: University of Pennsylvania Press.

Jackson, L. A. (1993) 'Friday the 13th University of Zimbabwe Mini-skirt Saga', *Southern Africa Political and Economic Monthly*, December 1992/ January 1993, 25–6.

Jacobs, S. M. and Howard, T. (1987) 'Women in Zimbabwe: Stated Policy and State Action' in H. Afshar (ed.) *Women, State, and Ideology: Studies from Africa and Asia* London: Macmillan.

Jagwanth, S. and Murray, C. (2002) 'Ten Years of Transformation: How has Gender Equality in South Africa Fared?', *Canadian Journal of Women and Law*, 14(2): 255–99.

Jeater, D. (1993) *Marriage, Perversion and Power: The Construction of Moral Discourse in Southern Rhodesia 1894–1930*, Oxford: Clarendon Press.

Klugman, B. (2000) 'Sexual Rights in Southern Africa: A Beijing Discourse or a Strategic Necessity?', *Health and Human Rights*, 4(2): 145–73.

Louw, D. J. (1998) 'Ubuntu; An African Assessment of the Religious Other', Paper given at Twentieth World Congress of Philosophy, Boston, MA, 10–15 August 1998. Available online at http://www.bu.edu/wcp/Papers/ Afri/AfriLouw.htm, accessed 3 May 2006.

Menon, U. (2000) 'Does Feminism have Universal Relevance? The Challenges Posed by Oriya Hindu Family Practices', *Daedalus*, 129(4): 77–100, Fall.

Miller, A. (2004) 'Sexuality, Violence Against Women, and Human Rights: Women Make Demands and Ladies Get Protection', in *Health and Human Rights*, 7(2): 16–47.

Mohanty, C. T. (1991) 'Under Western Eyes: Feminist Scholarship and Colonial Discourses', in C. T. Mohanty *et al.* (eds) *Third World Women and the Politics of Feminism*, Bloomington: Indiana University Press.

Mokgoro, Justice Y. (1998) 'Ubuntu and the Law in South Africa', *Buffalo Human Rights Law Review*, 4: 15–23.

Mutua, M. (1995) 'The Banjul Charter and the African Cultural Fingerprint: An Evaluation of the Language of Duties', *Virginia Journal of International Law*, 35: 339.

Narayan, U. (1997) *Dislocating Cultures: Identities, Traditions and Third World Feminism*, New York and London: Routledge.

Oyewùmí, O. (1997) *The Invention of Women: Making an African Sense of Western Gender Discourse*, Minneapolis and London: University of Minnesota Press.

Petchesky, R. (2003) 'Negotiating Reproductive Rights', in J. Weeks, J. Holland and M. Waites (eds) *Sexualities and Society: A Reader*, London: Macmillan.

Phillips, O. (1997a) 'Zimbabwean Law and the Production of a White Man's Disease', *Social and Legal Studies* 6(4): 471–92). Reprinted in J. Weeks, J. Holland and M. Waites (2003) *Sexualities and Society: A Reader*, London: Polity Press.

Phillips, O. (1997b) 'Zimbabwe: Venus Monstrosa and "Unnatural Offences"' in D. J. West and R. Green (eds) *Socio-Legal Control of Homosexuality: A Multi-Nation Comparison*, New York: Plenum.

Phillips, O. (1999) *Sexual Offences in Zimbabwe: Fetishisms of Procreation, Perversion, and Individual Autonomy*, unpublished PhD thesis, University of Cambridge, UK.

Phillips, O. (2000) 'Constituting the Global Gay: Individual Subjectivity and Sexuality in Southern Africa', in C. Stychin and D. Herman (eds) *Sexuality in the Legal Arena*, London/Minnesota: Athlone/University of Minnesota Press, 17–33.

Rubin, G. (1984) 'Thinking Sex: Notes for a Radical Theory of the Politics of Sexuality', in C. S. Vance (ed.) *Pleasure and Danger: Exploring Female Sexuality*, New York: Routledge and Kegan Paul.

Seidman, G. (1984) 'Women in Zimbabwe: Post-Independence Struggles', *Feminist Studies*, 10(3): 419–40.

Smart, C. (1977) *Women, Crime, and Criminology*, London: Routledge and Kegan Paul.

Spitz, R. and Chaskalson, M. (2000) *The Politics of Transition: A Hidden History of South Africa's Negotiated Settlement*, Oxford: Hart Publishing.

Shephard, B. (2000) 'The Double Discourse' on Sexual Rights and Reproductive Rights in Latin America: The Chasm between Public Policy and Private Actions', *Health and Human Rights*, 4(2): 111–143.

Susser, I. and Stein, Z. (2004) 'Culture, Sexuality and Women's Agency in the Prevention of HIV/AIDS in Southern Africa', in E. Kalipeni, S. Craddock, J. Oppong and J. Ghosh (eds) *HIV/AIDS in Africa: Beyond Epidemiology*, Oxford: Blackwell Publishing, 58–143.

Suttner, R. and Cronin, J. (1986) *30 Years of the Freedom Charter*, Johannesburg: Ravan Press.

Vail, L. (ed) (1989) *The Creation of Tribalism in Southern Africa*, London: University of California Press.

Van Zyl, M. (2004) 'Escaping Heteronormativity: Sexuality in Sexual Citizenship', in A. Gouws (ed.) *(Un)thinking Citizenship: Feminist Debates in Contemporary South Africa*, Aldershot: Ashgate, 148–78.

Vance, C. and Miller, A. (2004) 'Sexuality, Health, and Human Rights', *Health and Human Rights* 7(2): 5–15.

Weeks, J. (1989) *Sex, Politics, and Society: The Regulation of Sexuality since 1800*, Harlow: Longman.

WLSA (Women and Law in Southern Africa Research and Educational Trust) (2001) *Venia Magaya's Sacrifice: A Case of Custom Gone Awry*, Harare: WLSA.

Zimbabwe Human Rights NGO Forum (2001) 'Gendered Human Rights', *Human Rights Monitor*, no. 12 (March). Available online at http://www.hrforumzim.com/frames/inside_frame_monitor.htm, accessed 23 May 2006.

Chapter 14

Another look at Lady Bountiful: reform, gender and organisations

Judith Rumgay

Introduction

Since the publication of the Carter Review (Carter 2003), policy for the delivery of community correctional services in England and Wales has begun to move towards a new phase of privatisation. Carter envisaged a streamlined correctional service contracting for treatment services on a large scale, with the role of the probation service relegated to purchasing of programmes, and assessment, referral and enforcement in relation to the individuals passing through them. Much of the response to this proposal has concerned the impact on the probation service in terms of staffing, maintenance of service quality and morale. Surprisingly few have reflected for long on the implications of such a project on potential voluntary sector programme providers. In particular, the question whether the voluntary sector *wants* to become a key player in the delivery of community-based punishment, as it is currently conceived in policy terms, has been quite studiously overlooked.

This chapter explores the enterprise of one voluntary organisation in an attempt to illuminate a vision and spirit that were ultimately crushed even as the sector as a whole expanded. The Griffins Society pioneered a range of hostels in North London for women offenders over a period of 30 years between the mid-1960s and mid-1990s. As we shall see, judged by contemporary expectations of the voluntary sector, it appears to have been an egregious organisation:

elitist in its composition; anachronistic in its management style; and idiosyncratic in its approach to service delivery. Nevertheless, its ground-breaking development of hostels for the most challenging female offenders earned generous acclaim across the spectrum of observers from field practitioners to senior civil servants. Moreover, unlike many organisations that have responded to the unmet social and psychological needs of women during the past 30 years, the Griffins Society was cheerfully apolitical in its perspectives on gender relations. Yet, its accomplishments in rehabilitative services for female offenders anticipated many of the elements of 'gender-specific programming' (see, for example, Bloom 2000; Covington 2000) that have been hailed over the past decade as offering a new, enlightened approach to the treatment of difficult and damaged women.

What combination of factors brought about this unlikely advance in the provision of rehabilitative services for female offenders? Moreover, what can we learn from it about the essential ingredients of voluntary sector involvement in this field? In the attempt to answer these questions, this chapter draws on the retrospective evaluation of the Griffins Society's work, which was conducted after the organisation's withdrawal from service provision in 1996 (Rumgay 2006). The study collated and analysed rich archival data, observation at the three surviving hostels and interviews with the Society's Council Members, project staff and allied professionals. For the purpose of this chapter, illustrative quotations from the interviews are used.

While the evaluation project included a detailed examination of practice within the hostels and its outcomes, the present chapter focuses on the Griffins Society itself. The research is somewhat unusual in respect of its holistic approach to evaluation of an organisation's contribution to offender rehabilitation, which was informed by the extraordinary character of the Society. Feminist contributors to this field have tended to focus more exclusively upon either historical accounts of penal reform activity (e.g. Freedman 1981, 1996; Rafter 1985; Zedner 1991) or, more recently, the study of rehabilitation programmes in isolation from their organisational context (e.g. McMahon 2000; Zaplin 1998).

We begin by briefly describing the organisation's history, before turning to examine the qualitative characteristics of its enterprise and concluding with a discussion of its significance for theorising the role of the voluntary sector in the penal system.

Optimism and growth

> People had an idea for something and just said, 'Well, who can
> we get to do it?' Or we picked it up and ran with it, if we
> thought there was a gap.
> (*Council member*)

The Griffins Society was founded in 1965, when prison welfare, which
had been provided, hitherto, through a system of local Discharged
Prisoners' Aid Societies, was transferred to the responsibilities of
the probation service. Encouraged by the prison governor, Joanna
Kelley, the Holloway Discharged Prisoners' Aid Society, which was
possessed of relatively generous funds, reconstituted itself as a new
voluntary organisation to provide accommodation and support for
women after release. The Society's core council comprised a group
of upper middle class women acting in a voluntary capacity to
bring Joanna Kelley's vision into reality. The remarks of one Council
Member, above, illustrate the energy, opportunism and adventure
that they brought to their enterprise.

Renaming itself as the Griffins Society, after the heraldic beasts
that adorned the entrance to the old Victorian Holloway Prison, the
organisation's first premises opened in 1966. This voluntary after-
care hostel became the flagship of the organisation's enterprise.
Capitalising on its close originating association with Holloway
Prison, the premises pioneered a range of new services, including
accommodation for discharged prisoners, a meeting ground for
imprisoned women and their children, a psychotherapy group and
a coffee bar for women offenders isolated in the community. The
Society, with a youthful optimism and enthusiasm, immediately set
about purchasing the adjoining property to develop the project on a
larger scale after creating a unified building.

The Society rapidly acquired a reputation as a provider of
accommodation for the most difficult women offenders. At the Home
Office's invitation, the organisation developed the first, initially
experimental, women's bail hostel, which opened in 1978. In 1983,
a third property was opened, offering bed-sitter accommodation
to women who had achieved a level of independence that did not
require 24-hour support. In 1990, the bail hostel, now pronounced
a success, moved to larger premises. In addition, an agreement was
negotiated with a local private landlord for the lease of a 'cluster' flat

which could accommodate four women bailees who were capable of living independently, supported at a distance by hostel staff. In 1992, another property next to the original after-care hostel was opened, accommodating those who had progressed to a level at which they could cope with reduced support. Fortuitously, the vacated property of the original bail hostel became the site for the development of a project instigated by the invitation of the statutory organisation responsible for oversight of Special Hospitals. This last hostel, for women with severe mental health problems, opened in 1994.

At this point, the Griffins Society was running five hostels and catering for a total capacity of 65 women. Its commitment to securing further resettlement opportunities for its residents was reflected in successful negotiations with local authorities and housing associations for generous independent move-on accommodation for its graduates. It appeared to be thriving on its reputation as a pioneer of projects for the accommodation of the most challenging women offenders. Yet, only a year later, in 1995, it closed the two after-care hostels and reached the decision to withdraw from activity as a service provider. That decision was implemented with remarkable alacrity. The three surviving hostels – the bail hostel with its 'cluster' flat, the supported bed-sitter accommodation and the registered care home for severely mentally disordered women – were transferred to a larger voluntary organisation in 1996.

The downward spiral

> The *joy* went out of it for some of the trustees. It just became a *headache*.
> (*Administrative officer*)

With such qualities of enterprise and staunch commitment, bolstered by the evidence of their success, what misfortunes could trigger such a rapid spiral of decline that in the space of two years a vigorous organisation, with five pioneering projects to its credit, would withdraw from hostel management altogether? The Society's apparently abrupt withdrawal from service provision can be seen to be rooted in a series of disappointments accumulating over several years.

First, the Council committed considerable resources and energy over a substantial period in an attempt to realise an ambition to develop a mother and baby project. However, when a property was finally secured for the purpose after many abortive efforts, funding for the project by the Housing Corporation and local authority, which had appeared secure, was withdrawn. Reduced funding prospects necessitated revision of staffing plans to a level that appeared dangerously inadequate. Moreover, structurally, the property presented huge challenges to convert it to a safe environment for children. The property was never opened as a hostel for mothers with babies, but was redesignated, as we have seen, as a voluntary after-care hostel, intended for occupation by graduates of the original project who had achieved sufficient independence to cope with reduced support.

Second, however, this second after-care hostel never thrived, primarily because there were insufficient suitable graduates. Problems at the original flagship project were also accumulating. As a voluntary after-care hostel, it was the least generously funded of the Society's projects. As Home Office support for voluntary after-care hostels waned during the 1980s and 1990s, with policy interest re-focusing on compulsory post-release supervision for high-risk offenders, staffing levels became inadequate for its clientele of women with multiple problems associated with drugs, alcohol, mental disorders and involvement in street lifestyles. Moreover, expectations of supported housing were shifting in favour of smaller projects and self-contained accommodation. The Society found it necessary to draw heavily on its own financial reserves to sustain these two after-care hostels, a resort on which it could not rely indefinitely.

Decisions to close each of these hostels in turn were taken in 1995. Now, having already seen the collapse of one of its dearest ambitions in the mother and baby project, the Society found itself closing hostels instead of opening them.

Third, although the mental health project was initially the brainchild of the statutory organisation then responsible for the special hospitals, it became immersed in problems that threatened its survival for years. A cluster of factors conspired to produce difficulties that appeared at times insurmountable. Changes to the system of funding residential care, reorganisation of the central administration for the special hospitals, and hostility to the project from several psychiatrists, whose support in referring and supervising discharged patients was crucial, thrust an enormous burden of the fight for survival on to the Griffins Society itself. It is to their lasting credit that this project survives and thrives today. Even after the transfer to a larger organisation, the Society continued to assist in its funding until it eventually established viability. For the Council Members themselves, however, this was yet another struggle at a time when they were beginning to question both the worth of their philanthropic enterprise and the limits of their personal tolerance.

Finally, in some ways, the Society was a victim of its own success. Expansion and diversification brought with them new demands. As time went on, the transition from a charitable, value-driven perspective to a businesslike approach to management and development, which was characterising shifts in the voluntary sector as a whole (Taylor 1996), became a recurrent preoccupation. The increasing regulation and bureaucratisation of voluntary sector activity (Taylor 1996) imposed a great burden on The Council, who remained a small group of volunteer women. The lack of an infrastructure that would support the administration and development of the organisation with its three surviving hostels meant, ironically, that the Society was now too small to compete in the modern world of professional bureaucracies.

Lady Bountiful and organisational character

Some people will make political statements about the [council], its make-up, the way it operated and so on ... But I did get to see as warden, at first hand, quite how much work was involved, particularly for [the chair]. It was like a full-time job for which she wasn't paid. That side of it can easily be lost, in terms of being quite dismissive about these good ladies. Because some of them worked jolly hard and did a lot.
(*Hostel manager*)

The composition of the Griffins' Society Council is crucial to an understanding of its organisational character. This small organisation comprised at its core a remarkable collection of wealthy, in some cases titled, upper middle class women whose philanthropic spirit derived from the sense of *noblesse oblige* accompanying social privilege (Odendahl 1990; Ostrower 1995). Their social status empowered them with a direct access to influential policy-makers that is unusual for small service providers. They were, for example, assisted by an unusually close relationship with the Home Office, forged through social acquaintances with politicians and senior civil servants.

Council Members did not shy from exploiting their powerful connections in the pursuit of benefit to their projects. Indeed, their campaign to nurture their enterprise was conducted within the very social circles in which they routinely moved. Contrary to the common stereotype in which 'ladies who lunch' are assumed to quarantine philanthropic activity from the rest of a privileged, leisured existence untainted by connection to disadvantage, for these women the pursuit of their cause was an integral aspect of their social interactions (Daniels 1988). Meetings with potential donors, trustees of benevolent institutions, senior-ranking civil servants and politicians, which constituted common social encounters for Council Members, presented valuable opportunities for the solicitation of material, financial and strategic support. Council Members were adept at mining this seam of prosperity and advantage.

> If one personally had any connection with a charity, knew somebody, got a friend who's on the board of this or the committee of that. A lot of it was personal – what is *now* called networking.
> (*Council member*)

To observers, unfamiliar with the mysterious interactions of a social élite, the processes through which council members achieved their goals were naturally somewhat opaque. Nevertheless, there was unanimous agreement on their effectiveness.

> They seemed to have got their hooks into an awful lot of very senior Home Office officials. It wasn't just a case of writing a letter. They'd go and knock on their office door … It was the *scale* of things that was so impressive. It wasn't just a quick grant out of the mayor's charity. It was the Home Office and £23,000 for a new boiler … My perception was that once you got to the heart, the darker recesses of the Home Office, these mandarins would lock themselves away in offices. But they *couldn't* hide from *these* people! Because, not only did they chase them during the day, they also met them socially. So they *couldn't* get away, they *had* to commit – which was always rather amusing.
> (*Police officer*)

A second crucial feature of the organisation was the non-professional status of Council Members. Many Council Members were active in the lay magistracy, some were its representatives on probation service committees, and some were involved in Holloway Prison's Board of Visitors. They therefore were, collectively, experienced in contact with statutory criminal justice agencies. Their participation in the criminal justice system was, however, for the most part, conducted on a voluntary basis. They were not professionals in the field of offender rehabilitation. Their activity was marked by an earthy, common-sense practicality that was quite different in kind from the characteristic conduct of professionally trained and experienced players. Moreover, while acknowledged and admired by many witnesses to their efforts, this quality hardly conforms to the general stereotype of the impractical, superficial leisured lady. Indeed, Council Members' organisational competence suggests that they were pursuing 'careers' in voluntary service (Daniels 1988) analogous to those of the professionals to whom they were necessarily tied in pursuit of their objectives.

> There's *nothing* [she] doesn't know about hostels. Nowadays, if somebody suggested that she should be brought in on our committee with her qualifications, we'd be saying, 'What *for*?' But she was *spectacular*.
> (*Council member*)

The hostel environments that these women developed and nurtured reflected their status as socially influential, self-efficacious and lay volunteers in the criminal justice system. In particular, there were three hallmarks of the Society's enterprise that significantly flowed from this: it was maternal, 'hands on' and bold.

Philanthropic maternalism

> I believed very much that we should focus exclusively on women, because of the experiences that so many of the women had with men. I didn't want us to become a refuge. I didn't… want [to prevent] women who wanted to continue relationships with the fathers of their children … But … there was no doubt the women had been cruelly damaged by their relationships with men.
> (*Council member*)

Council Members' accounts of their involvement in the Griffin Society largely lacked a political, feminist perspective. The remarks of the Council Member above were among the strongest in terms of commentary on women's disempowerment. They believed, however, that they had a natural empathy for their residents' plights by virtue of their common womanhood. This appears to have been no optimistic fantasy on their part: many observers testified to their ability to comprehend residents' predicaments.

They were *very* committed. They came from very different backgrounds from the women, but had great *empathy* for their problems.
(*Hostel manager*)

The history of the Griffins Society is infused with an ambition to support motherhood. Pregnancy, childbirth and motherhood were constant features of the lives of hostel residents, thrown into stark relief by the gender-specificity of the organisation's clientele. In the early years of the first after-care hostel, women prisoners were granted temporary release to receive visits from their children on the premises. Moreover, a number of women completed their pregnancies while resident there. In all the hostels, unfulfilled motherhood was a recurrent theme among women whose relationships with their children were disrupted by their personal difficulties.

However, to describe the Griffins Society as a 'maternal' organisation implies more than a particular focus on providing for mothers, although this was the most obvious expression of the approach. The term denotes a perspective that is not only sensitive to multi-faceted needs of women, but, moreover, evokes responses that are also typically female (Koven 1993; Koven and Michel 1993). Thus, the maternal approach sprang from both the exclusive focus on female offenders and the female composition of The Council. One manifestation of this was the high quality of the physical environment that they maintained in each of their projects, at considerable recurring cost to themselves in terms of fund-raising, time and physical effort. Interviewees, reminiscing about their impressions of the hostels, returned to this theme repeatedly. Provision of material comfort of a high standard, however, was not a policy that Council Members consciously imposed upon themselves. It sprang naturally from their personal beliefs and assumptions about the intrinsic worth of a comfortable, homely environment. It might never have occurred to some Council Members that there was an easier and cheaper alternative in the provision of more Spartan accommodation.

This brand of maternalism has characterised many forms of female philanthropy and activism. Female philanthropists have traditionally favoured those aspects of social life which predominantly affect women, children and families in their charitable donations (Ostrower 1995), voluntary work (Prochaska 1980) and reform efforts (Koven and Michel 1993). Historical analyses of women's penal reform movements (Freedman 1996; Mahood 1995) and even of early appointments of women to the police force (Appier 1998) similarly identify a seam of maternal ideology that was not a merely coincidental characteristic of these female encroachments on traditionally male preserves but crucial to their legitimacy. While Council Members made no explicit appeal to ideology, this maternal perspective, rooted in personal experience, profoundly shaped the character of their project.

'Hands on' management

Our whole thing was based on a different – much more of an old fashioned *do-gooding*, as I see it now. But, you know, it *worked*. Well, it *seemed* to work.
(*Council member*)

Early in the life of the organisation, Council Members altered their management style from a restricted concern with the structure and furbishment of the property to include taking a direct interest in their residents. A system of regular visiting by Council Members was instituted that survived to the organisation's withdrawal from service provision. Moreover, Council Members made themselves readily available for personal support of staff during stressful periods, spending time in the hostels and making themselves accessible by telephone. Their 'hands on' approach to management became a crucial aspect of their organisational identity, both demonstrating the volunteer spirit and personal commitment of Council Members and symbolising the ethos of an organisation that sought connection between women from different social worlds.

Again, direct participation in the practicalities of service delivery has long characterised women's philanthropy (Prochaska 1980). Notably, penal reform has featured strongly among the forms of philanthropic activity that historically have offered opportunities for 'hands on' involvement by women with time to give. Indeed, in Victorian times, it appears that the proximity of middle class female volunteers to poor, wayward women was approved for its potential for communicating social values (Zedner 1991). Thus, whether they recognised it or not, the Council Members were extending a very old tradition of philanthropic activity by wealthy women of the leisured class.

A bold organisation

We were a very *determined* band of vocal volunteer women. *Not* to be trifled with, as some poor men at the Home Office

discovered. An assault by people like [us] was something to be wary of ... We had ... *push* and *determination* ... We were *never* ones to hold back.
(*Council member*)

The Griffins Society established early, and maintained throughout, a reputation for admitting women who were excluded from other hostels. This anti-exclusionary policy, however, was not a fragmentary occasion of daring, but reflected a deeper courage in the organisation. Each project on which they embarked broke new ground in the field of penal welfare, yet Council Members appeared to be undeterred by the risks they were taking. Several observers invoked the term 'bold' to describe their enterprise.

The thing I would say about the Griffins as an organisation, was that they always wanted it, they were always enthusiastic, they always stuck by it and despite the problems, they kept with it. That was important, because there were enough other things going wrong in other areas that were discouraging people. One needed some solid feature to it that one could rely on.
(*Senior administrator*)

Partly, perhaps this spirit was borne out of their personal experience of success and influence: as members of a social élite, Council Members generally expected, with good reason, to get their own way. It is unlikely that they were unaware of their ability to intimidate those from whom they sought help for their enterprise. Their self-confident ebullience was simultaneously charming and disconcerting, deployed to good effect in the service of their cause.

Philanthropic dinosaurs

It was a bit of *social* thing as well as ... running a hostel for the women. We'd have get-togethers after our annual meeting. Things like that. So it was good *fun*. I enjoyed meeting the people – both the people on the management committee and the women in the house. It was a good lifetime experience, really. I enjoyed it and I thought it was worthwhile. It was difficult, but it was worthwhile.
(*Council member*)

This reminiscence of one Council Member aptly captures the mood expressed by many. They frequently asserted that in their voluntary endeavour they were 'having fun', apparently oblivious to, or unconcerned about the potential connotations of superficiality. Just as they pursued their cause in the interstices of their routine social interactions, so they brought a distinctive sociability to the formalities of hostel governance. While their behaviour could thus appear to appeal to the stereotype of the frivolous leisured lady, it in fact infused the organisation with an ethos of mutual regard and respect.

> For all that I might not always agree with their philosophy, they were quite *solid* … The managers knew … so we were of the same feeling … There was a *commitment* to the organisation. It wasn't just to my little patch, or my little thing, so I can be seen as doing really well. It wasn't competitive and it wasn't divisive. There was a *fairness* that went through everything. That *must* have been the [council], because they were the solid constant thing, through all of us who came and went.
> (*Hostel manager*)

This ethos was infectious, enhancing the interest and support of many who might otherwise have rendered merely the level of support required by professional duty.

> It became more than just another committee to me. I was *involved* with them, spent a lot of time with them, was very *interested* in what they did. They were a nice bunch of people … a very dedicated bunch of people.
> (*Police officer*)

The changing ethos of voluntary sector activity had a strong psychological impact on Council Members. While in retrospect they generally adopted a robust perspective on their organisational demise, endorsing the need for a businesslike, corporate approach to the management in the voluntary sector, they were also hurt by the devaluation of their contribution.

> I remember one of The Members of our committee who left, saying she'd done her years and she was getting on a bit. When asked, rather pointedly by me, was she feeling a sense of disappointment – because I realised there was something

that she wasn't happy about – she said I was quite right ... It was that she was not welcome in the sitting room any more to sit and chat to the residents. She felt that was what her role was and that was what she was good at. When it was made clear that she was not welcome, she didn't want any more to do with it.
(*Council member*)

Much attention focused on this particular aspect of trends in voluntary sector organisational structure, which seemed to encapsulate professional denigration of their activity. Council Members found themselves under pressure to relinquish their cherished 'hands on' management style and to limit their involvement to fund-raising, policy and corporate issues. This was deeply felt by some members as a loss of the personal meaning that their endeavour held for them. For example, committee meetings within the hostels traditionally included brief accounts of individual residents' progress. Council Members were deeply offended on being advised that this practice constituted a breach of women's confidentiality.

It was a feeling that we weren't really doing as much as we could have. Maintain the projects, lay gardens for them and all this sort of thing. But one was *allowed* to do that. We could provide as much as we could for their well-being, but we had no input with the actual residents ... I remember getting quite fed up with the whole thing, saying it's quite ridiculous for [a staff member to say] that she's not prepared to tell us about something. She's not even prepared to tell us the *name* and, God Almighty, we *run* this place!
(*Council member*)

Furthermore, this small group of volunteer women could not sustain the bureaucratic workload that they now faced. However, they found it impossible to bring sufficient new blood into The Council to replenish their numbers. Council Members concluded that they had become dinosaurs of a bygone era, when affluent women *expected* to give their time, outside the support of their families, to 'doing good' voluntarily.

At this time, they were under pressure, as were all voluntary sector groups, to introduce greater diversity and expertise into their council. Yet, the style and methods of operation of a council comprised largely of professionals did not suit them, either practically or psychologically.

At the practical level, a *modus operandi* in which activity was fitted into the interstices of family life and other voluntary commitments did not match the expectations of paid professionals as to when and how they would fulfil their obligations to council meetings. At the psychological level, Council Members felt that the expertise that they had built up through 30 years of experience in running hostels was being devalued by virtue of their lay status and informal approach. Ultimately, they concluded that they were philanthropic dinosaurs.

Learning from Lady Bountiful

Unless you had an organisation like the Griffins, you wouldn't have had that championing of the cause of ... women in the criminal justice system. That was *completely* without doubt ... So they championed that cause. They were very professional in that cause and they got that cause right ... Unless *they* had championed that cause, it wouldn't have received the attention it did. Everybody knew that if you put a *finger* on [their hostels], then we had big problems on our hands ... I am a servant of the government ... Whoever the Home Secretary of the day is, I mustn't sail Jack Straw or Michael Howard into troubled waters unless there is a very good reason to do so ... So they *did* use their power, *political* power, effectively. They *did* get established in London those facilities for women which wouldn't otherwise be there.
(*Senior civil servant*)

These remarks offer an extraordinary testimony to the accomplishments of a small group of unpaid 'amateurs' in the political and professional world of the criminal justice system. In adopting residential rehabilitation for women offenders as their enterprise, the Griffins Society's Lady Bountifuls espoused one of the least popular causes for 'doing good' and befriended one of the most neglected deviant groups (Rumgay 2000, 2004). This study did not set out to laud them: indeed, there was an early anxious, nagging doubt that such an egregious bunch of privileged, powerful 'ladies of leisure' could truly have masterminded a successful project for the benefit of some of society's most disadvantaged and disenfranchised women. Ultimately, however, the research challenges some instinctive prejudices about the philanthropic activities of the wealthy.

It is an irony that an organisation that began amidst, and partly in

293

opposition to the professionalisation of prison welfare, should itself succumb to that pressure within the voluntary sector. The decision by Council Members to end their philanthropic enterprise reflected complex feelings arising from disappointment at project failures, relief of physical and mental exhaustion and a sense that their activity was devalued and outmoded in the late 1990s. For some, the demise of the last surviving Lady Bountifuls might not come a day too soon. Yet, such a reaction would reflect a reflex prejudice to the cut-glass accents, stylish costumes and easy references to influential acquaintances in public life that commonly comprised first impressions of Council Members. Certainly, Council Members of the Griffins Society never tried to disguise their class. Indeed, like many philanthropists from wealthy, upper middle class backgrounds, they regarded their status and connections as assets to be deployed in pursuit of their cause. Closer acquaintance with Council Members, however, revealed them to have a sharp, humorous and self-deprecatory perception of their social image.

Similarly, the behaviours associated with Council Members' lay status are too easily denigrated as unprofessional. Such a criticism implies that Council Members had pretensions to professionalism. Yet, it was the very essence of the Griffins Society that it was sustained by the unflagging efforts of non-professionals. In the current climate of voluntary sector professionalisation, the potential for devaluing the unique contribution of lay volunteers may endanger their very presence among the caring services. At a time when government policy seeks to regenerate the 'volunteer spirit', we must be prepared to ask about the nature of rewards for such activity and how those rewards might be preserved within an increasingly bureaucratised and professionalised voluntary sector.

As we have seen, the maternalist approach of the Griffins Society mirrored, albeit unconsciously, that of traditional female social welfare and reform activities. The historical maternalist enterprise, however, has left a curious ambiguity in the choices confronting contemporary women who seek progression along career paths traditionally dominated by men. Perhaps more poignantly, it has also produced ambivalence and division among feminist commentators on its legacy. For example, Appier's (1998) history of female involvement in Los Angeles Police Department shows clearly that the maternalist approach of early women officers offered a unique set of values and practices that became the very justification for their presence in the service. However, over time, women police officers moved from active infusion of maternalist perspectives as their conscious strategy for penetrating a strongly masculine culture, to deliberate rejection of their social work identity. Instead, their project became that of assimilation into the police department through adaptation to male conventions. Appier observes that this tactic achieved little in extending the range of women's activities into male preserves. Moreover, it contributed to the isolation of women police officers from a network of supportive female relationships in the broader field of social activism.

This example illustrates the pitfalls associated with a project of assimilation through adaptation, with its connotations of denigrating female attributes by comparison with male. Nevertheless, alternative feminist perspectives in the same field, such as Schulz's (1995) history of women's policing in the United States, argue for the achievement of equality through measurement against prevailing male standards. This ambivalence between championing distinctively female characteristics and seeking equality on male terms pervades much of the feminist criminological literature, both in respect of female career paths in criminal justice and of the treatment of female offenders. On the one hand, the achievements of women reformers in moderating the harsh treatment of female offenders and demonstrating the benefits of maternalism are lauded (e.g. Freedman 1996). On the other, critics remark upon the irony that in emphasising sexual difference, female penal reformers became locked into programmes that perpetuated gender inequality both for their own professional roles and for the recipients of their endeavours (e.g. Rafter 1985).

Griffins Society Council Members appear not to have troubled themselves with these ideological debates. Certainly, it did not occur to them to identify themselves as penal reformers, even though their enterprise unwittingly followed the repeated historical examples of individuals such as Elizabeth Fry (Kent 1962), Mary Carpenter (Manton 1976), Margery Fry (Jones 1966) and Miriam van Waters (Freedman 1996) in their adroit combination of practical, 'hands on' activity and political manipulation. Rather, they simply pursued their cause with the values and tools that flowed directly from personal experience. Nevertheless, Council Members of the Griffins Society had no need to engage in a philanthropic enterprise that exposed them directly to a challenging and often unrewarding clientele, and that required their constant attention and effort. They could undoubtedly have chosen an easier path of chequebook sympathy for worthy causes or sitting on fund-raising or grant-giving committees, from which to 'do good' at arm's length from the realities of disadvantage and deviance. This was not the Griffins' style. Instead, they unnecessarily elected a much harder route, which exposed them directly to unpalatable realities of the society in which they were privileged members, yet from which they did not flinch in their practical immersion in their endeavour. It is precisely because of this, that the effort to understand what motivated them offers an insight into voluntary commitment that is crucial to any successful attempt to revitalise volunteering by lay citizens.

Ultimately, the rewards that Council Members gleaned from their efforts seem to have emanated from their involvement with women passing through their projects. While they were not so naive as to expect radical reform in each individual resident, they appear to have derived pleasure merely from personal contact established within the hostel environment. In reaching out to women from alternative social worlds in this direct way, they transcended the many hours of academic reflection that have recently been spent on the causes of and solutions to social exclusion. It is a tragedy that their withdrawal has broken this bridge between the worlds of social affluence and social disgrace, and that such a result might be regarded by some as a triumph of professionalisation.

How long can sympathy for the plight of others beyond one's immediate social circle withstand the absence of direct personal contact? This question is particularly pertinent when the plight in question is that of an unappealing deviant group. As much research into public attitudes to crime and punishment has shown, empathy and tolerance do not easily spring from abstract principles, but rather flow from direct acquaintance with another individual's suffering (e.g. Stalans and Diamond 1990). By exposing themselves to the realities of women's lives within the hostels, Council Members nurtured their capacity for sympathy with individuals whose challenging, antisocial behaviour commonly served to intensify their exclusion from conventional society.

Finally, idiosyncratic as their methods were, the Council Members of the Griffins Society ensured that the voices of disadvantaged and neglected women were heard in corridors of power not generally noted for their receptivity to tales of human suffering. It appears unlikely that those voices have increased in volume through their replacement by professional bureaucracies for which access to those corridors is limited. Feminist critiques of female penal reform activity as serving the interests of sustained class inequality while instilling middle-class values in those who were doomed to serfdom (Mahood 1995; Rafter 1985) offer inadequate analyses of the Griffins Society's enterprise. Council Members made no pretence of political radicalism. Yet, they were well aware that they enjoyed access to, and could directly influence, sources of power that would impact, for better or worse, on the quality of their residents' lives. They chose to manipulate it for the better. Thus, they put their élite prestige at the disposal of women who would never themselves attain such extensive social capital (Farrall 2002), however successful their efforts at personal reform might be. This 'social capital by proxy' was the unique philanthropic gift of Lady Bountiful.

References

Appier, J. (1998) *Policing Women: The Sexual Politics of Law Enforcement and the LAPD*, Philadelphia, PA: Temple University Press.

Bloom, B. (2000) 'Beyond Recidivism: Perspectives on Evaluation of Programs for Female Offenders in Community Corrections', in M. McMahon (ed.) *Assessment to Assistance: Programs for Women in Community Corrections*, Lanham, MD: American Correctional Association: 107–38.

Carter, P. (2003) *Managing Offenders, Reducing Crime: A New Approach*, London: Home Office, Strategy Unit.

Covington, S. (2000) 'Helping Women to Recover: Creating Gender-specific Treatment for Substance-abusing Women and Girls in Community Corrections', in M. McMahon (ed.) *Assessment to Assistance: Programs for Women in Community Corrections*. Lanham, MD: American Correctional Association: 171–234.

Daniels, A. K. (1988) *Invisible Careers: Women Civic Leaders from the Volunteer World*, Chicago, IL: University of Chicago Press.

Farrall, S. (2002) *Rethinking What Works with Offenders: Probation, Social Context and Desistance from Crime*, Cullompton: Willan Publishing.

Freedman, E. B. (1981) *Their Sisters' Keepers: Women's Prison Reform in America, 1830–1930*, Ann Arbor: University of Michigan Press.

Freedman, E. B. (1996) *Maternal Justice: Miriam Van Waters and the Female Reform Tradition*, Chicago, IL: University of Chicago Press.

Jones, E. H. (1962) *Margery Fry: The Essential Amateur*, London: Oxford University Press.

Kent, J. (1962) *Elizabeth Fry*, London: B. T. Batsford.

Koven, S. (1993) 'Borderlands: Women, Voluntary Action, and Child Welfare in Britain, 1840 to 1914', in S. Koven and S. Michel (eds) *Mothers of a New World: Maternalist Politics and the Origins of Welfare States*, London: Routledge, 94–135.

Koven, S. and Michel, S. (1993) 'Introduction: "Mother Worlds"', in S. Koven and S. Michel (eds) *Mothers of a New World: Maternalist Politics and the Origins of Welfare States*, London: Routledge, 1–42.

Mahood, L. (1995) *Policing Gender, Class and Family: Britain, 1850–1940*, London: UCL Press.

Manton, J. (1976) *Mary Carpenter and the Children of the Streets*, London: Heinemann Educational Books.

McMahon, M. (ed.) (2000) *Assessment to Assistance: Programs for Women in Community Corrections*, Lanham, MD: American Correctional Association.

Odendahl, T. (1990) *Charity Begins at Home: Generosity and Self-interest Among the Philanthropic Elite*, New York: Basic Books.

Ostrower, F. (1995) *Why the Wealthy Give: The Culture of Elite Philanthropy*, Princeton: Princeton University Press.

Prochaska, F. K. (1980) *Women and Philanthropy in Nineteenth-century England*, Oxford: Oxford University Press.

Rafter, N. H. (1985) *Partial Justice: Women in State Prisons, 1800–1935*, Boston, MA: Northeastern University Press.

Rumgay, J. (2000) 'Policies of Neglect: Female Offenders and the Probation Service', in H. Kemshall and R. Littlechild (eds) *User Involvement and Participation in Social Care: Research Informing Practice*, London: Jessica Kingsley: 193–213.

Rumgay, J. (2004) 'Living with Paradox: Community Supervision of Women Offenders', in G. McIvor (ed.) *Women Who Offend, Research Highlights in Social Work* 44, London: Jessica Kingsley: 99–125.

Rumgay, J. (2006) *Ladies of Lost Causes: Rehabilitation, Women Offenders and the Voluntary Sector*, Whitby, ON: de Sitter.

Schulz, D. M. (1995) *From Social Worker to Crime Fighter: Women in United States Municipal Policing*, Westport, CT: Praeger.

Stalans, L. J. and Diamond, S. S. (1990) 'Formation and Change in Lay Evaluations of Criminal Sentencing: Misperception and Discontent', *Law and Human Behavior*, 14(3): 199–214.

Taylor, M. (1996) 'What are the Key Influences on the Work of Voluntary Agencies?', in D. Billis and M. Harris (eds) *Voluntary Agencies: Challenges of Organisation and Management*, Basingstoke: Macmillan: 13–28.

Zaplin, R. T. (ed) (1998) *Female Offenders: Critical Perspectives and Effective Interventions*, Gaithersburg, MD: Aspen.

Zedner, L. (1991) *Women, Crime and Custody in Victorian England*, Oxford: Oxford University Press.

Index